More Scenes from the Rural Life

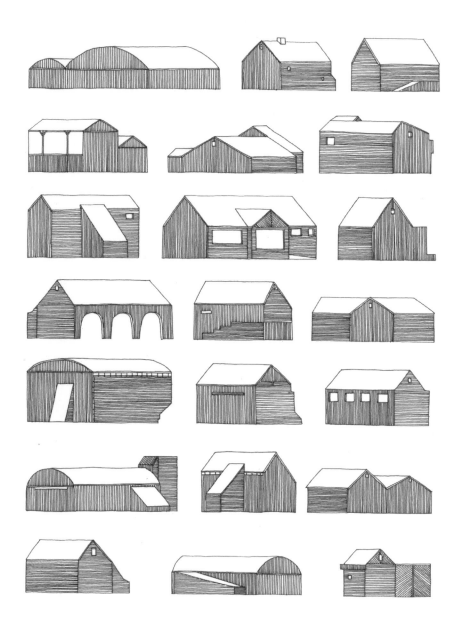

More Scenes

FROM THE

Rural Life

Verlyn Klinkenborg

drawings by **NIGEL PEAKE**

PRINCETON ARCHITECTURAL PRESS

NEW YORK

PUBLISHED BY
PRINCETON ARCHITECTURAL PRESS
37 EAST 7TH STREET
NEW YORK, NEW YORK 10003

VISIT OUR WEBSITE AT WWW.PAPRESS.COM

TEXT © 2013 VERLYN KLINKENBORG
DRAWINGS © 2013 PRINCETON ARCHITECTURAL PRESS
ALL RIGHTS RESERVED

PRINTED AND BOUND IN THE UNITED STATES BY THOMSON-SHORE
13 12 11 10 4 3 2 1 FIRST EDITION

EDITOR: JENNIFER LIPPERT
DESIGNER: PAUL WAGNER
TYPESETTING: BENJAMIN ENGLISH
DRAWINGS: NIGEL PEAKE

SPECIAL THANKS TO:
MEREDITH BABER, SARA BADER, NICOLA BEDNAREK BROWER,
JANET BEHNING, FANNIE BUSHIN, MEGAN CAREY, CARINA CHA,
ANDREA CHLAD, RUSSELL FERNANDEZ, WILL FOSTER, JAN HARTMAN,
JAN HAUX, DIANE LEVINSON, JACOB MOORE, KATHARINE MYERS,
MARGARET ROGALSKI, DAN SIMON, ANDREW STEPANIAN,
ELANA SCHLENKER, SARA STEMEN, AND JOSEPH WESTON OF
PRINCETON ARCHITECTURAL PRESS —KEVIN C. LIPPERT, PUBLISHER

LIBRARY OF CONGRESS
CATALOGING-IN-PUBLICATION DATA
KLINKENBORG, VERLYN.
MORE SCENES FROM THE RURAL LIFE / VERLYN KLINKENBORG.
—FIRST EDITION.
PAGES   CM
ISBN 978-1-61689-156-5 (HARDCOVER : ALK. PAPER)
1. NATURAL HISTORY—UNITED STATES—ANECDOTES.
2. COUNTRY LIFE—UNITED STATES—ANECDOTES.
3. NATURE. I. TITLE.
QH104.K577 2013
508.73—DC23
2012048882

TABLE OF CONTENTS

Prelude

———

When I was a boy—so these stories always begin—I spent a summer or two on my oldest uncle's farm in northwestern Iowa. It was the farm where my father was raised, and when I say I spent a summer or two there, I mean it's summer in all my memories of the place. The sun is hot on the cracked sidewalk leading down from the back door to the garden gate. The lilacs are long over. The grove is in full, ominous leaf.

But in photographs from my father's childhood it's often winter on the farm, and you can see in those photographs that the farmsteads in the distance have been joined, not separated, by the snow lying out on the fields. In the mudroom between the kitchen and the back door of the farmhouse, there were signs of winter even in the summers when I came to visit—enormous quilted coveralls, oil-stained at the cuffs, hung by the nape on hooks, like headless convicts all in a row. I knew that in winter the mud in the machine yard froze into unbelievable shapes, and I imagined, though I never saw it, that in the animal yards a fog sometimes lay dormant just above the backs of the cattle and that in the low houses where the chickens and pigs were kept the body heat was often oppressive, too liquid, too penetrating to tolerate for long.

On that farm were dairy cows, beef cattle, hogs, and both the laying and the cooking kinds of chickens. In my father's day there had been draft horses and sheep and geese and a goat or two as well. In other words, there had lived on that farm, at one time or another, bulls, steers, heifers, cows, calves, boars, sows, shoats, gilts, colts, fillies, geldings, mares, stallions, roosters, cockerels, hens, pullets, ganders, geese, goslings, rams, ewes, kids, and lambs. To each of these a breed name was also assigned, and each came in a color that could be named specifically, too. Some of these creatures also had personal names or an impromptu moniker that singled out a uniqueness, like a twisted horn or a hostile temperament. Of all these distinctions I was unaware. To me, even the difference between beef cattle and dairy cows was confusing at first.

But what wasn't confusing was the appeal of these animals, their power over my imagination. Even now, remembering those days nearly fifty years ago, I feel as though I'm looking past the horizon of my own life and into a painting by Constable. In the afternoons the dairy herd really did walk up an elm-shaded lane to a small, heavily trodden yard where they stood, meticulously aware of rank, waiting to be admitted to the milking parlor. The door would be slid back on its rollers, and one Holstein—always the same one— would make her way up the concrete ramp, swinging her rectangular head side to side as she came through the doorway, and then stepping along the barn to her stanchion with all the gravity of a town woman carrying a hot dish to a church supper. The air would soon be filled with barn swallows and the rhythmic, wheezing sound of automatic milkers.

Almost every day I found myself in a corner of the farmyard where the hog fence met the side of a granary. There, I could stand on one of the fence rails, being careful not to let my feet poke through to the other side, and I could look in on the life of pigs. Unlike the humid climate in the farrowing house next door, the atmosphere above the hogpen seemed to be filled with a molecular dust that held the light. There were bogs of mud in the low spots, as there are in every good hogpen. Yet this was an overwhelmingly dry place, the locus of an effete, hair-splitting rationalism espoused by thick-skinned philosophers who were also profound students of their own bodily comfort. The hogs lolled, they fretted, they batted their small eyes in the noontime light, they tried to convey their intelligence to one another, and to me, but failed.

All the wood in the pen as high as a pig's back was sanded smooth by their rubbing, which I didn't understand until the first time I stroked a mature boar's pompadour and realized that it was bristle. Cleanliness was a fetish among the humans in the milk room, where milk was filtered and cooled in a stainless steel tank, but it was no less a fetish among the hogs in the hogpen, though you had to look for it. Perhaps the cleanest spot on the whole farm—with apologies to my aunt Esther—was the hog trough between meals.

Its inner surface had been worn as smooth as ivory, as smooth as the trencher of an ascetic desert saint.

But it wasn't only the animals I noticed. It was also the humans among the animals. I was struck by my uncle Everon's fearlessness as he moved among the hogs, a fearlessness all the more remarkable because the hogpen had been represented to me as a terribly dangerous place. If a cow leaned too heavily on one of my cousins as he washed her bag before milking, he would simply thump her on her bony flank until she stood over.

I, who had grown up almost solely among people, expected to see human responses from these animals—resentment, outrage, peevishness. I didn't realize that the high disdain with which the cattle treated my cousins was a form of comedy or that the squealing of the hogs as my uncle moved among them was absurd self-dramatization. Do you suppose it was anyone's purpose, let alone the collective purpose of so many human generations, to breed so much dignity into farm animals? Who needed the intellect of the pig—its radical smartness? Who would set out to engender an eye as calm and unjudging, yet so capable of reflecting human self-judgment, as the eye you see in the head of a cow? Yet there they are, reminders of how utterly interwoven our fates have turned out to be. Farm animals are the product of coevolution with humans, or rather we're the product of coevolution with them. They are twinned with us. The word that applies to our link with them is neither *bond* nor *contract*: it is *covenant*.

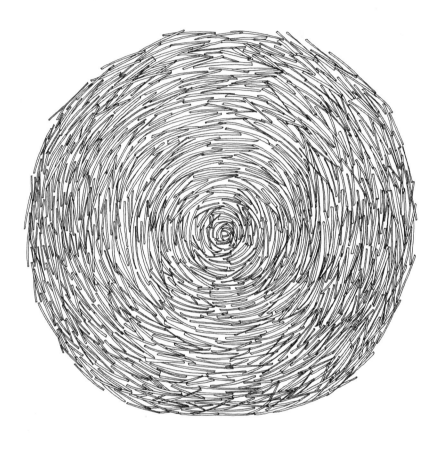

Year

ONE

April 5

A couple of months ago, I began getting up at four in the morning. I'd been reading a lot of William Cobbett (see Appendix), who believed that an hour in the morning was worth two in the afternoon. His idea of morning began at four. I don't usually imitate the lives of the writers I read—who would want to?—but for Cobbett, I was willing to make an exception. Once, when he was living in America, he met a wagon driver who was surprised at how much Cobbett got done during the day. A born explainer, Cobbett said, "I rise early, go to bed early, eat sparingly, never drink any thing stronger than small beer, shave once a day, and wash my hands and face clean three times a day, at the very least." The driver said, "That was too much to think of doing."

The dogs are thrilled to get up at four, because it means they can run around outside for a few minutes, have their breakfast, and be back in bed by four fifteen. For a few weeks in midwinter, I had the early morning darkness all to myself. The February sun seemed as lazy as that American driver. But week by week, the darkness has eroded, crumbling sooner and sooner every morning. And when dawn comes, the turkeys come with it.

They slip out of the woods in the middle pasture, a flock of twenty-some birds almost every morning. Some days they scratch their way slowly downhill, stopping here and there to wipe their feet the way the chickens do, wiping and suddenly staring at the ground to see what they've dislodged. Other days, the flock pours down the hillside, making their way to the spot where we spread cracked corn for them. In the early morning dusk, they look like low, hunched shadows, but as the light grows stronger it catches the copper and bronze and brass of their feathering. They move more sinuously than I'd ever imagined, their heads no larger than afterthoughts.

While winter lingered, it was hard to say just who was who in the flock. Spring settled that. I looked out in the pasture last Sunday morning and saw a tom turkey, fully inflated, bestriding a hen. He let himself deflate until he looked no different from the rest of his harem, who are slender birds. Then he blew himself up again. His body swelled and turned black before my eyes. He became globular. He turned blue and white in the face and red in the wattles. His wings fell to his side, and his primary feathers reached out to the ground. His tail fanned out and pivoted side to side as he shuffled forward, like a dancer in *The Mikado*. This was spring in all its glory, all its urgency. Then he trailed his way uphill toward the other male, and they dueled with each other as though they were dueling with a mirror. The hens kept after the cracked corn and never once looked up.

May 29

The other morning, I lifted a bale of hay from a loose pile of bales on the barn floor, and a fox jumped out from under it. The fox ran to the back of the barn and turned to watch me. It paced a few steps, uncertain, and then scurried under the door and out into the cold rain. It was a moment of pure transgression. All the old story lines broke apart—the ones about farmers and foxes and chickens—and just when the old story had been going so well. The fox had stolen a couple of our chickens. I had chased it off several times. It would lope up the hill in the middle pasture and sit on the ridge looking back at me, waiting for my next move. We hated to lose the chickens, and we hated the fox for taking them, but it was a conventional hatred, a part we knew we were supposed to play.

But there are no stories where the fox sleeps overnight in the barn on a bed of hay only a few feet from three horses in a run-in shed and a big, campaigning dog in his kennel. In all the traditional tales, the fox keeps its distance, a playful distance, perhaps, always respecting the invisible boundary between wildness and not-wildness. But the other morning, and on several mornings since, that fox ignored the boundary completely. The reason was obvious. It was dying from a terrible case of sarcoptic mange, an all-too-common disease caused by mites that infest the skin and cause severe inflammation and hair loss. Foxes with mange die from malnutrition or they freeze to death. The night had been frigid, with a blowing, soaking rainfall. Even the driest den would have been insufferable, and so the fox took refuge where I found it, in a burrow among hay bales in a dry barn.

My wife and I have been seeing foxes ever since we moved to this place. They skirted the far edge of the pasture at a businesslike trot, keeping a watch as if they knew that someday we'd give in and get chickens. But because they always kept their distance, they were platonic foxes, storybook foxes, with sharp muzzles and thick red fur and bushy tails and the gloss of wild health. They looked the way they were supposed to look, the way you imagine a fox looks. Every now and then, a fox would get hit by a car on the highway near our house, and one of us would wonder aloud if it was our fox and we would miss it in advance. And yet there was always another fox crossing the pasture.

But seeing this nearly hairless fox shivering at the barn door, its tail a pitiful file of vertebrae under bare flesh, I couldn't help thinking what a thin concept of wildness I'd been living with. The wild was where the archetypes lived, negotiating their survival. Each animal in the wild embodied its species, which means that it lived up to its portrait in *The Sibley Guide to Birds* or *Walker's Mammals of the World*. And though I had a rough idea of how creatures died in the wild, I'd never come across an animal driven out of the wild—across that taboo boundary and into my barn—by the extent of its suffering. The fox and I looked at each other, only a few feet apart. If it had been a dog, I could have helped it. But even the pity in my eyes reminded it that it had come too close.

September 23

I promised myself this year that I'd cut the thistles before they went to seed. But thistledown is in the air and lying in clumps at the base of the plants. Bumblebees are working urgently on the few thistle heads that still remain purple. For a few nights last week the sky caught a late glow behind the birch trees on the hill west of here. The light seemed to lift stray bands of clouds apart from the soft opacity of the blue behind them, a blue that memory alone can't do justice to. I go outside at night now just to admire how steep the temperature gradient has become, how the mercury seems to roll off the table once dark comes. Fall is here.

As it happens, I'm ready for fall, for once. Winter's hay is stacked in the barn. There's nearly enough firewood under cover and more right at hand. The old roof, which used to shed shingles the way our dogs shed hair, has been replaced. A brand-new furnace glistens in the cellar, awaiting only an electronic twitch from the thermostat upstairs. The new chickens have a new house next to the old chickens in the old house, and they're all secured in a fenced-in chicken yard against foxes, skunks, and weasels.

But the readiness runs deeper than that. Perhaps it's the suspicion, based on next to nothing, that this will be an early autumn. Suddenly the thought of autumn contains the promise of renewal I usually associate with spring. I have the feeling that a time of year is almost here when I'll again know just how to do what needs to be done. The sight of a school bus on the road suggests as much. So do the hardware store signs advertising wood-stove pellets for sale by the ton. The very briskness of the air seems to invite me outdoors and to work.

The temperature could well reach the 90s again, and summer could turn out to be deathless. The tomatoes may go on ripening for another month, or they could be bitten off in a hard frost tomorrow. There's no saying for sure, only a lingering sense of expectation, a hope for what lies ahead. For now, though, I walk past the pig house and look at the two young pigs nestled in the hay, and I find myself thinking not how hot they must be but how comfortable they look, ear-deep in bedding. They peer out at me, trying to judge whether I've got the feed bucket in hand. It's a narrow calculation on their part. They could get up, run to the door, and meet me at the fence. But if they stay where they are, piled next to each other, then nothing's lost if I just happen to be passing by.

October 31

The other day I noticed that I was walking down to the barn again. It sounds like a strange thing to notice because some days I walk down to the barn a dozen times without noticing it. My mind is on the tape measure I left on the workbench or the pile of logs cluttering up one side of the barn-yard or the way the horses watch me as I pass. Sometimes I get down to the barn and can't remember why I came. I never worry about those moments because there are so many things I could have walked down to the barn for that I'm sure to find something I need or need to do. All the tools live there as well as most of the things, like lumber and machines, that require tools sooner or later.

What I was really noticing that day was repetition. Apart from my trips to the barn, I'd also gotten on and off the tractor again and again, hitching up implements, opening and closing gates. Having grown up, like most Americans, in several different places, I often wonder what it would be like to live your life in just one place. It would mean, among other things, a depth of repetition I can barely imagine, and with it an attention to a subtlety of change that I can also barely imagine. When my wife and I first moved to this small farm, five years ago, I marveled almost every day at where we were and how we lived. It happens less than it used to, but when it does I feel like I'm walking along beside myself through a deep tunnel of habituation. Everything seems so familiar—the sugar maples and hickories, the brambles edging their way up from the rail fences, the steel fence posts leaning against the south face of the barn. It leaves me wondering how deep the reverie of living in only one place might really go—something I'll never know.

But even a little time in one place adds up. The chores never go quite the same one day to the next, because the wind is up or a truck backfires on the highway just as the horses were about to settle down. The seasons never proceed along quite the same path. Even something as categorical as the first frost comes in the most uncategorical ways. Some years it drops like death on the garden, blackening everything in sight. This year the frost waited and waited and then took only the morning-glory blossoms along the road before returning a week later and taking everything else. We live up here within the circumference of change, and every year the circle gets a little bigger.

Some things almost never change, of course. At dusk the chickens take to their roosts, my wife says, like ninth-grade girls at the high-school basketball game. We moved the pigs to fresh pasture last weekend, where they're hip-deep in still-green grass, but they still come loping over to visit when we walk out their way to check on their feed and water. And no matter how the day has gone, night never really begins until I walk up from the barn for the last time.

November 23

A couple of weeks ago I found a small settlement of lice on one of the pigs. I got out a stiff horse brush and gave that pig and her companion a serious brushing, which is one of the great joys in a pig's life. Then I raked out all the old hay in the pig house, closed the two pigs inside with a fresh hay-bale to tear apart, and hauled the house off to a different part of the pasture. I brush them every time I feed them now, and I haven't seen any lice since. I brush, and the pigs flop over on their sides and lie there, barely breathing, eyes closed, legs quivering with pleasure. I try to remember to watch just how much affection I let myself feel for them.

Affection is what we're really farming up here, farming it mostly in ourselves. Snow fell late the other afternoon, and as it thickened all around me, I realized that there's nothing more definite, more substantial in the world than the topline of a red pig against the snow. That's the kind of thought I carry around for days on end, until it explains something I didn't know I was trying to explain. I can always see the self-interest in the animals, and perhaps they see it in me, too. But there's always something else as well. The horses drift their flanks in my direction when they muzzle up to their hay. Is it just a scratch they want or do they have something to tell me? The chickens crowd up against the chicken-yard fence as I approach with the feed bucket, and I have to admit that this is small-town self-interest at its purest, the look of the line in front of the payroll office. Most of the birds flutter away from me as I toss out the cracked corn, and then they fall on it greedily.

But there's always one, a Speckled Sussex hen, that will let me pick her up and hold her under my arm. Why she lets me do that I have no idea. Why I like to is easy: the inscrutable yellow eye, the white-dotted feathers, the tortoise-shell beak, and, above all, the noises she makes. "No inhabitants of a yard," Gilbert White once wrote, "seem possessed of such a variety of expression and so copious a language as common poultry." I don't know what the Sussex is saying—perhaps only "put me down"—but it sounds like broken purring. She was a day-old chick on Memorial Day and now, like the rest of the flock, she's beginning to lay in the dark of winter.

A clean barnyard is its own reward, and the way the pigs exult at feeding time is itself a source of exultation. But there's still no chore as pleasing as gathering eggs. Most of the serious chicken books have charts that measure cost-effectiveness in the poultry yard, the ratios of feed to eggs to dollars and cents. None of the books say anything about gratification, even though a newly laid egg looks exactly like something for nothing.

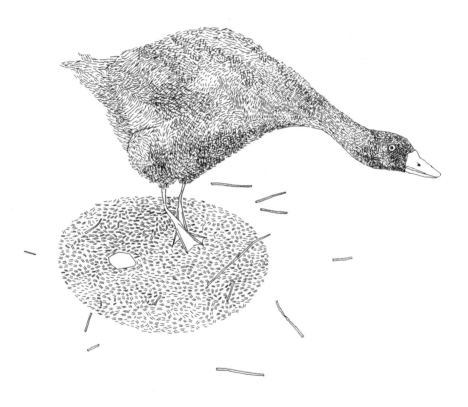

Year

TWO

February 8

For the past few weeks, I've been wondering, just how sharp can an icicle get? In early afternoon the icicles outside my office window lengthen themselves drip by drip, and I conclude that an icicle can only be as sharp as a drop of water. But in the morning, when the rising sun turns that curtain of ice lavender, the icicles look as sharp as needles. They're ridged along their stems like the spine of some ancient reptile, and yet they quiver in the wind. On the west side of the house, they reach from the ice dam in the eaves all the way down to the frozen deck. *Icicle* is too delicate a word for those constructions. They're the stalactites of a deep, hard winter in a cave of cold.

One morning last week, the temperature was twelve below zero at six A.M. A few days later the temperature at the same time was twelve above. To a thermometer, the difference between those two readings is twenty-four degrees. "An old-fashioned winter," you hear people saying, as though the snow were falling or the mercury dropping to the sound of sleigh bells. On a bright blowing day, the air fills almost invisibly with particles of snow that catch the sunlight. They look like the stars you see in your eyes when you stand up too quickly. At night the moon coasts through the sky like the source of cold, shedding its beams on a frozen world that the sun is powerless to warm when it finally rises.

All around us on this small farm we have the makings of a glacier. Every step we take compresses the snow a little more, and the pressure slowly turns new-fallen powder into ice, just the way it does in a real glacier. If spring comes, the last thing to melt will be the ski tracks along the fence line. When I walk across the pasture with Badger, a big, loping mix of Airedale and Australian shepherd, I can feel the history of this winter underfoot. Sometimes the snow crust from the Christmas storm bears me up so that I'm walking only calf-deep through the January snow, and sometimes I break all the way through to November. Badger skims across the snow, plowing it with his nose, until suddenly he holds a paw up, whimpering in the cold. Then we run for the house. In the chicken yard, the hens and roosters stand on one leg, then another as though they were marching in extreme slow motion down the alley between snowbanks.

On a twelve below morning, the ones really having an old-fashioned winter are the animals. Snow falls on the horses and never melts, because their hair is so thick. I imagine they look stoic, but I know that the idea of stoicism is all mine. Compared to a summer full of flies, a cold, hard winter with plenty of hay and fresh water is nothing to complain about. The pigs spend most of the day bundled in their house. They look naked, but they're like land-going whales, serene in a coat of blubber that keeps them warm through the worst of it. The animals see me come out of the house hooded, gaitered, mittened, and balaclaved and wonder what poor creature is this.

March 8

At last the starch has gone out of the snow. The hillsides and pastures have begun to slump. After a day of warm rain, a circular hollow forms at the base of every tree, and when the clouds drift apart, the afternoon heat the trunks absorb enlarges those hollows. Last week, a bare patch of ground opened up on a south-facing hill and along the south-facing ditches. The call of birds at the feeders began to change almost a month ago. You could tell that something had been added to the perfunctory songs of winter, even if you couldn't say just what it was. I never think which way the shadows fall as the sun moves across the morning sky, and yet I can't help noticing that the angles have changed. The shadows on the snow seem bolder, more definitive than they did a few weeks ago.

All of this is encouraging, and yet the garden catalogs lie in an undisturbed heap. The top layer of soil is still a good foot and a half beneath the snow, and the gardening zeal I should be feeling lies buried well below that, down where the beetle grubs doze. Every time I get ready to start making seed lists I should have made a month ago, we get another six inches of light powder, which hurls me backward in time. The thaw is as fickle as the blonde coyote my wife saw in the pasture the other day. It stood there boldly for a while, driving the dogs crazy, and then it vanished into the woods, leaving only its canine musk behind. Spring is going to have to come this year not with hints and prognostications but with a solid blow to the head, a slap across the face, a sharp poke in the ribs. Otherwise I won't believe it.

The surest sign of the changing season up here is the blacktop roads. In mid-January the highways seemed to be full of mild corrugations, ripples rather than bumps. The ripples sharpened into ridges over February, and as rain began to fall and freeze in the night, the frost began to shear off whole layers of asphalt. Just up the main road from our house, an axle-deep, car-length pit has opened. The road crews marked it with flashers, but only the locals know how spine pounding it really is, and by March we know every heave in our stretch of road. We weave up and down the highway, trying to keep out of the alignment shops, trying to avoid the bone-rattling shocks that nearly jump you into the other lane.

I keep a long list of things that need doing this spring mainly because keeping a list itself is an accomplishment. It's been too cold to build pasture pens for the chickens or a house for the ducks and geese that are coming in May. It's too cold to begin building a farrowing pen for the sows we have coming later this year and too early to start seeding the pastures. So I'm trying to figure out how to treasure these days of utter suspense, before the winter goes. There's never any telling what spring will bring.

March 18

I'd like to be able to hear the snow melting. A low whoosh would do, a sigh from the snowpack as it yields to the sun's insistence. I'd settle for a barely audible scream. The sound the snowmelt actually makes—the aural glittering of a dozen rills—is too diverting to suit my darker emotional needs. We had more than a hundred inches of snow this winter. It's not enough that it should melt. It should suffer as it melts. For the past five months I've walked back and forth to the barn over a sheet of polar ice. Now it groans as I step along it. I enjoy the sound. I send the horses up and down the ice sheet, then I follow in the tractor. I'm breaking up winter while I have the chance.

Reports say that robins are near and that red-winged blackbirds have arrived only a few miles south of us. The snowdrops and aconites lurk somewhere under the sagging drifts. Last Sunday—the first really warm day in months—the rain gauge in one of the garden beds suddenly reappeared, as if reporting for work. Plowed snow still stands in peaks all around us, looking more geographical than ever now, an Earth in miniature. Since the big melt began last weekend, those alps have broken apart into separate island continents, divided by a rising sea of gravel and matted sod. The runoff cuts deltas into the rotting ice. Whole Ganges flood the low spots.

I admire the animals we live with, their keenness, their toughness, the completeness of their sense of self. But what I really admire right now is their ability to shed. I stood in the barnyard the other evening with Nell, the mustang. She eats half what the other horses do and hairs up twice as thick. She's been rolling fretfully in the snow for the past couple of weeks. When I scratched her back I came away with whole fistfuls of red horsehair. By the time I finished scratching, the ground around her looked like the floor under a draft-induction barber's chair. She squared her legs so I could lean into the work.

This time of year makes me wish I could slough my skin entire, like a snake, just walk away from that old integument and step out new into the air. Humans thrive on metaphors of rebirth and regeneration, but it's the actuality of spring that overwhelms us. Every hour peels back another layer of snow and shrinks the dominion of ice. The ground gives and the sap streams upward. The finches molt into their mating colors. I walk out among it all hoping to change with the season, too.

March 24

A couple of weeks ago, I was in the agricultural midland of the San Joaquin Valley, where geometry rules. Almonds, grapes, English walnuts, and apples stood in careful ranks beneath the warm sun, the apples blooming, bees working the blossoms in every grove. Then I came home. The passengers on the plane let out a collective groan when we dropped below the clouds over Albany and saw a layer of ice over everything below us. The ice was just a fleeting reminiscence of winter, melted the next day. Winter's real reminder was the look of the land itself. The earth had been flattened by the cold compress of all that snow. The grass was leveled. Where leaves had blown up against the stone walls last October, there was now an indiscriminate mat of partial decomposition. Any natural order in the landscape had been eradicated.

You know what happens next. Spring comes at last. It makes a terrible story, because we've heard it so often, and yet it's the best story any of us know, always worth repeating. Last Sunday, the pasture in front of the house greened up. The pasture grasses reasserted their ascendancy. They climbed out of the dead thatch, through the overlay of dead leaves, and took on the color of hope itself. The earth seemed to blush green. You could practically smell the photosynthesis. All the markers of spring had come and gone—the snowdrops, the aconites, the sap lines where the neighbors collect sugarmaple sap.

After checking the fences, I turned the horses into the pasture. They trotted through the gate with the high-headed carriage they use when advancing into new ground, breasting the world around them. Then they ran, leaping and farting and kicking. They circled back around and lowered themselves into a flying hand gallop, almost squatting as they stretched out to speed, clods flying from their hooves. Then they stopped and bounced straight upward, all four feet in the air, the way a fox does when it pounces on a vole. They half-reared and feinted, pirouetted and bucked, rolled once or twice. And suddenly it was over. Remedy stood at the southwest fence line and sighed at the neighbor's horses across the road. Nell and Ida began to graze on the new grass. In a moment they lay flat out on their sides, basking in the sun, stone dead to all appearances.

I stood at the fence, watching the horses turn into their emotions. As much as I admire the rationality of horses—the quality that allows us to ride them—I admire just as much the way they come unhinged with something that humans would have to call joy. There are days when it feels as though we carry our bodies around with us, separate, confusing, demanding, the distant province of our being. But spring brings days when we can almost emulate the horses, when the body acts on its own thought, which it receives directly from the sun bearing down, the grass bearing up, the whole surface of place itself coming to life again.

May 18

"Living as we do, in the eternal NOW! it is but faintly that we can mirror on the mind, the existence of this country, as it was but a little while past." So writes a regular correspondent in the September 1, 1853, issue of *The Country Gentleman: A Journal for the Farm, the Garden, and the Fireside*, published by Luther Tucker in Albany, New York. Recently, a reader sent me an old bound volume of *The Country Gentleman*, which was published every Thursday and read far and wide. Since then, I've been putting off the eternal NOW! as best I can and contemplating the existence of this country as it was but a little while past.

It was a time, 150 years ago, when there were weekly cattle and grain markets in Albany, when Cooperstown reported regularly on its hops production, and when the Democratic Party in New York—the Hunkers and Barnburners—were divided into Hard Shell and Soft Shell tickets. Long forgotten breeds of animals filled barnyards and pastures. In those days a hungry person, coming in the right season upon a barn floor covered with apples, could choose from Pearmains, Pippins, Greenings, Lady Apples, Spitzenburgs, Maiden's-blushes, Baldwins, Tewksburys, Russets, and the wonderfully named Seek-no-furthers. At the state fair in Saratoga Springs, one exhibitor displayed 175 varieties of pears.

The America glimpsed through these pages was a rural laboratory, a place where farmers and gardeners experimented constantly. Butter, it's reported, tastes best when churned at fifty-two degrees. One reader describes the best way to strip osiers or basket willows. Another corrects the notion that "Minnesota is too cold for profitable farming." Yet another defends "scientific farming," which, he argues, is nothing more than "patience, perseverance, energy of character, and a determination on the part of the farmer that he will make his farming a 'living witness' to all reasonable men, that his theory and practice is a reality, and not a 'humbug.'"

But *The Country Gentleman* wasn't just farming news. It was a digest of events from around the world, with special attention to English farmyards, railroad accidents, and the news from California, which still lay a little more than three weeks away by the fastest ship. The paper reported the fact that "the celebrated Kit Carson has arrived in California from across the plains, with some nine thousand head of sheep." It excerpted uplifting speeches and always included a reflective essay called "The Fireside." It featured a literary column, which noted in one week the appearance of the sixth volume of Coleridge's works, the newest number of *Bleak House*, and a groundbreaking book called *The Hive and the Honey Bee* by Rev. L. L. Langstroth.

I can't help imagining the day each week when *The Country Gentleman* arrived by mail. (In 1853, when it began, the paper cost $2 a year.) Mr. B. V. French in Braintree, Massachusetts, would check to make sure his ad for Devon cows had been properly printed. Another reader would notice the strange statistic—ironic, of course—that "there are eight hundred ways of earning a living in New-York. The number of expedients for getting your living earned for you by others, has not been mentioned in any census." And I, a reader coming a century and a half later, am struck above all by a set of figures derived from the census. "The village, town, and city population of the United States, is 4,000,000. The rural population reaches 19,263,000." That, as much as anything, defines the difference between now and then.

June 18

When I first moved to the country, a realtor showed me a grand old farmhouse with an attached barn. The realtor was dreaming to think that I could afford it. But the memory of that place has stuck with me, especially the thought of walking through what looked like a closet door off the kitchen and being swallowed by the cavernous maw of a beautiful, well-worn dairy barn. If you owned the place, I suppose the surprise of it would wear off one day. But to me it felt like walking out the kitchen door and directly into the tree-tops. Like most New Yorkers, my first thought, then, was "convertible space." The reason I still think about that place is for the pleasure of having the animals so close, so collectively, so cooperatively housed.

There's a house and barn where I live now, attached by a road. And what I've discovered over the years is that unless you also have a machine shed, you don't actually have a barn. Even more than animals, machines require shelter. The local farmers I admire pride themselves on never letting their equipment spend a night outside. That means machine sheds with sliding doors. There's no such thing as a free-range tractor, at least not in the northeast, whereas most of the animals we raise do best when free-ranging. But they all require some housing, even the ducks and geese.

As time passes here, we're accumulating a lot of small animal shelters, most of which I've built myself. It begins to look like musical chairs. Until the new pigs come next month, the ducks and geese, only a few weeks old, are borrowing the pig house. The old and new chicken houses are vacant now so the winter chicken yard can get some rest. The birds are out on pasture, which they share with the horses.

The first thing I built when we got chickens was a chicken tractor—a small cage designed to be moved daily to fresh grass. I read the books and built what I saw there. It was way too heavy and not very chicken-like. I took it apart the other day and rebuilt it according to my knowledge of chickens, not books. It comes as a surprise to realize that I can now predict what chickens want in the way of housing, but it's true, as far as it goes. I show

25

them just what's in their price range, nothing more. How far down this road I've gone became plain when I realized, with satisfaction, that I'd built the new chicken tractor entirely out of scrap. The chickens seem proud of it, too.

Domestic animals are the ones we build houses for. Wild animals make their own arrangements, consulting only their own needs. The point was brought home to me a couple of days ago. I'd been waking up in the middle of the night, wondering just how to refashion that chicken tractor. I'd worked up a dozen different versions in my head. One morning last week, my wife and I walked around the garden, just to see what had grown in the night. We stopped to admire a Korean fir she got me for my birthday last year. Whenever I stand next to it, I feel like Paul Bunyan, as tall as the trees I survey. Together Lindy and I looked down into the boughs and there, in a fork near the trunk, was a bird's nest with four tiny azure eggs inside, a demitasse of horsehair, grass, and lichen, perfectly wrought and all from scrap.

July 27

I don't think of wasps as particularly domestic creatures. They cause in me, and in most people, a swift revulsion—not only a fear of getting stung but of getting stung by an insect that looks so alien. But while I was fixing up the pig house the other afternoon—the new pigs were waiting in the back of the pickup—I saw a pair of paper wasps delicately dabbing at the edges of a small nest hanging from a single stem under the pig-house eave. Something about their movements, embroidering their way around the circumference of cells, struck me as downright *broody*, which is a word that has recently come into common use up here. The wasps and I were at work on the same task, fixing up the place, and I've concluded that they're not as alien as humans think. According to one researcher, paper wasps recognize each other not only through the chemical scent on their exoskeletons but through visual identification of facial patterns.

Nature seems to offer the same two lessons to humans over and over again. The first one is this: no matter what form life takes, no matter how alien a creature appears at first, it turns out in the end to be close genetic kin, with similar concerns as ours. The other lesson is best summed up by the animal behaviorist, Elizabeth Tibbetts, who studied the recognition behavior of paper wasps. "They are more sophisticated than we thought," she concluded. That's always the conclusion. Some people seem to think that more sophisticated wasps must mean less sophisticated humans, as if behavioral sophistication were a zero-sum game. In fact, there's plenty to go around.

Someday, as a measure of our own sophistication, we'll come to the blanket conclusion that all creatures are more sophisticated than we thought.

The stripes on the paper wasps are the color of midsummer, a shade that in some lights is golden, in others almost orange, like mullein and asters and black-eyed Susans. Mid-July comes and the palette of blossoms shifts to hotter colors, as if in their vividness they were reflecting the sun. My own wishfulness makes these weeks seem a perpetual season, a part of the year when time almost pretends to stop. Out by the mailbox, the Queen Anne's lace has come into bloom, flat white discs of galaxies spinning far out in space. It seems as if those blossoms have always been there, but that's the memories of other summers filling in for the shortness of this one.

What makes this summer different around here, besides the fact that this year's pigs are real talkers, is the presence of a broody hen. The natural eagerness to sit on eggs has been bred out of most chickens, but we have one hen from an old breed—a Dorking—who will sit on anything even vaguely egg-shaped. Three weeks ago we set her on a clutch of eggs from another old breed—an odd number for good luck. She has barely moved since then, except to reverse direction in her nest box and shift the eggs beneath her. Her comb has gone pale, and she's looking a little bloodshot around her beautiful amber eyes. When I stop by to check on her—waiting for that twenty-first day—she looks out at me with surprising certainty. To me it looks as though she knows she's in the home stretch.

August 7

Look deep enough into the history of almost any Iowa town and you come to the primordial nineteenth-century tale of breaking the prairie, as if it were a herd of wild horses. Breaking the prairie took special plows and large teams of draft animals. The first step was skinning the earth, turning over the sod, exposing the fertile soils that lay beneath it. But what really broke it was ending the cycle of wildfires and then draining the prairie, ditching the sloughs and laying tile to carry away water that was good for wildlife and thick stands of native vegetation but not so good for alien row crops. In a modern Iowa soybean field in midsummer, it's easy to see that fire isn't much of a threat anymore. What's hard to see is the drainage network that underlies much of the arable land in the state. Farmers are adding to it even now.

The Iowa prairie was well and truly broken. Eighty percent of the state was once prairie and now it's all but gone, replaced by what used to be mixed farms and are now corn and soybean fields. A couple of weeks ago, on a beautiful windswept day, I turned off the blacktop in Cherokee County, in northwest Iowa, onto a gravel road not far from the tiny town of Larabee. Down that road, two small pieces of land interrupted the symmetry of soybeans and corn. They totaled two hundred acres, a little more than half the average size of an Iowa farm last year. A sign identified this as the Steele Prairie Preserve. Another said, "Do Not Spray." There was a wide spot in the road with room for one car. That was it, except for the wind and what that small prairie remnant implied.

Standing at the edge of that swath of unmowed, unsprayed, untilled vegetation was like visiting a small body of water preserved to commemorate what an ocean looked like before it was drained. Two hundred acres barely permits the word *prairie*, which implies a horizon-wide stretch of grassland. And yet for all its meagerness, the Steele Prairie Preserve suggests the grandeur to which it had once belonged. It had been kept alive by a family that cut wild prairie hay from it well after their neighbors were planting hybrid corn and alfalfa. Biological complexity and diversity sound like abstractions, until you see them flourishing beside the monotony of a soybean field, a whole county of soybean fields. These acres could only hint at the way real prairie would reflect the wind—catching its oceanic sweep— and yet the wind was different here. Instead of the rustling newsprint sound of corn and soybeans, there was a breezy hush that seemed to merge with the birdsong rising from the community of tallgrass plants. It was a richer note than anything you hear in a pasture or a hayfield, if only because no one ever lets a pasture or hayfield grow so tall.

There are tiny stands of native prairie all across the Midwest, in graveyards, along rail lines, in parks, and in floodplains. Most are only a few acres, and it takes work to keep them from being invaded by nonnative plants. In states where the prairies were richest, like Iowa, those last stands serve as much to remind people of oxen shouldering the plows forward as to preserve the species that once made up the great sweeps of grasses and forbs. It's always been easier to see the wealth of the black soil that lay under the prairie than the wealth of the prairie itself. I saw that soil freshly turned by a moldboard plow at a threshing bee in Granite, Iowa, and its blackness was exhilarating.

There's no getting back to the prairies, of course. The time for preserving a greater share of them slipped away even as modern agriculture was coming into its stride. The great figure in preserving Iowa's prairies was Dr. Ada Hayden, and she died in 1950, after canvassing the state for remnants worth setting aside. And though the prairie restoration movement has gathered force, it takes more than the right collection of species and the best of intentions. It means regenerating the elemental forces of nature, unleashing a biological synergy that dwarfs what we usually mean by that word. To this day the Steele Prairie Preserve is maintained by fire. Standing at its edge, I wished I could be there to see it burn.

August 23

I don't remember when I gave up. Perhaps I still haven't. But so far, this goes down as the summer I grew no vegetables. Potatoes volunteered and so did some garlic and chives and a single cornstalk. Last year's radishes did all they could. The blueberries set fruit copiously this year, but then all they ask is acidity and mulch. In mid-May I spent the better part of two weeks preparing the soil, creating a seed bed in the upper garden and tilling the lower one. Then the deluge came. Lindy worked in the perennial beds in a rain-suit for the entire month of June. I discovered I'm a fair-weather gardener. I want to plant my garden seeds in rows, not runnels. Still, I notice that local gardeners who weren't deterred by endless rain are reaping the benefits now.

Every day the vegetable plots nagged at me. One of them still does, its perfect vacant tilth preaching a stern lesson about timeliness. But the lower garden has taken matters into its own hands. It has rioted. Every weed seed that lay dormant has sent up a skyrocket of growth. If you can just get past the ethical question—these are weeds in what was a vegetable garden last year—there's real beauty in the confusion. Mullein spikes tangle with branching thistles. A hummingbird browses the jewelweed thickets. Bees clamber everywhere, rummaging in and out of blossoms. A hops vine has run its way to the top of a column of motherwort and dangles there, with nowhere higher to go. The goldenrod are just coming into their late summer color, looking almost cultivated in their elegance compared to the rest of this menagerie. The vegetation has locked arms. It says, "Keep Out." And so I do.

This mess has reminded me of the true generosity of a well-kept vegetable garden. By late August, tomato plants or cornstalks or cucumber-vines are making offerings everywhere you turn, saying, "Here," presenting perfectly wrapped packages of ripeness. Compared to the bristling self-determination of a full-grown burdock, a tomato plant dangling ripe fruit looks a little over-eager. Can a bed of mesclun really be as ingenuous as it seems?

Of course, the tangle in the lower garden is no more natural than the perfectly ordered beds of a true potager, and no more unnatural either. It merely announces the absence, the expiration of human labor. I think about reconquering that plot, and the thought of it wears me out. But I have a pair of allies who will make all the difference in the end. In a week or two, long before the worst of the weeds have gone to seed, I'll move the pig house into that garden and turn the boys loose. It will be a joy to see them doing what they do best.

October 27

One of the Saxony drakes in our flock—five months old—died last Sunday, on a bright fall afternoon. Why he died, I don't know. Not a feather had been ruffled. No blood or broken bones or signs of distress. He lay in the duckpen, relaxed, half-hidden by nettles, while the rest of the flock marched back and forth across the lawn, as they always do, stopping to agitate the grass with their bills and probe the roots to see what's stirring. The only thing unusual was death itself, which lies invisible on the other side of each of the creatures on our small farm, and of us, too, of course.

The ducks have never liked being picked up, not even when they were a day old and living under warm lights in the basement. They have a sense of personal autonomy and flock coherence that's much stronger than it is in chickens, who are wily individuals in comparison. So I took the opportunity to hold the Saxony under one arm and look him over closely. It made me think of the days, long ago, when being a serious ornithologist meant being a good shot.

I opened the webs on the Saxony's feet, which had relaxed in death— as if on the forestroke while paddling—and ran my fingers over his covert feathers and through his deep down. I could see the hornlike reinforcement on the prow of his bill, called the bean, and the fringing along the back of the bill—a kind of bird baleen—that allowed him to filter water. I could feel the sudden, mournful density of his weight. His massive bluff gray head and neck had lost its arch in death, but some strange new dignity had come to him, too. The inherent comedy of his everyday manner—the way his feet waddled around his barnyard keel, his depth of body—had been replaced by the staggering intricacy and beauty of his feathering seen up close.

We often think of stone as the great revealer of time, the preserver of geological patterns and fossils that teach us how ancient this world really is. But even something as ephemeral as the finger-thick down on this drake's belly and the feel of subcutaneous fat beneath it seemed utterly suffused with time, the evolutionary time needed to create them. In our lives, we make steady, categorical distinctions between the present moment and the past, as if the two could never meet. And yet the beautiful brown cape on this Saxony's shoulders, each feather tipped with a band of white, carried the deep past of evolution directly into the present, where I stood with the drake under my arm, watching the leaves whirl away from summer into fall, while the rest of the flock grazed nearby as if this were just another good day to be a duck.

November 28

Life is full of things you'd never think of doing until someone tells you not to. Casting pearls before swine is one of them. I've never owned pearls, but I do own a pair of swine. They're handsome pigs, energetic, cheerful, full of advice when I show up with the dinner bucket. My wife has no pearls either, but over the past few months she and I have cast lots of things before our swine—fresh apples, pineapple rinds, buckets of roasted peanuts, bruised melons, a whole pickup load of spoiled sweet corn. The pigs snuffle it all up. I'd like to think that if we had pearls in the house, we'd toss them into the pigpen just to see what happens. What stops us is having been taught all these years never to cast pearls before swine. And no pearls.

Even as a child I knew that the "pearls" in the phrase were really one's own good qualities or talents. Don't waste them on the rabble was the gist of the saying. But I lived in the Midwest, where something that sounds like a farm saying usually was a farm saying. Swine may be a figure of speech in other parts of the country, but where I grew up there were many more swine than metaphors. The pigs I knew best belonged to my uncle Everon. When I was young he seemed like a stern man to me, sterner and sterner the closer we got to the pigpen. He wasn't about to throw pearls before swine or let me do so either. Keeping pearls away from the pigs was just practical advice—the start of a long list of things to keep out of the pigpen, including batteries, lightbulbs, and baby brothers.

It's worth remembering that this warning about pigs and jewelry first appears in the Sermon on the Mount. It dates from a time when swine ran free and when, just walking down to the mailbox, you could find yourself cornered by pigs demanding pearls. In those days, casting your pearls before swine might have been a good idea.

I've tried over the years to apply this saying to humans and their behavior, to cultivate the cautiousness and the reserve it suggests. But it never really works. At its heart that saying contains an arrogance I'm not really comfortable with. Separating the sheep from the goats is one thing when it comes to humans. Separating the sheep from the goats from the swine is something else entirely. I'm just not up to it. Especially because the saying seems to take it for granted that pigs are nasty, brutish animals, incapable of appreciating the finer things in life.

But I've found swine to be tolerant creatures, trusting, sincere, and completely honest. They repay kind treatment—an extra apple, a bellyrub, a squirt from the water hose on a hot summer day—with real joy. And if they mainly associate me with breakfast and dinner, that's my fault. I don't spend nearly enough time in the pen hanging out with them, trying to see things as they see them. They see me coming and, frankly, I look like a bushel of pig feed. But the moral is really this. You don't want to hoard your pearls unless you're sure they're pearls. And you don't want to decide that the world is full of swine until you're sure you know what you mean when you say "swine." I'd be proud to think that my pigs saw only the best of me.

December 6

By 2:30 the other morning, the moon had dropped well down in the west, behind the birches. Just enough snow had fallen to reflect the moon's light. While the dogs ran around the pasture, hoping it was already breakfast-time, I looked at the stars, which were washed out by the vaporous glow in the sky. It was almost as light as it is on a dark December noon, when the clouds look like snow and the chickens are already thinking of roosting. By early afternoon, the two turkeys, Tom and Pearl, flutter up to their high roost above the chicken-yard fence. The horses are already giving me significant looks over the pasture gate. The ducks have laid a trail of cuneiform footprints back to the duckpen through the snow. My day too contracts with the natural light. I become just one of the animals.

For the past couple of weeks, a flock of wild turkeys has wandered down from the woods just as I go out to feed in the mornings. They make a beeline for the corral where the pigs last lived. So do the chickens and the ducks and Tom and Pearl when I turn them out. The ducks and geese always cluster together. The chickens work the fringes, darting in and out among the wild turkeys. Pearl looks like a pale version of the wild hens that surround her. Tom spends the better part of the morning completely and futilely inflated, so dizzied by the presence of so many females that he can't remember to eat. Food is the one thing on the wild turkeys' minds.

32

And yet every afternoon at dusk the wild turkeys glide back up the hill, and Tom and Pearl walk back into the chicken yard, reenacting the drama of domestication. I watch it with a feeling of gratification. Some mornings, Pearl drops down from her roost and lands outside the chicken yard. She waits till I open the door and then walks straight in, piping an electric song. This is something more than domestication on her part. It's courtesy. I wonder if she can feel the tug to wildness and whether day's end comes like a surrender to her. All I know is that this morning she dropped down outside the fence again, and when I last saw her she was walking up the hill in the midst of the wild turkeys. She gave me a look as if to say she'd be back before dark.

December 16

Like half of America, I came down with the flu recently. That means quarantine at the top of the house in a spare bedroom with a view of the sugar maple and the pasture beyond it, where the horses are standing in falling snow. I was raised to believe that sleep is a sovereign remedy for everything but death, so I drift between waking and sleeping, visited mostly by one of the cats, who likes the third floor—a converted attic—as much as I do. I wake just long enough to see the snow falling, and to judge how sick I feel, before drifting off again. The pleasure of it—waking only long enough to know you're dozing—confirms something one of Ishmael's shipmates said in *Moby Dick*: "Damn me, it's worth a fellow's while to be born into the world, if only to fall right asleep."

Wet snow blows in from the east, and then after a day or so, the weather pivots and a hard wind strikes up from the west, gusting from its heels. That's when I can feel the age of this house. The windows rattle. The attic exhaust fan clanks open and shut. The mudroom takes on a chill that lasts till spring. Sometimes when I wake in the middle of the night, I go down to the kitchen and feed the woodstove. But in quarantine, I might as well be sleeping on the roof. That's how far away the woodstove feels. Every now and then the furnace fires up as if to say to me that it's on my side.

The horses stand blanketed in snow, and from time to time they lope around the pasture just to listen to the icicles on their flanks. It takes a foul night to drive them under cover. The wild turkeys stroll down out of the woods and along the driveway and right up to the mudroom door, as if they were going to knock and come in to get warm. I have yet to see the weather that makes any difference to the ducks or geese. Only the chickens shy away in the snow. They stay snug on their roosts, darning their socks, and, for some reason, our tom turkey has decided to join them.

The wind rises, snow twists in the air, and the old honey locust on the edge of the garden cracks and booms like it's being detonated from within. I expect it to go over any minute. Everyone finds the lee of something to stand in until the wind drops again. As for me, I lie here in the lee of the flu, astonished by the health, the vigor of everything around me, including the crows that huddle on the sugar maple outside, dark clumps of shadow in a white world.

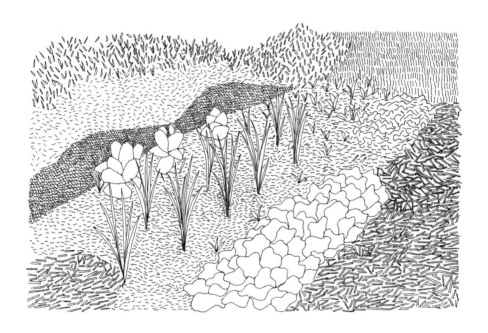

Year

THREE

❧

March 9

You don't really notice a skunk's smell. It notices you. It loiters in the air, nearly sentient, waiting to knock you down, strong enough to make you wonder how a skunk can smell anything but itself. I walked into a fresh scent on my way to the barn one morning just past. There were no tracks or signs of digging in the snow. But in the warmth of that afternoon I heard the sound of bees, and I saw where the sound was coming from. The skunk had attacked a corner of one of the hives in the night. Its claws hadn't done much damage, only enough to open a crack. The bees were trying to patch it with propolis. They wouldn't have been out without the skunk's provocation. But there was the answer to one of winter's most pressing questions: Are the bees still strong in the hive?

A farm is naturally a place of bold scents, though most of them seem to have been bottled up by the sharp cold of this past winter. A thaw releases them. Late winter smells like a very old barnyard. It suddenly hits me how long it's been since I cleaned the henhouse. But the real sign of a February thaw is the skunks. They begin to come out into the margins of daylight in the same week the highways start to heave with frost. To drive around here is to feel your way along a lurching roadway from one slick of skunk scent to the next. Sometimes I pass a skunk just changing its mind at the edge of my headlights. More often I see those that kept right on going and didn't make it. They leave in the air an immortality all their own.

I knocked together the corner of the hive that had been clawed apart. A couple of bees spurted out and droned around my head. But they weren't serious. This is a gentle colony. Whether the skunk found them so gentle I don't know. I've heard that a skunk will disturb a hive not to get at the honey but to eat the bees that mob him. I've also heard that a skunk's smell can travel well more than a mile downwind. They say, in fact, that skunks in winter don't really hibernate. They den up, five or six females with one male, and sleep deeply through the cold weather. The least thaw rouses them to hunger and desire. They stir from their nests and amble down to the road, as if drawn there by something only skunks can know. They wait in the night, trying to decide whether the highway selects for boldness or hesitation.

April 9

Until a few days ago, the biggest tree on our farm was a century-old honey locust at the edge of an embankment overlooking the lower pasture. There are other big trees on this place—hemlocks and hickories and one old sugar maple that looks like something out of *The Faerie Queene*. But a few years ago the honey locust began dropping major limbs after windstorms, and with each dropped limb it seemed to reach higher and higher into the sky. What kept it standing I don't know. The core of the trunk had decayed into dirt-red frass. The tree leaned into the northeast, where the worst of our storms begin, and perhaps that made a difference. In the end, it was only the strength of the wood itself, a kind of cellular will, that kept it standing.

But last Wednesday two men in a white pickup pulled into the driveway. It was a quiet consult. They walked around and around the tree while Lindy and I watched. "One scary tree," the older man said. The younger started his chainsaw and let it idle on the ground while he walked down to the spot where we hoped the tree would fall. With the saw he nipped off the Virginia Creeper vines running up the trunk, each one as thick as my upper arm. He inscribed a few lines in the bark at the base of the tree where he wanted to make his incisions. Then the saw began to scream in earnest.

The horses watched from the round pen in the big pasture, locked away from this sudden change in the scenery. The chickens lined up at the edge of their yard and watched, too. It was a still day, but suddenly in the branches high above us there was an abrupt lurch—more earthquake than gale.

38

Then a pause. The locust began to give in to gravity, and fell. I don't even remember the sound. I expected the earth-shaking whump I'd felt when I'd felled sounder trees myself. But the locust had been ready to come apart, and come apart it did. The three dimensions of its crown crashed into two dimensions on the ground, leaving its silhouette scattered across the garden. I wrote a check, thought again about buying a log splitter, and went inside to work.

That afternoon I climbed the locust where it lay. The stump was now nothing more than a hollow atoll surrounded by a grass-green sea where waves of snowdrops were cresting, about to break. I peered inside the riven trunk and found a red desert of dry, tunneled heartwood, adult beetles entombed at the end of each tunnel waiting for the fullness of spring to chew their way out. I pulled a squirrel's nest out of the bole, high up. Above me the crows sat in the hickory tops, considering this fresh hole in the sky.

April 21

In the Northeast the word *bench* doesn't mean much as a description of landscape. The terrain is simply too tangled and wooded, the views too short. But the word comes into its own in Montana. The mountains there dominate the view, their ranges rising almost naively against the sky: the Madison, the Gravelly, the Tobacco Root. Where the mountains stop, the benches begin, great alluvial fans that shelve outward from the base of the mountains to the middle of a broad, shallow valley. There, a river is trenching its way between the benches.

I drove not long ago along the edge of the enormous bench that sweeps westward from Ruby Mountain and overlooks the Beaverhead Valley. Down in the thick of the valley, the river seemed to be slowly choking itself, twisting this way and that, hiding its true extent in bogs and alders and brush. If you looked at Beaverhead Rock, you could almost imagine the valley as it looked when Lewis and Clark came through. They found that "beaver were basking in great numbers along the shore."

But up on the bench, flocks of sandhill cranes courted each other in the shadow of giant irrigation rigs, which were dwarfed by the ground they had to cover. Tractors were working the earth into a dustlike tilth, and in the ranchyards rose great mounds of seed potatoes, which were being loaded into semitrucks bound for Idaho and planting. The bench beyond—that broad swath of dry grass—created an optical illusion. Without a point of reference—a line of utility poles, a house in the near distance—it was almost impossible to judge how far the bench ran. It was just short of prairie, open range for the wind.

Down in the pastures, closer to the river, it looked as though the sky had rained calves a few weeks earlier. Once every day or so, a rancher would drive a tractor through his pastures, pulling an implement that shaves hay off a round bale. The mother cows and their calves stood along that line of hay, grazing, and they bedded down along it, too. From the sky you would have seen great underscorings of black cattle all across the county. A couple of fences away, Angus bulls waited placidly for the coming weeks, when their call will come.

We always think of ferocity when we think of bulls. But in herds of their own sex, they can be perfect gentlemen. While fishing one day, I watched a group of bulls make their way down to a triangle of fence that reached into the river. There was room for only one bull at its apex, and they took turns edging into that corner and backing out again so the next bull could drink. I wondered if they noticed the tiny mayflies—the Baetis—making their way downstream in the film.

At some point, most anglers begin to wonder why they fish. Over the years the reasons pile up into a beaver dam of arguments, tangled this way and that, some more reasonable than others. I've come to a point in my fishing life where I simply like walking down the drainage—seeing where the streambed goes, where the tributaries enter, where the view rises from. Standing in the low spots is a good way to see the world. Nearly everything comes down to the water sooner or later.

And along the river, the landscape shrinks. All that's left is the rim of the benches and the mountains beyond them. After a day on the river, the world seems to be reduced to its essentials—light along the peaks and motion in the stream itself. But then daylight begins to tail off and, after hours of hard fishing, you start to see motion wherever you look, as though the river had gone still and a current were now flowing through the sagebrush and the rocks beyond. The only way to stop that illusory flow is to go back up onto the bench where nothing seems to move except the sandhill cranes flirting in the distance.

May 21

About a month ago, a Phoebe began building a nest of moss on a light fixture under the eave above the kitchen door. It looked like futility. Every time the door opened, she fluttered away, and there always seemed to be as much moss on the threshold as there was on the nest. But now the nest is done, and she broods happily, only her beak and tail visible. Sometimes on a still evening, her mate perches on a stone pillar at the edge of the deck, tail dipping up and down. He looks over at me, where I sit, and then flutters upward to take a bug in midflight. I go in after the bats are on the wing. I look up at the nest just above my head, and I close the door as quietly as I can.

Under the old chicken house, the Ancona duck is brooding, too. It's hard to know when she found time to build a nest. As a flock, the ducks and geese walk a mile a day. I'd always thought of them as aquatic creatures, but then I'd never seen a drake run after his mate in breeding season. All winter the poultry live in a fenced run. When bare ground shows through the snow, we throw open the doors for what we've come to call a "poultry holiday." But now the grass is green, and every day is a holiday. The ducks and geese waddle off down the drive, into the lower pasture, around the back of the barn, over the high ridge into the middle pasture, where one of the quarter horses—Ida—herds them back down the hill to their yard. Meanwhile, the Ancona sits, deep in a caldera of down and straw. A Wyandotte hen sits in a galvanized tub in the new chicken house, too. She has been fooled by an old glass nest egg, put there to show the young hens where to lay.

The phoebe's chicks will be altricial—hatched nearly naked and immobile, with eyes closed. They'll need the constant attention and feeding of both parents—and we'll need to stop using the kitchen door. The ducklings will be precocial, alarmingly alert, downy, and dependent on their mother mainly for heat. We got our annual lesson in precocial last week when the baby chicks we'd ordered arrived from Iowa. When Lindy picked them up from the post office, they were a day old, still ingesting the last of the yolk. We dipped their beaks in water and turned them loose on the floor of a water tank with a heat lamp overhead. They rocketed around the tank as fast as they could run—stretching their legs after the flight. A fly cruised over the tank, and all the chicks looked up, hoping it would fly a little lower.

June 1

For nearly as long as there have been humans, there have been laws defining the status of animals, reserving them for certain uses and for certain people. Those laws, some of them unbelievably cruel, are meant to pattern human behavior without any reference to an animal's autonomous right to exist. If the game laws implicitly acknowledged the value of a pheasant's existence, it was only as an item of human property. America's hunting laws have the same idea behind them, if more democratically expressed.

It's a dramatic shift to put laws on the books that assert an animal's property in itself and protect it from any human use whatsoever. The Endangered Species Act is an extraordinary monument to human self-awareness and our awareness of the world around us. It says that for certain species—determined by vulnerability, not by any obvious human value—we're willing to place their interests ahead of ours. As an act of conscience, it's hard to beat.

What got me thinking about this was an endangered sea turtle, a Kemp's ridley female. She lay in the back of a pickup truck on Padre Island, Texas, a few miles north of the national seashore. Her shell was nearly circular, almost exactly the size of a manhole cover, and there was an unexpected concavity on her left side. The truck bed was lined with a blue plastic tarp, which kept slipping under the turtle as she tried to climb out. She had just laid a nest full of eggs, and as soon as the scientists on hand had taken a blood sample and inserted a tag, the turtle would be lifted out of the bed and released on the beach—bound for the Gulf of Mexico a few dozen yards away.

An endangered species sounds like an item of arbitration, a bureaucratic pigeonhole. But there was nothing abstract about this turtle. She showed a painful determination to get out of the truck bed and back onto the sand. It had taken the same determination to stride out of the surf, walk across the sea-wrack—a ridge of seaweed cluttered with plastic debris and stranded Portuguese men-of-war—and lay her eggs up the beach. A marine biologist lowered her from the bed onto the sand. I helped hold her in place while the final tag was inserted. I kneeled directly in front of her and placed my hands on what I thought of as her shoulders. She drove against me, the last human obstacle between her and the gulf. The wind blew, and behind me the surf roared. Then it was time to let go.

When she moved at last, she marched briskly down the sand, between a double cordon of onlookers—beachcombers and tourists who had happened upon the scene. The turtle rested for a few minutes, then struck out again. She nosed her way over the tidal debris, and then the biologist lifted her over a driftwood log that lay in her path. From there it was a clean break for the sea, down the slick sand and into the pooling backwash of the surf. I watched until the crest of her shell had gone under and the last swirls caused by her powerful strokes had been gathered up in a new in-rush of water.

It was one of those rare moments when you suddenly realize, viscerally, the profound otherness—the astonishing sufficiency—of nature.

Habitat barely suggests the convergence between the turtle and the sea she re-entered. It was more than aptness, more than fittedness. It seemed, at the moment of reentry, to have the force of an atomic bond.

June 18

The most famous line in Voltaire's *Candide* is the final one—"We must cultivate our garden." That is Candide's response to the philosopher Pangloss, who tries again and again to prove that we live in the best of all possible worlds, no matter what disasters befall us. Maybe so, Candide says, but we must cultivate our garden. Ever since *Candide* was published in February 1759, that line has seemed to express a reluctance to get involved, an almost quietistic refusal to be distracted by the grand chaos of earthly events. That reading might make sense, if Candide hadn't already lived through a lifetime of woe. In fact, that line is the summation of Candide's wisdom: no matter how you choose to explain the world, the garden still needs cultivating.

I thought of Candide the other morning at 6:15, on hands and knees in my own garden. I was transplanting tomatoes and peppers. It takes some practice getting on hands and knees at first. The hard part is psychological. Walking through the garden, I can maintain a certain aloofness, as if I were about to be called away by the telephone. But to kneel in the straw-bedded pathways, plucking lamb's quarters from among the kale, is a powerful form of submission. The first time I surrendered to my garden work this season, I remember thinking that none of this seemed very important, the weeding, the watering, the planting. It's such a tiny gesture to pull up a mallow or an oxalis before it gets away from you. Surely there were more important things to do—calls to make, writing to be done, news to follow.

Candide's most important lesson comes from a Turk who sends his fruit to be sold in Constantinople. "Work," the Turk says, "keeps us from three great evils: boredom, vice, and need." But even this is too much explanation. As the garden takes on substance, as the peas begin to shroud the sticks they cling to and the beans begin to climb their trellis, the garden grows in imagination, too. It wakes me up at first light, when the air is still cool. I go out with a basket of seeds and a small hand-hoe, and nothing seems more important.

July 12

Some previous owner of this place thought it would be a good idea to plant mint and Virginia Creeper around the garden. The nettles came on their own. All three plants lay down long, trailing roots—a telegraph line that runs from outpost to outpost. Pulling up those runners in loose soil is truly gratifying. Tug on a single nettle, and you can end up with an entire network of roots in your hand. You can hear them coming unzipped from the earth. Sometimes, working deep in the mint thicket, I follow a runner trail to what must have been an ancestral root cluster, a daunting mass of subterranean plant fibers. I feel as though I've suddenly stepped into a science fiction movie. I admire the native intelligence of this uncouth organism, its resourcefulness and its ability to replicate. But I know I must destroy it before it threatens civilization as we know it.

Each year the garden promises that next year will be easier. The beds will already be laid out, waiting for seeds and transplants. The drip irrigation lines will be ready to lay once the ground thaws. But so far, each year in the garden has been harder work than the year before. And because this year has been the hardest by far—new raised beds and deep, wide hay-covered paths—I'm tempted to believe, once again, that next year will be easier. I don't think I can work much harder anyway.

But the work, like the garden, has its own architecture. Some days it's just a relaxing visit to the tomato beds and the scent of late summer that comes from nipping new tomato shoots with your fingers. Other days it's dawn to dusk, sometimes on the tractor, sometimes on my knees, but most often with a garden fork in my hands, reclaiming the open ground I lost last year. It seems hard to believe that this simple tool—four steel prongs and a wooden handle—could be such a taskmaster or that it could repay skill in handling. But so it is. I found the fork's rhythm a couple of weeks ago, and now it won't let me alone.

July 14

I cleaned my saddle on a hot afternoon in Wyoming recently. It's a slick-fork western saddle, made for me nearly a decade ago by a saddle maker in Billings, Montana. At the time, I was spending part of every summer in the West, trying to learn as much about horses and horsemanship as I could. The days on horseback were always a strange tangle of joy and nervous anticipation. The horses were mostly strangers to me, and I was supposed to be imparting something to them, not merely taking what they had to offer. I rode, I learned a lot about horses, and the saddle darkened with use.

I took off the cinches and stirrups. I removed the breast collar and laid it in the sun. I brushed away the dust and oiled the latigos and worked over the fine tooling on the skirts and fenders with a soft rag. I removed a plywood splinter wedged between the oak frame of the stirrup and its leather lining—the result of a collision in a Colorado round-pen. I even spent a couple of hours polishing the nickel-silver bindings on the stirrups, trying to restore the mirrored shine they had when they were new. But they'd been nicked and dinged too many times to ever gleam again.

I'd spent part of that week in the saddle again. I was riding with old friends, including Buck Brannaman, and once again I was riding an unfamiliar horse, feeling in the way he moved how all the riders before me had responded to him. The horse's name was Eddie. He'd spent part of his life trying to decide just what his numerous riders were trying to teach him. But since he rarely had the same rider twice, Eddie decided to stick with what he already knew. That's why he felt the way he did under the saddle—a little stubborn, a little sluggish, but not unwilling. I spent three days getting him soft in the mouth again, easy to bend, light in my hands. In return, he reminded me how much I'd learned from horses. Eddie made me want to clean my saddle and come home and ride my own good horse, a quarter horse named Remedy, who has had plenty of time off.

You'd think that a man with his own horse and saddle would ride every day. You'd be wrong. I took a job—this one—that has made it hard to haul the horses west for the summer. And somehow the East to me seems too full of excuses and inhibitions for western riding. Too much work to do. Too many trees and highways. Not enough sky-wide spaces or antelope. Even the pleasure of watching the horses grazing in their pasture became an excuse not to interrupt them. And in the end I lost track of the time. My saddle sat in the horse trailer. The stirrups tarnished in the damp eastern climate. Mold turned up on the cinches. And Remedy, who was nineteen when I bought him, slowly turned twenty-six.

So I discovered when I got home from Wyoming last week. I put my newly clean saddle in the horse trailer and brought the horses down to the barnyard. Remedy usually leads the way, head high, a straight-up walk toward the feed pan and the hay rack. He's always the first to catch a stray sound, the first to trot toward trouble. But this time he came last—stiff and visibly thinner than he'd been two weeks earlier. At his age a horse that loses mobility begins to lose flesh as well, and he'd begun to lose both while I was gone. The vet thinks it's a matter of sore feet—a chronic condition with some aging horses—so I'll do everything I can to ease his pain and build his muscles again. That means lots of riding on my part.

45

Horses live a long time, long enough to make their owners believe they'll always be there. What they ask from humans is an incremental relationship—consistency, steady work, small changes that build up over time into big changes. In the West, I'd watched my friend Buck help a horse get over being herd-bound. It took about twenty minutes of loping and trotting. And when it was over—horse and rider standing relaxed at the far end of the arena, away from the rest of the herd—Buck quietly remarked that that horse had just changed the way his life was arranged in twenty minutes. Not many humans could do that, he added.

I don't know whether horses have any consciousness of time. But I know that in his pain Remedy seems to be deep within himself. That's not his way. In full health he is pure awareness, boldly alert. He can make you feel like an adjunct of his presence, as if he were vouching for you with the pasture gods. Now it's my turn to vouch for him, to get him healthy and ask him, before it's too late, to tell me all the things he knows once more.

August 6

The other afternoon I walked out to the vegetable garden and saw a woodchuck inside the fence. It was standing on its hind legs with its back to me nibbling lamb's quarters. This was like a burglar breaking into the house to shampoo the carpets. I watched for a minute or two, hoping the woodchuck would move on to some hairy galinsoga, another persistent weed. But then it turned and caught my eye. Instead of freezing like a cat about to pounce, it did a Tim Conway double take, dropped to all fours, and waddled out the back of the garden. I found the gap in the fence and fixed it.

The woodchuck had bypassed all of the ripening vegetables in order to eat a weed that grows thick on this place and is as edible to humans as it is to woodchucks. Some people and some woodchucks take a special pleasure in eating what's wild, but for me the pleasure is eating what I've cultivated myself. It's a habit I learned from my parents, who grew up on farms where the kitchen garden was nearly as important as the crops in the fields.

Those gardens were a matter of common sense, a way of providing for oneself. Like nearly every choice that humans make, they had an implicit political content. But the political content of our garden here, and our pigs and chickens, is overt—to step aside even a little from the vices of industrial agriculture. Our purpose is summed up in the words of an old victory garden poster, meant to encourage Americans to produce their own food during World War II. It says simply, "Grow Your Own. Be sure!"

The victory garden movement came to an end when canned food no longer needed to be rationed. But in 1943, 60 percent of Americans grew victory gardens producing some eight million tons of food. Many people abandoned their vegetable plots when they were no longer a national necessity. Many others realized that fresh food and the pleasure of gardening more than justified the labor. Some were able to pass that realization along to their children. What my dad called "gardening," I called "weeding." I've learned few of the details of how he gardens, especially because he gardens in California. But I learned from him the feeling that something is missing without homegrown vegetables.

Think of all the millions of houses across this country raising only grass and swing sets. Imagine turning up a corner of those lawns for lettuce and tomatoes. There's plenty of use for the extra food in every community. Gardeners have always found ways to make their gardens tithe, if only because part of the pleasure is sharing the harvest. A national crisis turned America, for a few years, into a nation of gardeners. They planted victory gardens then because of a lack of canned food. We should plant victory gardens now because of a lack of victory gardens. How else will the habit get passed along?

September 4

The other night, just before dusk, I walked across the pasture with a bucket of grain. Two dozen chickens followed me in a mob. Some came running toward me, wings flapping, as though given enough room they might actually take off. I led them into their pen, scattered the grain, and closed the gate. Then I drove the ducks and geese into their yard. *Drove* is too strong a word. I hinted at the direction I wanted them to go and they went. I opened another gate and led the horses down to the barnyard. When they'd been fed, I stepped into the pigpen. The gilt came over for a rubdown, and the barrow flopped down beside her. They lay back to back, eyes closed, pale pink bellies available for scratching.

Some evenings I notice the haze that settles in the valley or the big orange moon coming up over the trees. But that night I noticed how we all fit together, animals and humans. The piglets arrive pretty wild. Baby chicks clatter about the brooder house in fear. But time passes, and they all settle down. They seem to tame themselves somehow.

That night I saw the ways that they've tamed me. I never rush the ducks. It only confuses them. I never ask too much when herding chickens.

47

The horses expect a certain presence from me, which changes with every situation. The pigs want joy and vigorous scratching. None of the animals seems to want me to be other than human. But they do want me to be a human who knows how the world looks to them and respects it.

All of our animals were raised among humans from birth. Except one—Nell, the mustang. We bought her nearby, but she was adopted as a weanling in Nevada—part of the federal wild-horse adoption program. I've seen other mustangs captured, so I have a good idea what it was like for her. She's seventeen now and has lived the last decade with us. She's been trained, trailered, ridden, and cared for. And yet it's always a toss-up whether she'll let me catch her.

Our animals show their trust in us every day. But sometimes Nell trusts us, and sometimes she doesn't. The freeze-brand on her neck isn't the only sign of that long-ago capture. All the rest of us, animal and human, live together in a single place. Nell lives in her own. She reserves the right to withhold herself, to stand apart. The chickens grow placid, the pigs get to like us, and the other horses go on with their lives. And yet the most meaningful moments, after all these years, are when Nell crosses from her world to ours. She walks right up, as if to ask where I've been, and settles her head in my arms. I feel the choice she has made every time she makes it.

September 24

The merest touch of frost the other morning brought down the potatoes in the lower garden. It seemed all the more surprising because the vines had been so rank with growth. Suddenly all the green was gone and I could see the lumps where the new spuds—ready to be gathered—lay hidden under the straw. I began lifting potatoes. Wherever I pulled a plant I found earthworms thriving in the borderland between straw and soil, writhing in their sudden exposure. The potatoes looked overexposed too—still thin-skinned, their brilliant white flesh visible through their jackets.

There's really no getting used to the biological miracles on a small farm, the simple fecundity of the earth. A couple of months ago I scattered seed potatoes on raw, bare ground and buried them in old hay. The vegetation seemed like recompense enough, but now I have more potatoes than I know what to do with. I planted a dozen Steuben bean seeds in June. Now the pods have dried on the plants, and my dozen seeds have been repaid forty or fifty times over with new Steuben beans—white with a caramel eye—drying on the sideboard. Like most gardeners we've nearly fed ourselves sick on

48

fresh tomatoes. Now they march directly into the kitchen, through a food mill, and into a pot of slowly condensing sauce, to be frozen for a winter day when fresh tomatoes are just a memory.

There's not a sign of stasis anywhere. The goldenrod, so vivid a couple of weeks ago, has faded to rust. That means the bees are tapering off as well. The past couple of years have been hard on honey bees—a combination of mites and bitter winters—but this hive is now in its second year. On a warm day the air thrives with bees outside the hive entrance. A strong smell of wax and honey and propolis drifts out of the frames. It adds just the right quality of darkness and sweetness to the complicated scent of this place.

The floral traces have mostly vanished, replaced by the burlap scent of decay in the wild fields around us. But the strong scented notes are always the smells of manure and the animals that make it—the horses and the chickens and ducks and geese. What ties it all together is the smell of pig—not the toxic, scalding scent of an industrial operation but the much friendlier odor of two pigs who move often to new pasture. Our Tamworths are nearly full-grown. The barrow is as round as an overgrown cucumber. I forget how complex that farm scent is when I've been in the city for a couple of days. But when I get home, just after dark, it hits me all over again. I stand in the twilight, looking out over the pasture, wondering how those smells in the night air can seem so vital and so welcoming.

November 24

Darkness seems to collect at this time of year, as though it had trickled downhill into the sump of November. Fog settles onto damp leaves in the woods—not Prufrock's yellow fog or the amber fog of the suburbs, but a gray-white hanging mist that feels like the down or underfur of some pervasive beast. White birches line the slopes beyond the pasture as if they were fencing in the fog, keeping it from inundating the house in a weightless avalanche. The day stays warm, but even at noon it feels as though dusk has already set in. The chickens roost early. The horses linger by the gate, ready for supper.

Usually I feel starved for light about now. But this year I've reveled in these damp, dark November days. It's a kind of waking hibernation, I suppose, a desire to live enclosed for a while in a world defined by the vaporous edges of the farm. My ambition extends all the way to feeding the woodstove and sitting with Tavish the Border terrier in my lap, which perfectly suits his ambitions. The frenzy of the spring garden has long since faded.

My plans to refence the place have been put on hold for another year. We're just sitting around waiting for the ground to freeze.

This isn't how it's supposed to be, I know. I keep an endless mental list of things that need to be done. But when a gray day comes, when the horses stand over their hay as though there were all the time in the world to eat it, one of the things that needs doing is to sit still. The ducks and geese are especially good at that. They come out of their yard in a rush in the mornings and forage across the pastures and into the garden debris. But an hour or two later they lie on the lawn like ships on a green sea, some gazing at the world around them, some with their heads tucked into their wings. I consider myself a student of their stillness.

November 25

It occurred to me the other day, on an old familiar stretch of highway out West, to think of all the old familiar stretches of highway in my life. Not as a metaphor of some kind, or as a way, somehow, of seeing where I've gotten in life—the answer, in asphalt, being exactly nowhere—but just for the fun of it. If I had a more graphical imagination, I'd draw all those strips of road side by side in an oversized scrapbook or cut them out of the folding maps and glue them into a single discontinuous journey.

The thought of all these highways occurred to me somewhere between Crow Agency, Montana, and the Wyoming border—part of the longer drive from Billings to Sheridan. In the past dozen years I've driven that stretch of highway dozens of times. It rolls up out of the lowland along the Yellowstone River—past the refineries and the Billings livestock auction—into a great sweep of wheat-land. It cuts across the Crow Reservation, over a shoulder of the Rosebud Mountains, and down into the Tongue River drainage.

There are times on that highway when I feel motionless even at eighty miles an hour. And there have been night drives when it felt like every mile had to be won against my own fatigue. Often, the car begins to buck whenever it gets crosswise to the wind, which has no impediments out there. When I first began making that trip, it still had the feel of a mythic journey, pushing backwards in time. It wasn't the Crow Reservation that made me feel that way or the signs for Little Bighorn. It was the lay of the land, the rimrock, the grasses, the antelope racing across the plains.

But if you spend enough time in the West, the myths erode, and what you're left with is an actual landscape. In a dry year, a vast swath of wheat burns black. Another year, the radio is suddenly full of Christian stations, a mixture of salvation rock and hometown choirs coming over the air. On one trip, a golden eagle nearly lands on the hood of the car. On another, I wake up from my daydream and find myself closing in fast on a sugar-beet truck headed for Billings, a single light flashing slowly on its tail. The beets look prehistoric, like lumps of matter waiting to be formed into walking, breathing creatures eager to know their creator.

I'm only an occasional traveler on this road, of course. I've missed the blizzards that shut it down from time to time, though I've caught more than enough of the thunderstorms, black as a burned wheatfield in the sky. A couple of months ago, I drove all the way from Hardin to Garryowen under the most violent rainbow I've ever seen, a dense wall of color shimmering overhead.

This last time, I left Sheridan after a hard autumn frost. In the pastures along the highway, the horses seemed to have frozen solid overnight. They held themselves motionless, broadside to the rising sun, in all of the postures available to their kind. One stood with eyes closed, ears pricked backwards. Another lay with front legs folded under, its neck arched so that only its muzzle touched the ground. Some stood clumped together in frozen bands amid frozen herds of cattle. There was no breeze to sweep their tails or manes. Mile after mile, pasture after pasture, the illusion held, as if I were driving through a land of cryogenic beasts. Then the morning sun took hold, and they all came to life again.

December 15

Every year I try to figure out what it means to be ready for winter. Every winter brings a different answer. One year the chimney gets cleaned, one year the rain gutters. One year I stack enough wood to heat us through May, and one year the garden gets put to bed properly. But I've never managed to make all these things happen in the same year. The only constant is hay. There's always enough of it, stacked well before the leaves have finished falling. The horses insist.

Somewhere in the back of my mind I'm always preparing for a different winter than the one that comes. I discovered that you can muddle through a hard winter. The power mostly stays on. The oil man comes on a regular schedule. The phone never goes out. Sometimes, well below zero, the yard hydrants freeze up, but with a little heat tape they thaw again. Even in the dead of winter the wood man will make a delivery, though calling him feels like a sober confession of failure.

The last two winters in the Hudson Valley were brutal. Yet they weren't as long or hard or dark as I expected them to be. The winter solstice comes and goes before the real cold begins. No matter how bitter it gets in January, it won't be getting any darker. The season is always more transitional than it seems, as fleeting as summer. Every day is headway toward spring.

Sometimes I imagine preparing for a winter you can't muddle through. It's a deep arboreal season. Time pauses and then pauses again. The sun winks over the horizon, glinting on a snow-swept lake—just enough light to wake the chickadees. The eave is low all around the house this winter comes to, and I've surrounded the entire house with cordwood, leaving gaps for the windows and doors. Winter will go nowhere until I've burned it all. I have no plans except to rake the snow off the roof after the next big blizzard and carry out the ashes from the woodstove and read everything I've ever meant to read.

A daydream like this isn't really about winter or snow or firewood or even the feeling of having prepared every last thing that needs preparing. It's about something far more elemental, the time that moves through us day by day. It's an old human hope—to have a consciousness separate from the consciousness of time—but it's always a vain one. I'll never get that much cordwood stacked and I'll never need to. Winter comes and goes in the same breath, condensing right before your face on a day when the temperature never hits twenty.

Year

FOUR

January 13

There's really no counting the roads you never expect to find yourself on. But you know it when you suddenly find yourself on one of them. I came upon such a route a couple of weeks ago in the midst of a cross-country drive— US Highway 84, from Lubbock, Texas, to Clovis, New Mexico. Once you're in Lubbock, the odds of ending up on Highway 84 are pretty good. We'd planned on cutting across Texas farther north, through Amarillo. But a powerful winter storm pushed us south from Little Rock, Arkansas, where the ways divide. Instead of going through Oklahoma City, which was coated in ice, we drove through Texarkana and Dallas and Abilene instead, bound for Santa Fe and points west. Hence, Lubbock.

So says the logic of the roads. We got up three mornings in a row, drove all day, and turned up in Lubbock. That city was nowhere in my thoughts when we pulled out of the driveway at home. Yet there we were, and happy to be there after another day spent in the interstate backwash of a wet winter storm. We glimpsed a patch of blue sky for a moment in central Tennessee, but never once the sun. It was dark when we pulled into Lubbock, late, and it was dark when we rose the next morning in a dense, freezing fog.

Lubbock lies at the eastern edge of the Llano Estacado—the Staked Plains—one of the strange, dire places in the American imagination. It was trackless once, a nearly featureless, grassy plain between the Canadian River to the north and the Pecos to the west, a place where the very idea of direction seemed to vanish, where every heading seemed equally unpromising. Coronado crossed it in his delusory wanderings, bewildered by its scale. To me it had been only a beautiful name—Llano Estacado. I'd filled in the promise of so much bareness, such a flat expanse of grass, with grim imaginings, wanderers doomed to lose their way and their horses and their lives.

But there was no losing the track out of Lubbock even in the fog. US 84 angled northwest, and as the sun begin to regain its grip it became clear that the inhabitants of the Llano Estacado had found plenty of water by mining the Ogallala Aquifer beneath it. This is one of the few places in America where you can still find a windmill repair shop. Dark brown cotton fields stretched away in every direction, the even terrain broken only by enormous loaves of cotton—bales the size of semitrailers—covered with blue tarps. In some fields the bolls still clung to the plants, and now and then a drift of cotton came rolling across the highway like miniature, bleached tumbleweeds.

Where the cotton fields ended, there stood enormous dairies, cows grazing on smooth, sodlike plains irrigated by prehistoric water from the aquifer below. It was as though the hillside pastures of Vermont had moved westward with the herds that once grazed them. Despite the expanse of the plains—perhaps because of them—agriculture here is as industrial in its nature as the oil fields farther south near Midland and Odessa.

Overnight the trees had taken on a thick coating of ice. The sparse groves around distant farmsteads glowed white in the accumulating light. Towns like Sudan and Muleshoe were overshadowed by their cotton gins, by the feel small farm towns always give off on a cold morning, no matter what the local crop happens to be. Day was rising with new energy. By the time we got to Muleshoe, the hopes of seeing real sun—a blue sky, horizon to horizon—seemed more than just a pipedream for the first time in nearly two thousand miles.

The wonder of a road like that is its actuality. You can pull onto the shoulder, stop the car, and walk over to feel the cotton bolls or take in the effluvial aroma of the dairies. You can drive up the main street of Clovis and feel the bricks on the roadway rumbling under your tires or contemplate the enormous "Santa Fe" sign marking the railroad tracks as you head back to the highway. No matter what you may think of where you are, no matter how you once imagined it, you are implacably there—not where you used to be, not where you're going, but there. What you see along the way gathers inside you like a dust storm or a haystack or any other metaphor that seems appropriate to this tail end of the high plains.

January 20

My wife and I recently drove from the farm to California. The trip had a narrative. It was called *Middlemarch*, by George Eliot. We slipped the first cassette into the car stereo somewhere near Albany—"Miss Brooke had that kind of beauty…"—and we finished the last one—"and rest in unvisited tombs"—somewhere between Bakersfield and Fresno. In heavy traffic, or when one of us wanted to sleep, we turned the novel off. The rest of the time we listened. It so happens that America is as wide as *Middlemarch* is long, at seventy mph along the Southern route.

A novel is really a temporal creation. It's as much about the ways in which time passes in the story and in the reader's awareness of the story as it is about anything else. If you sat in a room and read *Middlemarch* or listened to it being read, you'd become very aware of the time it took. But for us the novel became a spatial creation. It was as though we were driving along a pavement of Eliot's sentences laid end to end across the country, the ink as black as asphalt. Now and then—Eliot does have occasional longueurs—we found ourselves working our way up a difficult passage, climbing a switchback from clause to clause. But for the most part it was smooth sailing. It felt as though the occupants of Middlemarch, that provincial town, were riding along with us in the back seat—Peter Featherstone and Mary Garth and poor Lydgate.

I'd read *Middlemarch* several times, but I'd never heard it. No matter how well you remember a novel you've read, hearing it read aloud is like finding another book within it. I'd forgotten how vividly Eliot captures the gossiping life of Middlemarch—how distinct the voices of even the smallest characters could be as they talk about the coming of the railway or the chances of reform or the troubles of the evangelical Mr. Bulstrode. Lindy and I rode along, cocooned in the voices we were hearing, and the acoustic space within the car became a psychological space, a place where we could watch Eliot dissect, with a surgeon's grace, the inner mind of Dorothea Brooke.

Outside the trucks roared past, or we roared past the trucks. The Virginia countryside gave way to Tennessee and Arkansas and Texas and finally New Mexico, Arizona, and California. Wooden fences gave way to barbed wire and welded pipe. The landscape was American, of course—an America adulterated by the effects of I-40. And yet we also drove from New York to California by way of Loamshire, the fictional county in which *Middlemarch* is set. It should have seemed incongruous to be hearing about "the hayricks at Stone Court" while looking out at the brush of west Texas, and yet it wasn't. The weather seemed to darken whenever we entered Mr. Casaubon's thoughts, and it brightened whenever Dorothea appeared, no matter how hard the rain was falling.

The human mind has a natural propensity to give in to the story at hand. We stop reading aloud when the kids get to a certain age, and yet there's a craving for the sound of a story that never goes away. I suppose that if adults still read aloud to each other the way they did in centuries past, we would get a lot less reading done. I can certainly read *Middlemarch* much faster than I can listen to it. But when we got to California, one of the first things I did was get a copy of *Middlemarch* from the library. I seemed to recognize every sentence, as if this one were the water tower of a small Tennessee town and that one were a pasture in the oak hills of California.

February 17

We came over the mountains and down into Los Angeles a little more than a month ago. The heavy rains had subsided, and the hills were stationary again. Most of the roads and highways had reopened, though it was impossible, on certain routes, to get to San Juan Capistrano or Ojai or drive up Topanga Canyon. In Malibu, a landslide has nearly closed off a residential street and, beside it, steel buttresses keep the rest of the slope from coming down. Here and there blue tarps have been thrown across the hills to keep the slips from slipping further when the rains return. Up the coast, just south of Santa Barbara, the earth is still settling over the edge of La Conchita, where ten people died in a landslide last month.

I felt a sudden claustrophobia when we came over the mountains, as if we'd left the mainland behind. I felt it again when we drove up Mount Baldy at night and looked out over the lights of the San Bernardino valley. The passes leading out of this great basin are so few, the mountains steep and brittle. But most of that unease has worn off. This is the wrong season for fire, and I think of earthquakes only when I'm idling under a freeway overpass, waiting for a light to change. I can feel the roadway rumbling overhead.

What never goes away is the dread of real estate. It's an utterly anomalous feeling. I meet perfectly pleasant people here—people whose lives differ from mine only in ordinary ways—and yet they seem extraordinary to me because they're vested in California real estate. I think of it as a fable. You wake up one morning and find that overnight a giant beanstalk has sprouted under your house and lifted it high off the ground. The next night it happens again, and soon you're in the clouds. The view would be terrifying—the plain earth is so far out of sight—except that all around you are other houses on other beanstalks.

Most of our friends here live in modest houses—fifteen hundred square feet and under. But they live in immodest places. It's literally nothing to come across a laborer's cottage in Santa Barbara—built in the days when laborers could still afford to live there—appraised at nearly $1 million. A friend in Brentwood says that her sense of her house's worth is always a decade behind the times. I think this is a sober defense against an unsettling unreality. What can it mean when the houses on one block in La Jolla are worth more than all the real property in the western half of South Dakota?

I've been trying to decide whether this extraordinary escalation of property values produces hypermobility or immobility. The answer is probably both. One person trades upwards as quickly as he can. Another stays put, in the depressing assurance that even if she sells her two-bedroom bungalow for $1.2 million, she can only afford to buy the place next door. One thing is certain. Without the enormous equity bubble that seems to be floating California's economy, all the Hummer dealerships would go out of business.

In Los Angeles, time is equity. The money—swelling like a zucchini in August—changes everything. It brings a strange formality to the act of selling real estate, which here has become one of the theatrical professions. There's something august, almost sacramental about the transfer of real property. It's one of the grand rites of capitalism. Here that rite attains its highest pitch. All across town realtors peer down from billboards the way personal accident lawyers peer down from the billboards of Albuquerque. The photographs are meant to impose trust but what they really seem to be saying is, "Have You Seen This Woman?" A realtor and his clients stand in the drive of a house on San Vicente Boulevard. They look as though they've come for a wake. But they're not in the presence of death, they're in the presence of money. Not even present money. Future money.

I suspect that there's a symbiosis between these extraordinary inflating prices, which have a life of their own, and the potential for natural disaster. By any real logic, the threat of wildfires and the collapse of sodden hillsides whose vegetation has been scorched away, not to mention the possibility of the Big One, should dampen the real estate market. But what reminds people of the Big One every day is the fact that it hasn't happened yet.

February 24

The steady rain makes no difference to the sea lions and surfers. It seems to make no difference to the cattle grazing the coastal pastures. The oldest barns along this stretch of road—the coast highway an hour north of San Francisco—show a pale green, like a wash of sea-water, over the gray of the barn-wood. The sheep along the fence lines look almost as though they were fleeced with the Spanish moss hanging from oaks along the highway. The light is as variable as the rain and the salt breeze. Moisture catches in the manzanita and sage. Pastures stream with water, and creeks rumble down the cliff-face, making for the sea across open beach.

So much water seems natural enough on the northern coast. Terrestrial life is half-aquatic there. But it's been the same in Southern California, and not just on the coast. Last weekend, the whole of the Los Angeles basin looked and sounded like a sheet of tin roofing being pounded by rain. The region absorbed the rain about as well as a sheet of tin. At times, every street in the shadow of the San Gabriels was a desert wash choked by a deluge, the current sucking at the curb as it ran for the ocean, miles and miles away. In the aftermath, the streets have been scoured clean, but the sidewalks have silted up in the low spots. Fallen magnolia blossoms dam up pools of water along my walk to work.

For the last two months, the local news in Southern California has been about nothing but houses tumbling downhill and highways blocked by mudslides, about yellow tags and red tags and the threat of evacuation. But there's another news here, whether the sun shines or not. It's the green of the hills. No one remembers this much rain, and no one remembers this much green. *Green* is beginning to fail as a word. It begins to feel unmeaning, a word you can imagine Caliban practicing on the beach, trying out the sound of it over and over again. To look at the hills and say the word *green* is ridiculous. The question is which green on what plant and in what light and facing in which direction and are we talking about new growth or old? The blue of the sky— even in the profligate light of Southern California—is simple in comparison.

Where the freeways cut through the low hills, there's a sudden sweep of prairie. It feels as though you could pull onto the shoulder, get out of your car, and walk to Nebraska knee-deep in spring grass with the broad sun on your back. But the real complexity of color emerges where the hills fold inward, hollows and canyons falling away from the highway toward some hidden termination. Crossing the Grapevine in a downpour a few days ago we came up short against a rockslide that had spilled across the road. The highway—beige and gray—seemed to have trapped us in a monotonous band of color, as if we were only allowed to drive along one or two wavelengths in the spectrum of visible light. But beyond the roadway, out across the hills, the new grass intensified toward a green that seemed to surpass human vision, as if it were visible only to grazing beasts.

In the last few weeks, I suppose I've seen every green I've ever seen. All except one, and that was a vermilion moss growing along a streamside on a glacier in Iceland. Even that green is probably growing here somewhere. But there's also a green here that I imagine I'll never find anywhere else. We saw it south of Bakersfield just after sunrise a few days ago. The last violent storm had flung itself apart, and the clouds over the Sierras had lifted just enough to show the snow that had crept far down their slopes overnight. Rows of grapevines ran in perfectly even corridors from the highway to the foothills, miles away, where the morning was just beginning to take hold. The sunlight caught those hills just so. The distant oaks broke the light. The moisture in the air above the pastures diffused it. The storm clouds restrained all but the lower rays of the sun. I'd give the color of those hills at that moment a name if I knew it. And that's just one of the names I don't know when I look up into the hills.

March 9

Ever since I got to Southern California, people have been reminding me that this part of the world has its seasons too. I always agree. I can think of at least four seasons in Los Angeles—rain, fire, escrow, and the Academy Awards. There's an old Midwestern guilt in that need to account for the seasons here. I think of all the Iowa families that moved to California about the same time my family did, in the mid-1960s. Most of them, in that first generation, found it hard to spend an extra cent. Lying in the sun—just lying there!—seemed an unaccountable waste of time. They could barely allow themselves the pleasure of eating outdoors without fussing over the pleasure of eating outdoors. Telling the ones who stayed in the Midwest that there are seasons here too was a kind of cultural negotiation, a way of saying, "We're not all that different just because we live in California and eat artichokes now." A growing season 365 days long felt like a plenary indulgence, even if you were Methodist.

Any place with as many climates—or as much climate, allowing the word its salutary overtones—as Southern California doesn't really need seasons. Drive from San Juan Capistrano, over the Santa Ana Mountains on the Ortega Highway, up through Riverside to the snowpack on the San Bernardino Mountains and you cross any number of climatic zones, each enjoying a season unto itself. Southern California reminds you that climate is a function of place and season is a function of time.

A climatic zone may be tiny—no larger than a damp winter creek-bottom in an otherwise arid landscape. And a season here may be only a matter of days as well. One day feels like sodden winter, and by the evening of the next day, the middle school girls are playing soccer under the field lights, the shriek of referee whistles cutting through the warm night air. Summer comes over and over and over. As a result, everyone is equipped to seize it the instant it appears.

I sense the encroaching season here readily enough—the way a plum-blossom spring overlaps with the constancy of agave and yucca. But I miss the Northeastern sense of time. The days are longer than they were when we got here. And yet it's hard to feel their lengthening, thanks to the orange perma-glow in the urban sky at night. But it's also because light isn't the cue my students are really waiting for. They are keenly and hormonally sensitive to climatic disturbance, and they're waiting—the whole region with them— for warm nights. Here, every night, unless it's pouring, is a convertible night. But with real warmth, the stoicism of keeping the top down will give way to the sybaritic pleasure of merging with the biotic city, all those beings feasting on air.

Whenever I think of where we are in the year, I think of home and the winter it's been having. I can imagine the operatic movement of the light, the way each day reaches a little farther into the darkness of morning and evening than the one before. Those extra minutes of dawn and dusk are almost pure emotion this time of year, as though something had been reclaimed that was in danger of disappearing forever. It seems sometimes as though that place—its snowy pastures, its huddled woods—is on a separate globe, pursuing a more elliptical path around the sun than planet Los Angeles.

The irises are in bloom here in Southern California. But what's an iris? It's something won back from the cold and the snow, a rigorous assertion that winter may come again but only by going through summer first. That's not what the irises say here. They're blooming along with roses and oranges and birds of paradise and rosemary and lavender and camellias. To me it makes no sense, no matter how beautiful it is. Something is always blooming in this nectared city.

May 20

Over the past few months in Los Angeles, old memories have come back to me. Most of them aren't really memories of the place as it was when I last lived in the area thirty-some years ago. They're memories of illusions. The otherness of other lives weighs heavily on my imagination, and to drive, as a young man, along elevated freeways, peering out into the palm-dotted neighborhoods was to be overcome by other lives. Los Angeles seemed far stranger to me then than it has these past few months. The difference may be age, but it may also be Los Angeles.

It was a less respectable city, as I remember it. It was the great city for starting over, where you could repair your respectability or ditch it, once and for all. I had relatives who tried both, who became school teachers and settled into the middle groove or turned John Birch and stopped paying income tax. You never knew how that city would take an Iowan. People always seemed to be moving up or down, not in wealth or status, but in the moral freight their lives carried. The city made room for every version of those lives.

You can still find plenty of moral friction in Los Angeles. People still save a little vitriol for people who live those other lives. Los Angeles is still a city where a bad toupee or the wrong lipstick sets off entirely different reverberations than they would in New York. It's still easy to glimpse here what would happen if your life went off the rails and it became a struggle to keep up appearances to the outer world.

But it's a different city now. It has an earnestness and a tolerance it once lacked. Everyone aspires to own a house—real estate is respectability itself—but there's no agreement on what the lives being lived in those houses will look like. What passes for American culture has been divided and subdivided, split into hundreds of channels, and reinvented in thousands of ways. A few blocks of tract houses or turnkey mansions—it makes no difference—may turn out to contain dozens of one-family neighborhoods that agree in only one thing—the day the trash goes out.

In thirty years, though, some of the underlying illusions of this place have changed very little. There's still a profoundly American faith in the exceptionalism of the present generation. I've spent the past few months on the edge of one of the fastest growing counties in Southern California. Big-box malls have sprung from the earth and around them streets and streets of houses built by enormous corporations. The houses crawl over the hills and up to the edge of ravines. They roll over the desert and infringe upon the wetlands and grasslands. And yet the people who occupy them are still surprised that theirs wasn't the last development, that the open fields a few blocks away are now only houses and more houses.

Americans have always had one good story to tell—the next city, the next county, the next house—and no one really knows yet how to tell the new story, the one where the frontier collapses in upon itself. Perhaps one version is simply this—the respectability of the settled regions suddenly coexists with the violence, the lawlessness of the real frontier, and both change as a result. We know how that story goes when it's told as a western. I think we're only figuring out how it goes when it's a fact of life being worked out as new houses cascade outward toward a final limit, where there's no longer room or money or tolerance for more new houses.

I like to remember the stories of that one Los Angeles relative of mine—the one who went right wing. I saw him only a few times after that transformation. There was no particular bitterness in his voice. He knew how to talk about other things. He'd come to a place where he could fit in while not fitting in. I think that was his secret. He knew that Los Angeles was no frontier for him, that it wasn't so much a question of starting over here as of finishing out. There were plenty of open fields in the Iowa he left behind. Los Angeles was the place to forget them.

June 6

When it feels like time—no matter what the clock says—I walk the horses down to the night pen from the pasture where they've spent the day. I whistle when I open the gate. Their heads turn abruptly to the sound. I rattle the grain in the bucket, and, if they show any reluctance, Remedy begins to drive the other two horses toward me. Ida makes a feint toward the pigs in their enclosure, and they dart in circles round and round, barking and snuffling as they go. I lead the horses down the drive and into the corral, never looking back to see whether they follow or not. It's part of the contract. They trot the last few steps and settle over their sweet feed.

This is the fly time of year. We spray the horses, and some days they wear mesh face-masks to keep the flies off. I look out in the pasture, and there are our horses, strangely disguised as if for some long-ago game show.

But nothing really keeps the flies away. On the bad days, I walk into the night pen just ahead of the horses, and the flies that envelope them suddenly envelop me. I swat them away, thinking it's a case of mistaken identity. I'm not a horse. But at a moment like that, the distinction is academic. To the flies, I'm a horse, a particularly pale, thin-skinned, succulent one, and lacking a horse's ability to quiver its skin in just one spot.

In that moment, the sense of human separateness slips away. It happens again and again here on this farm. Every day, for example, I make a point of sitting on the threshold of the portable pig house hoping to make friends with two young Tamworth gilts. We're going to breed them, and we want them as tame as they can be before then. Every day, they ease up to me a little sooner. Yesterday I could touch them on the forehead. In a month, they'll flop on the ground to have their bellies scratched.

There's still an elemental distrust in their eyes. They stand broadside to where I sit, looking sideways and a little backward toward me, as if positioning themselves to breeze right past if I make a sudden move. But they turn and rub their flat wet noses against my knuckles. They glance at me and then drift away, grazing as they go. I sit and watch them, hoping to find the grain of their domesticity, the way to enlarge their trust. But I can see in the look they give me—the almost human gaze—that they're studying me, too, waiting to discover how dependable I really am.

June 15

In and out we come all day long, and so do the dogs—to the pastures and the corral, to visit the ducklings and goslings in the horse trailer, to admire the new gilts in the hogpen, to feed the chickens and gather eggs. We learned early on to leave our boots in the mudroom and to check ourselves for ticks at night. We like the bats that nest in the eaves, and we don't so much mind the chipmunks that sometimes disappear through the cracks in the foundation. We no longer really hear the sound of mice and flying squirrels in the walls at night. We all seem to live in each others' margins.

But the other day I found a forest tent caterpillar climbing a computer cable in my office. The creature had ridden one of us into the house. Its presence was oddly revolting, if hardly surprising. Forest tent caterpillars are everywhere this summer. I find them on the fence rails. They drown in the duck tank. Wherever the hand goes—to a gate-latch or a bucket handle—it's sure to find a forest tent caterpillar, sometimes the tiny ones—barely an inch long, as thin as a tightly spun yarn—and sometimes the big ones—two inches long and nearly as fat as a pencil. Considered solely as a contrivance of nature, they can be quite beautiful. A line of ivory-colored keyholes runs down the back, and the sides are demurely brushed with an eye-shadow blue.

But I rarely think of them this way, not during an outbreak as serious as this one. I brush them off my shoulders and hat and sunglasses as I mow the pastures. I shake them off the windshield wipers to keep them from being squashed against the glass. And every now and then I come upon a tree where they've massed on the trunk, a somber congregation of caterpillars holding themselves still along the bark while around the edges one or two twitch with the promptings of some holy fire. In such numbers, they actually look like bark, as though the surface of the tree might begin to writhe.

I don't know why this causes such revulsion in me. Forest tent caterpillars don't bite, they don't stink, they don't carry diseases, and they aren't personally unhandsome. It isn't the thought of their numbers—millions and millions of them from the upper Midwest eastward—or the extensive defoliation they cause. But everywhere they go they lay down trails of silk, as though they were wiring the woods. A high wind brings the silk kiting down from the leaves, suspended in midair. To walk outdoors is to wind oneself in gossamer, as if you were being spun into one of the yellow cocoons they leave behind. I hope the poultry eat caterpillars. Some days the birds seem like our last line of defense.

August 8

One of the reasons I moved to the country was to try to have a more deliberate awareness of time. I imagined a tree—a sugar maple—coming into bud in spring, then leafing out and darkening into an overshadowing presence in midsummer. I imagined watching it lose its leaves in fall and somehow banking what I'd seen, as if those images would help me experience time as a continuum and not as the balking, lurching beast it so often seemed to be.

But I had no idea how much time the country contains. I'm hip-deep in it always. I thought the seasons would come and go and that's what I'd pay attention to. Instead, I find myself watching what the seasons leave behind, the steady accumulation of change. When we moved here, nearly eight years ago, an old honey locust loomed over the vegetable garden. Its ashes have long since been spread. The ancient crabapple on the corner has been pared back to a few stubs of branches. Nearby, a pair of white spruces are beginning to tower over me, though I planted them as whips. There are finally apples—eleven of them—on the young trees along the driveway.

The posts in the rail fence beside them have just about reached the end of their useful life.

Naturally enough, I think of myself as the still point amid all this change. My leaves never fall. If I lie fallow for a while, I'm not suddenly overcome with nettles and jewelweed and vagabond hollyhocks, like the vegetable garden. The ducks and geese molt, the horses hair up and shed, but my coat is constant. I notice the changes in myself only when I set my hand to a familiar task. A couple of weeks ago, I stacked 354 bales in the barn loft. It was surprising how much knowledge there was in how I handled them, though there was none at all compared to the old dairy farmer who was throwing them to me.

I've banked nothing, or everything. Every day the chores need doing again. Early in the morning, I clean the horsepen with a manure fork. Every morning, it feels as though it could be the day before or a year ago or a year before that. With every pass, I give the fork one final upward flick to keep the manure from falling out, and every day I remember where I learned to do that and from whom. Time all but stops. But then I dump the cart on the compost pile. I bring out the tractor and turn the pile, once every three or four days. The bucket bites and lifts, and steam comes billowing out of the heap. It's my assurance that time is really moving forward, decomposing us all in the process.

September 11

Earlier this summer, I emailed my brother a list of the animals we're raising on this farm. I called it an inventory, but it was really a way of acknowledging that perhaps we've gone too far. There are now five pigs in various stages of growth and a large, comic parade of ducks and geese. There are chicks in the basement and chickens in the mulch. And there are the longtime partners in this enterprise, horses, dogs, and cats. My brother—who has three pigs and four goats—wrote back and said, "Wouldn't it be great to know the real inventory?"

That phrase has stuck in my head for the past few weeks. I sent my brother a list of the animals that Lindy and I are responsible for, the ones we need to feed and water every day. But I hadn't even begun to count the creatures that are responsible for themselves. Even among those, the animals I think of first are the ones that have a direct relationship with us— the Phoebes that nest above the kitchen door, the fox that steals hens from our coop, the wild turkeys that troop into the pasture in winter, the red-tail hawks that screech overhead, driving the poultry to cover. There are others, of course—hummingbirds in the bee balm and hollyhocks, pileated woodpeckers in the deep woods, catbirds in the elderberry. But these too belong to a circle of animals that seem scaled to human powers of observation.

What makes the real inventory interesting is all the rest of the organisms that live on this place. Sometimes I get a vague sense of how vast that inventory might be—nights when the crickets ring in my ears, evenings when the low sun is refracted in the wings of thousands of insects in flight over the pasture. But it's still only a vague sense, a catalog of life forms whose numbers I have to guess at. I imagine the abundance of life here in the shape of a pyramid—the kind of illustration that might appear in a schoolbook—with a pair of humans at the peak and legions of soil bacteria at the base.

But one of the things I've learned living here is that life isn't a pyramid with humans at the peak. It's an interrelationship far too complex to diagram so anthropocentrically and so simply. There's a map of need here that I can't read but that governs me as well. I go about the endless tasks, the chores, the feeding and grooming of animals, and I pretend that I'm separate and in charge. The pigs and geese remind me that that's not exactly true. If I wrote up the real inventory, I'd have to include myself as well.

October 7

One of my favorite E. B. White essays is the one called "Memorandum," written sixty-four years ago this month. I never understood it until I'd been living on this farm for a while. "Memorandum" is White's list of the things he ought to do on his own much larger farm along the coast of Maine. The essay begins with the words "Today I should" and it ends not because White has run out of things that he should do but because it's getting dark, and he's spent the day typing, and his piece is already plenty long.

What drives that essay is October. Every warm day, every day without rain or a killing frost feels like an opportunity stolen from harder weather. And in the opportunity of a warm October day—like the past week up here—you suddenly feel the pressure of the coming season. White never says it, but he's talking in "Memorandum" about the pleasure of not doing the things that need to be done. He's talking about resisting October—not by pretending it's an appendix of summer but by refusing to think of it as the foreword to winter.

I'd like to have gotten the lower pasture refenced this summer, and right now, like White, I need to take up the chicken fences and think about where the pigs will go when the ground freezes. I need to bring wood scraps from the back of the barn up to the house for kindling and get the log splitter back under cover. I could go on and on with this list, but you're better off reading White's. It was—as farms go—a more interesting time. And it's pleasing to read a list of chores from sixty-four years ago. Not one of them needs doing today. My list needs doing right now.

So why don't I get up and do them while the weather's good? And why didn't White stop typing and at least "carry a forkful of straw down to the house where the pig now is?" There's the writer's work, for one thing. But there's also the counterpoise of all those tasks that need doing. Starting one means not starting any of the others. It feels better to put everything off evenhandedly. The fog is low to the ground these mornings, and in the lower pasture a sugar maple that has already turned casts more light than the sun. It's going to rain for a few days. And when the next good day comes, what needs doing here will no longer be merely a matter of should. It will be a matter of must.

November 23

Now that it's winter again—wind-chill in the single digits, ice and snow on the ground—I can tell where the cold air leaks into this house. A couple of weeks ago, I began pulling apart the walls in the oldest part of the house, the mudroom and laundry room. As I worked, I felt a forensic hostility. The laundry room had been built around the washer and dryer, making it impossible to replace them without taking the room apart. So I took the room apart. I found what appears to be the oldest beam in the house—dating back to the late eighteenth century. I found miles and miles of BX electrical cable. And I found the cold spots, which I'm slowly plugging.

The most satisfying part of all of this has been burning the house from inside. By the time I finished tearing out the laundry room, which was renovated sometime in the 1980s, there were stacks of scrap wood on the deck. I've enjoyed cutting them up and feeding them—nails and all—to the woodstove. The carpenter who built that room and its cupboards and closets stinted nothing when it came to lumber and nails and, especially, screws. In the evening, lengths of his handiwork crackle in the fireplace. In the morning, those dry scraps get the woodstove roaring in no time.

Behind all that work—all that Sheetrock—there's another house and another set of lives. When we reroofed the house a few years ago, the contractor reported that there had once been a serious chimney fire. The other day, I found its scars on a log beam hidden beneath the false ceiling in the mudroom. I wish, in fact, that the house were more articulate or that I was better at hearing what it has to say. I can hear the most recent occupants pretty clearly—they hated the thought of exposed wooden beams and brickwork. But the ones who lived here before them—all the way back to the first settlers—are nearly inaudible to me.

I often marvel at the decisions the previous owners made. We have enough wiring hidden in the walls for a commercial office building. I wonder who will marvel at the decisions I'm making now. The trouble is that you can only see what remains—not what's been erased. When I'm finished with my work, an era in the life of this house will have vanished, gone up in smoke. I'll rebuild from the bones of the house outward.

Year

FIVE

January 2

I've learned enough about farming—or living on a farm—to begin to understand the wisdom of the old farmers I know. They're wise because everything has already happened to them. The barn has burned down. The cows have trampled the cornfield. The combine has eaten a finger. The soybean market has gone south. If the worst hasn't happened to one farmer, it's happened to the neighbor down the road. A lot of the surprise has gone out of life. One of the reasons farmers like talking to my wife and me is because we still have plenty of surprise left in us.

In my worst nightmare, all the animals have gotten out and they're all tangled in the fence and they're rolling in a ball down the highway. So I'll just say this: the other day Magnus, the 300-pound Tamworth boar, got out. I looked out the attic window, and Magnus was loping after the horses in the big pasture. This is where a book like *Five Acres and Independence* really lets you down.

I'd like to claim that Lindy and I got Magnus back into his pen. But it was really the horses. They can be histrionic at the most inopportune moments, but that afternoon they were creatures of good sense. Remedy, the retired cutting horse, cut left and right, agile as a cat, flaring and snorting, keeping Magnus at bay. Nell, to whom Magnus was chiefly attracted,

showed us what it meant to have been raised in the wild. And Ida, the glut-
ton, led us all back into Magnus's pen, where there was a heap of grain on
the ground. Lindy and I shut one gate behind us, opened another to let the
horses out, and there we were. Order restored.

We now give the horses their hay in the morning beside Magnus's
pen. We throw some to Magnus so he can pretend to be one of the horses.
A quiet companionship has sprung up among them. Lindy says she saw
Magnus batting his eyes at Nell. But when he raises his snout and starts
snuffing the air, what he's smelling is his two prospective brides living down
by the barn, awaiting their nuptials. Their names are Suzanne and Cheryl.

While I was doing the chores that night, I kept hearing Wordsworth's
phrase about emotion recollected in tranquility. That's the wisdom of old
farmers. All the whooping and cursing has died away, and the gates are
latched and the lights are off and Magnus, who is as tame as tame can be,
has bedded down in his hut full of hay, wondering, as I do, just what had
happened that afternoon.

January 18

When I started gardening, I thought I'd find my way into a pattern that
would repeat itself year by year. But no two years have been even remotely
the same. I don't mean the weather or the quantity of rainfall. I mean just
what vision I have in mind when I think about planting the vegetable garden. It nearly always begins as the same vision—something between a regal
potager and a completely demotic garden allotment, the kind pictured, for
instance, in Louisa Jones's *Kitchen Gardens of France*. I can almost feel the
kind of enclosure I want the garden to offer, and how it feels to step out
of that enclosure—out from among the tomato poles and the sweet-corn
stalks and into the plantations of lettuce and basil. And yet no matter what
blueprint I begin with, an unintended theme seems to emerge each year. I
remember a year I can only sum up as "borage."

The hard part isn't choosing the seeds. Ordering seeds is like ordering fly-tying materials. Most are so cheap that you can afford a wide variety, as long as you can also solve the problem of where to plant them. For
me, the hard part is resisting the architectural urges of spring, the desire to
reorganize the beds, to sift the soil, to move the blueberry hedge that runs
right down the middle of what could be gratifying rows of Steuben beans.
I try to concentrate on two things: a simple diagram of what goes where, in
already existing beds, and putting the seeds in the ground when the time is

right. Somehow each year seems like a reinvention of the garden instead of a development of what came before. Perhaps it's that way for most vegetable gardeners. Aside from the rhubarb and the sorrel and the horseradish and—God forbid—the mint, not much survives from year to year except the hope of a garden that grows more and more complex, more involuted and worldly at the same time.

January 27

The snow that fell a couple of days ago seems to have polarized itself as it accumulated. Some patches catch the sun and throw it back in your eyes. Other patches turn a gray face to the world, as if the light were catching them on edge. The wind no longer pokes through the ribs of the house. After a while at their hay, the horses make their way across the pasture and stand among a row of felled saplings. I'll collect them in another month and turn them into bean-poles.

I've been thinking about a hotbed that Gilbert White was making 222 years ago. A hotbed resembles a cold frame, except that the seeds are planted in a bed of slightly composted manure, which gives off heat as it composts further. The best account of how to make a hotbed comes from the ever-pungent William Cobbett, who devotes half a chapter to it in *The American Gardener*. Cobbett, writing a generation after White, begins by saying, "I am not about to lay down rules for persons who can afford to have cucumbers in March." White wanted cucumbers in May, which meant making hotbeds in January. By early July, he could take apart and store the frames and sheets of glass. He also filled his hotbeds with melons, squash, and maize, which he grew mainly as an ornamental. White wasn't the only one who loved a hotbed. Mice nested in them, and he sometimes found snake eggs in the straw.

So what became of hotbeds? The better question is, what became of dung? How many gardeners have immediate access, as White did, to long manure (with straw and bedding mixed in) or short manure (without the straw)? We seem to be caught, in America, somewhere between the extremes of bagged compost—a finished product that gives no heat to a hotbed—and toxic oceans of liquid manure in the lagoons and holding tanks of factory farms. By White's standards, too, we all live in hotbeds. We grow seedlings on window-sills, safe in the knowledge that there will be no "ice in chambers," as White puts it. It's strange to think of it this way, but in our world, electricity has replaced dung. I looked up hotbeds in one of my favorite books, *Build It Better Yourself.* What it showed was a cold frame with an electric heating cable snaking through the bed.

I'm not suggesting you run out and make a hotbed. On this place, we have the straw and the horses and the dung, and I won't be making a hotbed either. But it's one of those practices that crystallizes the shift from White's time to ours. What always strikes me about White and Cobbett as gardeners—what always strikes me about all good gardeners—is their ability to take care. When it comes to hotbeds, Cobbett says, in a phrase that applies to nearly the whole of the garden, "The labour is nothing, the trouble very little indeed, and all that is wanted is a small portion of care."

February 14

The robins that were here a week or so ago haven't been seen again. The ground that was softening is hard underfoot. What snow fell in the big storm was perfect for plowing. It fell dry and light, over bare ground. We were out in the pasture near dusk yesterday and came upon one of the spots where the horses had lain during the afternoon. It looked like a buffalo wallow—a dusty hollow—except that the dust was snow and there was a thin glazing of ice where the body heat of one of the horses had melted the snow. The fresh snow is like a photographic plate recording a sudden exposure. We tend to think of the tracks in the snow as narratives—after all, they're the imprints of creatures who are going somewhere with some reason. But the tracks were so vivid yesterday that their stories seemed to vanish. What mattered wasn't the coming and going, the prints that seemed to begin and end abruptly, with no foreword or sequel. All that mattered was the visible impression in the snow, the strokes left behind.

Writing these words, I make it sound as though I go out into the pasture as blank as a photographic plate myself, waiting to receive impressions from the world around me. But that's never the way it works here. What sticks with me so often is what I've glimpsed out of the corner of my eye. It's the noticing I do without noticing that seems to register. And yet there are also moments like yesterday when I came upon the spot where the horses lay. It's dumb luck. I stand beside it and think "Huh!" That's as literate as it gets. Then the dogs move on, and the geese, seeing them, send up the alarm in the poultry yard, and a pickup comes down the road with its lights on and in the distance I can hear a freight train rumbling past. All the while I'm wondering what's for dinner and what I'll write tomorrow and how I'll ease away from the concentration it takes to write a book, now that the book is out.

76

And always there is the real issue—where will the new run-in shed go? The geese settle again and the moon comes up orange.

February 16

Once a week I drive south to the train station through what is still, for the most part, a farming valley. The fields along this route haven't yet been wholly abandoned, as they have across so much of the landscape north of New York City. Farmers still spread manure on the corn-stubble in the middle of winter. And in the middle of a winter like this one, you can even see a tractor and a manure spreader sunk to the axles in mud. These are mostly conventional farms, by which I mean that they're still dairying and raising grain in a pattern that would be familiar in Iowa, if anyone were dairying in Iowa. The difference is the quality of the soil and the scale of the operation and the size of the subsidies.

There's been a groundswell of unconventional farming up here. I mean small farms, usually organic, that have learned how to connect directly with consumers. It's a new model of farming based on an old model, one my grandfather would have understood back in the days before cheap transportation—whose real costs we choose not to notice—changed the way farmers and consumers think. On the road to the train I pass the outlying fields of large dairy farms, a few of which look very well managed. The beauty of one small clover pasture in late summer astonishes me. It's part of a rotation of pastures for a herd of Holsteins. The whole farm is beautiful, but that one pasture—never overgrazed, never undergrazed—embodies the care that goes into the place.

Lately someone has added pigs to the landscape. Two pigs, to be precise. I round a bend, look off to the right, and there they are. One pig is a Tamworth and the other looks like a Duroc. They have a quarter-acre field to themselves, tightly fenced, and a well-built house. Seeing pigs in the landscape was a huge part of my childhood in Iowa. They were everywhere, sometimes housed in small, portable quonset huts, sometimes in farm-built A-frame sheds. The pigs I saw when I was a kid had the keys to those houses. They could come and go as they liked. What you see now is white prefab buildings full of pigs all across the Midwest, with locked doors and feed bins and a single pickup parked outside. No pigs on the land.

It's been a joy to come across these pigs along the road to the train. I look for them every time. It's not that pigs are a novelty. I've seen plenty of pigs at home. They're part of the habit of our lives. I visit them across the pasture, behind the barn, below the garden, wherever we've moved them. The pleasure of the pigs on the road to the train is this: if I look up at the right time and the pigs are grazing in the right place, they appear to be standing on the skyline. I often see Holsteins along a pasture ridge with nothing but blue sky behind them. There's hilarity and solid comfort in the sight of those pigs on the horizon. I don't know why.

March 1

Some days I suspect that the objects around me are aging faster than I am. I put on a jacket to do chores and realize that I bought it in 1987. Here's a fly rod I made in 1981. In the stairwell hangs the mounted head of a mule deer my dad shot in Colorado a couple of years before I was born. The ears are coming apart at the edges, though the glass eyes are as bright as ever. They've been looking at me since I was an infant. How did these things get to be so old?

But nothing meters the passing of time like paperback books. I began buying them when I was in high school. I kept a small stack of them—Twain, Faulkner, way too much Aldous Huxley—beside the clock radio on my bed-side table. I bought each book with much consideration, and each one felt like another stone in the raising of a free-form house. I'd grown up on public libraries, but cheap paperbacks made it possible to have a library of my own.

Now those paperbacks are coming apart. The pages have yellowed. The glue in the bindings has turned brittle. The edges are crumbling. I reread a Dorothy Sayers mystery a couple of weeks ago and found myself using one of the middle pages as a bookmark. Nearly all my old Penguin classics—the ones with the black spines—are dis-binding themselves. St. Augustine fell into my lap not long ago. Defoe was one of the first to go to pieces. You wouldn't believe how sallow Samuel Butler looks, how debilitated Flaubert has become. Even poor Kierkegaard, published by Princeton, snapped in two the other day.

The books themselves aren't really worth restoring. Their texts may be of permanent value, but the physical objects themselves are not. Rubber bands might hold them together, but rubber bands decay even faster than books. There are only two solutions. One is to go on handling the books ever more carefully until all that remains is neatly organized piles of yellow dust on the bookshelves. The other solution is to honor the ephemeral nature of paper-backs and replace them, as if they were vinyl LPs waiting to be replaced by CDs and then by "remastered" CDs.

But here's the trouble. My Penguin copy of Jane Austen's *Mansfield Park* is identical to the tens of thousands of other copies that were printed when that edition first appeared. Or it was when I bought it. But replacing it means abandoning all the marks I made in it when I read it in graduate school. The marks have almost everything to do with who I was as a reader in the late 1970s and almost nothing to do with Jane Austen. They're probably worth abandoning for that reason alone.

But to me *Mansfield Park* is that one edition. Like many readers, I have a surprisingly visual memory for books. It's easier for me to remember just where a passage appears, spatially, than exactly what it says. Replacing that old familiar edition means learning a new map of the text. That's the peculiar thing about living with so many books. I can often picture just where I need to look inside a book, but I can't remember where the book is actually shelved. The thought of remapping my literary memory is simply too much to stand.

In the late 1970s, I worked as a curatorial assistant at the Pierpont Morgan Library, and in the shelves behind my desk stood books that were hundreds of years old, the paper crisp and white, the ink still precise. Jane Austen's letters to her sister, Cassandra—the actual, original objects—weren't quite as fresh as the day they were written, but even they were fresh enough to last another few centuries. The point of publishing was more than simply to emit a book—it was to give a text a kind of permanence.

For paperback prices I shouldn't have expected a lifespan longer than my own, especially given that paperbacks really came into their own during my lifetime. But I didn't expect such a synchronized collapse. This may not be the burning of the library at Alexandria, but it's a slow, steady combustion.

And as for you who say, Aha!—this only proves the value of digitizing books, let me say that it's not possible to digitize a book. You can digitize its contents, photograph its binding, record every last scrap of penciled annotation it contains. And yet the book can't be digitized any more than the feeling that I know where that quotation is if only I could find the book itself.

March 22

Winter turning into spring is a long, slow earthquake. The roads heave with the frost, and so does everything else. I notice it especially along the fence lines. The posts begin to cant away from the vertical. The rails begin to slip their joints. A long straight fence line creates the impression that this piece of ground, this bounded field, is somehow a unit, a single thing. Winter comes along, then spring, and it becomes clear that each fence post is rooted in a place of its own, completely separate from its neighbors only a rail or two away. Once I got the picture of a long, slow earthquake in my mind, I found myself marveling at the futility of fences. Thirty miles down the road, someone has put up a white plastic post-and-rail horse fence, as clean and bright as the fencing in a child's barnyard toy set. After one winter, half the rails have bucked free of the posts. I've begun to think of a fence as a line of buoys floating on the surface of a stiff sea.

A couple of weeks ago, the poultry yard went wild, and it's remained so ever since. No foxes or skunks or weasels. No goshawks. Just the onset of the spring rut. Normally, a flock of ducks and geese is like a glob of mercury on a glass plate. It wants to cohere. There's nothing easier than driving a flock of ducks and geese—a little patience, a hand gesture here and there, a sense of anticipation. But the coming of March has torn the flock apart. Some of the courtship is graceful, almost entrancing. I watched a Saxony duck and an Ancona drake bob their heads in time as they walked to the tank to drink, and as they drank they kept on bobbing. But courtship is hardly the word for the rest of what goes on. Suddenly there's no flock. There are only small clusters of birds who resist being driven together. This will pass. But not soon enough.

To ease the hens' lives, we've been killing the extra roosters. I caught a Welsummer the other morning and before it could protest I'd broken its neck. Here's what I think about as that happens. I wish I had the skill of the farmwomen I saw when I was young, who knew the trick of giving a chicken an instant death with their hands. I need a certain rage in order to kill the rooster, a cold dose of rage, if that makes sense. I'm undone by the arbitrariness of it, the way one rooster wanders into my path and is suddenly gone in the unceremonious morning light. And I'm no less undone by trying to understand what happens in that death, what vanishes besides the Welsummer's baleful stare. I feel where the vertebrae have separated. I think of my own neck.

April 26

The other morning, I looked out the south window to see if the flag had dropped on our rural mailbox. I saw a fox just beyond it, standing in the downfall of last year's goldenrod. The fox paused long enough for me to get the binoculars, and then it moved to the base of a rock outcrop, part of the orbit she uses to approach our poultry. Three—perhaps four—young kits followed her. She turned and led them back to the lip of the den, where they crowded around her. She bent down and licked one of them. They were only a few pounds each—thick with soft, mottled fur. In another week the grass will be tall enough to hide them. A week earlier, and they would have been too young to leave the den. The vixen slipped up the hill again, and her young didn't reappear.

The den is dug into the sunken foundation of a long-vanished outbuilding. I'm only a few steps away from those kits whenever I gather the mail. A few weeks ago I walked over to that old foundation to see if there was any fox sign, but it's far easier to trace the vixen by her cries in the night—circling around our pasture—than it is by footprint during the day. I wasn't even sure the den was really there. Now I know. I won't go back again until midsummer, but I can't stop watching.

The grace of wildness changes somehow when it becomes familiar. When I say the grace of wildness, what I mean is its autonomy, its self-possession, the fact that it has nothing to do with us. The grace is in the separation, the distance, the sense of a self-sustaining way of life. That vixen may rely on us for a duck or a chicken now and then, and to keep the woodland from closing in. How she chose to den so close to us is beyond me. The answer is probably as simple as an available hole. Our only job is to leave her alone, to give her enough room to raise the next generation.

May 1

Reading Gilbert White's entry for this date, which says, "men pole hops," I'm struck as always by the economy of his journal. That is, I'm struck by the scale and complexity of the world, barely visible to us, that lies behind his brief notes. Behind that one phrase—"men pole hops"—you have to imagine the change this activity would have brought to Selborne. The parish was filled with small hop-gardens, many of them carefully protected from the wind by hedges. Each garden was planted in mounds laid out in a checkerboard pattern (sometimes a quincunx). By now, the farmers would have opened the mounds and examined the roots of the hops, choosing the strongest shoots—the ones that aren't "worn out of heart," as one early writer puts it—and adding new mold and compost to them.

Then comes a day when everyone in the village turns to the labor of carrying hop-poles, made of ash or chestnut, into the gardens and erecting them. These poles were often twenty feet long and set firmly in the earth. As John Worlidge puts it in *Systema Agriculturæ*, "It is esteemed an excellent piece of Husbandry to set all the Poles inclining towards the South, that the Sun may the better compass them. This is most evident, that a leaning or bending Pole bears more Hops than an upright."

So imagine the transformation. Suddenly in late April the parish sprouts a forest of bare poles. When the wind is high, they sound a note all their own. Before long, women will come into the hop-gardens and tie the vines to the poles. By mid-June, the vines will have "run out" the poles, turning each of these gardens into a patchwork of light and shade. By mid-August, the bloom has begun. Each year brings its own variation. Some years the hops—the flowers themselves—"promise well," as White puts it. Some years, like 1773, a tempest blows up and makes "sad havock among the hops," knocking down the poles and tearing the vines. Some years, like June 1783, it's sultry and misty, "weather that men think injurious to hops." By late September the hops have been picked (an extraordinary thing in itself), and "the whole air of the village of an evening is perfumed by effluvia from the hops drying in the kilns." In early October, the bagged hops are carried to Weybridge Fair and put up for sale.

I add, merely as a note, that Worlidge recommends a tea made of water and pigeon dung for fertilizing the hop hills.

June 5

On the ground was a young woodchuck not half the size of a full-grown one. It lay on its back, feet spread evenly as if for dissection, fur still lustrous, bright curving teeth. There was also a profound hole at the base of its neck and a collar of blood. The grass seemed to suspend the woodchuck. Behind me in a birch tree stood a vulture that flushed when I came around the corner. It seemed to be trying to stand on one leg with wings raised, tipping side to side almost the way it does in flight. Sometimes it nearly lost its balance. A pair of crows complained from a higher branch. I had nothing to add.

What was interesting wasn't the dead woodchuck. It would have eaten my beans later this summer. What was interesting was seeing the vulture come out of its column of flight and make a long, curving landing behind the barn. I knew there was something dead in the grass only because of the vulture's hunching presence. It knew something was dead in the grass while it was high overhead. Death to me is still a curiosity, even after all this time here. To the vulture it's simply a way of getting a living. The vulture lifted its wings again, as if to feel the breeze beneath them. I took a step closer and it flew away.

There was nothing mournful in any of this, and cruelty isn't really a word worth using when talking about nature. The death of that woodchuck seemed surprisingly economical, considering what was happening on the rest of the place. The forest tent caterpillars—who knows how many of them?—have made their way up into the canopy of the trees, and they've erased May. Where there were young leaves there are now nearly empty branches. The roses are bare and so are the blueberries. So is the paper-bark maple. The walk down to the barn is littered with scissored leaf fragments, like a jigsaw puzzle waiting to be assembled. A strange light makes its way down through the trees—not spring, not summer. I can't quite capture the mood the light causes because I've never seen its kind before.

And yet some plants have gone untouched—the hydrangeas and a striped-bark maple. Perhaps there's something unpalatable in their leaves, just as there seems to be something unpalatable in the caterpillars themselves. Nothing wants to eat them or to bother them in any way. Their destruction lies in their own numbers, I suppose. I heard the electric fence snapping clear across the pasture the other night—grounding itself on a fallen tree limb, I thought. But no. The caterpillars had crawled up a neutral brace wire at the fence corner, so many caterpillars that the current leaped from the hot wire into the gob of them, sparking.

June 28

Lately I've been thinking about the volume the birds around us occupy. I don't mean the vast migratory territories they mark out over the course of a year. I mean the spatial dimensions of their ordinary lives among us. This is a thought that's been working away in my head for a long time now, ever since I saw a red-winged blackbird perched on a cattail and realized that the bird and the wetland in which the cattail was rooted were essentially synonymous. *Habitat*, as a word, sounds awfully general. It turns out to mean not some willful choice—the kind a human makes deciding to live in Dallas rather than Denver—but a profound correlation. The marsh is who the red-winged blackbird is. The fence post is the meadowlark.

When I first began to notice birds, I thought of them as autonomous creatures whose habitations were simply unconnected matters of fact, as though the pictures of the birds in my bird book could somehow fly free of the book itself. But recognizing what you see means taking account of where you see it. It becomes clear that we live in a world of infinitely overlapping and abutting habitats. We're one of the rare creatures that is unbound, except in the broadest sense, by place and vocation. It takes a conscious act of will on our parts to remember how profoundly and how beautifully bound to habitat the other creatures around us really are.

This thought occurs to me again and again on a fine summer evening, when the phoebes are fluttering after bugs, sometimes pausing on the grass, but swiftly coming to rest on the back of a lawn chair or the end of a twig. Where the phoebes won't fly, the barn swallows take over, also pursuing insects. Sometimes a swallow will cruise past my head. Compared to the swallow's manner, the phoebe flies a parenthetical flight. And as the two of them are taking bugs from very different regions of this place of ours— before they retire in favor of the bats—I can hear the catbird hidden in the densest shadow, mewing away. It shows itself just at the edge of the thicket, peering off into the clearing where a human sits hoping that the good weather lasts for a while this time.

August 2

I've tried growing tomatoes in page-wire cages and in stiff-wire cones. One year I let the plants flop along the ground, the way they seem to want to do. The past few years I've grown them on seven-foot stakes, a single stalk working its way upward. I've skipped most of the modern tomato technologies—red plastic mulch and water-filled girdles that keep young plants from freezing. I don't even try to raise the seedlings myself. A friend raises them for me—heirlooms mostly. I put them in the ground around Memorial Day and wait.

I'm a ruthless pincher. Off go the suckers—sprouting in the joint between branch and stem—and off goes any branch that looks like it's going into business for itself. Last week, several of the plants topped out their poles, and I pinched back the growing tips as if to say, "Vegetation is over. Time to ripen." I wash my hands and the water is green. My other skill is tying up tomatoes. A couple of years ago I found the knot I needed—a loose, open overhand knot around the stem and then a square knot around the stake, the whole thing shaped like an 8. I use baling twine, of which I have an infinite supply, cut into forearm lengths.

As skills go in this complicated world, these are as simple as they come. And yet I can't explain how much pleasure it gives me to examine each stem for suckers, to know that I've really looked those tomatoes over. As I tie up the stalks, I think about the storms that blow through this time of year—bruising rain, sudden downdrafts—and it's good to know that the tomatoes are safely moored. I know there's a harvest somewhere in my calculations. Other people's vines have ripe tomatoes on them. But earliness isn't everything.

The truth is that I'd rather grow tomatoes than anything else, with the possible exception of pumpkins. In a hard rain, pathogens may spring from the soil onto the lower leaves, corrupting them, but the tomato stalk pushes upwards, rampant, always probing outward, feeling its way, almost disregarding the fruit it was meant to bear.

August 25

A couple of weeks ago, the hayloft was nearly empty—half a dozen bales in the northwest corner, a hay elevator, and a pair of young swallows in a nest above one of the light fixtures. The sliding double doors were open at both ends, adding to the emptiness. We feed a bale a night to the horses this time of year, and having only six bales on hand is a little worrying. But the grass has been especially strong this year. And besides, we knew the second cutting was already being baled. On Saturday we would stack 650 bales.

There's nothing venerable about the barn. Internally, it's a truss and plywood affair, built by the previous owners back when plywood was cheap. Every barn was new once upon a time, but the barns I knew in Iowa were already in their third and fourth generations of use. They'd been gnawed by time, sanded by the hides of so many milk cows coming in to stand at stanchion. Those barns feel more forceful, more solemn, the emptier they are—on the milking floor and in the hayloft—because their architecture is more visible. Our hayloft, on the other hand, seems raw when it's empty, just a long slender plywood box.

But then the hay wagons come. I winch the elevator down onto a wagon-end. The farmers, who have lived their lives with hay elevators, make a few adjustments to the machine. They plug it in to see how it goes. The teeth chink their way up the incline. The bales, when they come, are like roller-coaster cars getting a lift up that first big hill. I catch them at the top and fling them back into the loft where two young men—eager for the workout—stack them. In a couple of hours there's only enough room to slide the elevator back into the loft on edge. Later that afternoon, I remember to climb up to the loft and pull down the bales around the swallow's nest so the barn cat won't get the young ones.

The end doors stay open for a few weeks until the hay has dried completely. The newness of the barn vanishes when the loft is full of hay, because the hay itself feels so old, even though it came out of the fields only a day or two earlier. What's old about it is the way it leads right back to my childhood and beyond. And yet every year I'm surprised again at how new the hay stays. Those last six bales? The ends of one or two of them were bleached by the sun, and they all had a spidery feel to them, as if they'd been bound with silk instead of twine. But the loft kept them dry and well aired, and when I fed them out in flakes for the horses, we were all pleased to see how the summer inside them had lasted.

September 12

My dad called the other night to tell me that my cousin Myron had died of a heart attack. I was in upstate New York, and my dad was in the San Joaquin Valley. Myron was at the Clay County Fair in Spencer, Iowa, when he collapsed and died. He had turned 61 in August. I last saw Myron a little more than a year ago. My uncle's steers had broken down a section of fence, and we all went out into the night to herd them in and fix the spot where they escaped. Myron has been seven years ahead of me all my life, which means he always seemed like one of the grown-ups. It felt the same way that night. Myron was helping. I was conscious of helping. There's a world of difference between those two things.

I seem, to my own surprise now this late in life, to have grown up in a world full of men I admired without knowing how to admire them. They lived near the home farm in northwest Iowa, and we lived in a small town a hundred miles away. What we had in common was that home farm, where I spent parts of several summers, and also the Sunday and holiday dinners my grandparents hosted, where the common language was pinochle. I thought at the time that Myron was shy and untalkative—a tall young man with a big smile and a red face, clearly a part of the grown-up world. He ran the corn-sheller, the most dangerous piece of machinery I'd ever seen. But what does any eighteen-year-old have to say to an eleven-year-old, especially when one has grown up farming and the other has grown up reading books?

I thought of this at the edge of a bean field talking to Myron and his younger brothers a couple of years ago. We were talking about the genetically modified crops growing all around us. Myron invited me to come out for bean picking one autumn and run the combine. He knew how that would impress someone who is still, essentially, a town kid. I wish I'd taken him up on it.

But there's something I wish even more. It turned out that Myron wasn't the least bit untalkative. The night we rounded up the steers I'd already listened—happily—to an evening-long monologue of his. It was about nothing, but it was also about all the kinships of land and family and commerce in the country around us. One name led to another, one place to another, in the present and the past. The real measure of how empty the countryside is depends on who is doing the telling. To hear Myron tell it, we were having cake and coffee in the midst of a richly peopled land. I've been looking forward to hearing the rest of the story ever since.

October 14

For the most part our animals don't have many secrets from us. The reverse is probably true too, except for the one big secret we keep from the pigs. The horses and poultry are always in sight, and together we all belong to something that's larger than any one of us—the daily routine of this small farm. Morning and evening I can feel the animals leaning toward what they know comes next—a walk down to the barn, hay and grain, layer-mash, egg gathering and the filling of water tanks. The livestock clocks in and out as surely as I do. I can always feel the weight of their scrupulous attention.

But sometimes I take the animals by surprise. I catch them without expectation and witness how deeply they reside here. It happened the other noon. We awoke to the first frost of autumn, a clear bright day that had not lost its chill when I walked down to the end of the driveway to get the mail. In the big pasture—all of an acre—the horses stood rigid, broadside to the sun. The ducks and geese lay sound asleep in the threadbare shade of a hickory that had hastened to lose its leaves. Some hens had sprawled in a dustbath, and there was a subcommittee meeting going on in the entrance to the portable chicken house.

Here I was, cutting my narrow vulpine arc to the mailbox and back, and all around me life seemed to have stopped. We think of time as an abstraction, an equation, a cold transparent thing without substance. But here, in this mid-day pause, time seemed to be giving off as much warmth as the sun itself. The horses were basking in the heat of the sun, keeping themselves perpendicular to its rays. But they were also basking in what I can't help calling their continuity, their presence in the long, floating, unscheduled middle part of the day. Nothing about their manner suggested that this was a private moment, partly because I find it easier to believe in a horse's sense of justice than its sense of privacy. And yet I felt that I was looking into a private moment.

The reason is simple. Whenever my life intersects with theirs, it's all expectation, a concern for what comes next. Among the animals, I feel as though I carry time like a bacillus, and we share the infection. But in the middle of the day, equidistant from morning and evening chores, the animals drift away into a life all their own. But if I stepped into the pasture, hoping to still my own clock, to pause in the sun, the horses would wander over—and the chickens would rush my way—as if to ask, "What now?"

November 10

By now, the wind has emptied the milkweed pods. The goldenrod has gone mousy. All the leaves are down, except for a few tenacious oaks and beeches and an ornamental dogwood that's a reprise of the entire season. Each tree looks more solitary—and the woods more intimate—in this bare month than in the thickness of summer. The memory of October seems a little lurid from the perspective of mid-November. The sumacs down by the road might have been reading Swinburne the way they caught fire and expired, vaingloriously, in the light of last month. But now that drama is over, as if the year had come up against a plain, Puritan truth and was the better for it.

I used to hate November up here—a month of freezing rain and inconclusive light. It brought out my most urban sentiments, a reluctant longing for the enclosure of the city, its containment and warmth and distraction and all those lights. Up here we're no more vulnerable to the prevailing wind now than we were in August, when the trees still had leaves, but that's not how it feels. I still can't get over the size of the November night. And yet my old disgust with the month is somehow slipping away.

I suppose this is partly the snobbery of place. October's vivid colors are a public spectacle. You can take them in even through the tinted windows of a chartered coach lumbering down the road. You can track the peak of the foliage as though it were just another commodity fluctuating in price. But nobody really chronicles when the lights go out in the goldenrod or when, all at once, the most luminous color in the landscape becomes the green of the moss on the ledge outcrops in the woods. These are private gratifications, the kind that come not from passing by but from staying put.

I've been replacing fence up here this fall, and the other morning I walked along the western property line, where the next stretch of new fence will go. This is the edge of the hemlock woods, where the ground is either bedrock or fungus. A few yards further in, there's a gorge with an intermittent stream. Most of the time the water goes underground well above our land, leaving the rockfall dry, but after heavy rains the gorge sometimes flows with the sound of a heavy wind. That morning was one of those times. In that somber place, as dark and deep as the month we're in, a stream was now rushing, not in flood, perilously, but working its way down the rocks, carrying the broken light of the sky with it. Another day or two, and the gorge will be dry again.

December 22

The heavy winds that blew through the Northeast a couple of weeks ago mostly missed our place. They took only the dead boughs, which now lie scattered along the edges of the pastures like porous old bones. The farmers up here will have a lot of cleaning to do along the fence lines before they make hay next June or they'll be baling kindling. In the woods across from our house, the wind snapped off the top of a sugar maple. The crown lies jagged on the ground, not yet weighed down by gravity or moss. It exaggerates the disorder of nature, which seems so apparent in the absence of snow this time of year.

Nearly every image of nature I've ever come across misses the sense of intricate confusion underfoot in the woods, the thickets of goldenrod collapsing into each other along the roadsides, the rotting tusks of fallen beeches broken against the western hillside. It almost never makes sense to talk about the purpose of nature. But until the snow comes I could easily imagine that the purpose of nature is to create edges, because every edge, no matter how small, is a new habitation. As purposes go, that could hardly be more different from my own, which is to reduce the number of edges here so that the big pasture is bounded by four clean lines only, free of interruptions from sumac or knotweed or shattered maple limbs. Left to itself nature is all interruption.

These are the thoughts that crowd around during the shortest days of the year, when the sky is the color of flint and the sun, when it appears, seems to have lost its candlepower. Even the feeling of dormancy—a harvest of rest—is incomplete without snow. But disorder is as much in the mind as order. I drive across the county, brooding on confusion, and come upon a towering single oak—stripped of leaves but still symmetrical—mocking the sawmill that lies across the road. The sight of that one tree is enough to banish sorrow.

Interlude

If you walk to the edge of a small Iowa town in mid-August, now or in the days when I was a child there, you come to a wall of corn or a low, continuous border of soybeans that reaches as far as the horizon. Town ends and country begins just that quickly, and the nature of country in central Iowa is so extremely orderly—the crop rows so meticulously laid out, weeds so thoroughly discouraged—that the edge of town always looks a little disorganized. Whatever else an Iowa town may be, it's only a clearing in the corn.

I lived in small Iowa towns from 1954 until 1966, when my family moved to California, as so many Iowans did in those days. Those years, and the years immediately after, reaching into the mid-1980s, brought a sea change in American agriculture. My mother's side of the family once farmed, and my father's side still does in the northwest corner of the state. The little I knew about farming when I was a boy I learned from my father's brothers and my cousins, though for me farming meant teasing the animals and pretending to drive the tractor and climbing in the barn. The thought that farming was really an economic activity—something done for money, with far-reaching social and environmental implications—never crossed my mind. I was surrounded, even in town, by the economy of farming, but it was a little like Iowa's summer

91

humidity—I noticed none of it. To this day, farm-town banks still post corn and bean prices along with the temperature and time on outdoor electric signs.

It would never have occurred to me to call what I saw in the fields outside town "conventional" agriculture. No one else I knew, young or old, would have called it that either. It was just agriculture. My grandfather, in Lyon County, had been something of a pioneering farmer, one of the first to buy a tractor, one of the first to experiment with hybrid seed and the new postwar chemical fertilizers. His sons and their sons followed his example. If I'd been asked to choose an adjective to describe the agriculture I saw around me, it would have been "progressive," a word that's an advertisement not a description.

In 1985 I began a book about the farming life called *Making Hay*. After nearly twenty years away, I returned to my uncles' and cousins' farms in northwest Iowa and spent part of June helping them cut and dry and bale alfalfa. That, I now think, is a little like going to an auto factory and studying how the cafeteria works. Alfalfa is a marginal crop in Iowa, where dairying has disappeared and cash grain is king. Unlike corn and soybeans, alfalfa usually stays in the ground for three years. It increases the amount of nitrogen available in the soil. (Soybeans do this too.) To me, there's something beautiful about the act of making hay. It never occurred to me to wonder, while I was writing my book, what role hay played in the broader agricultural economy of the state. It is, in most senses, a nostalgic crop.

Making Hay was for me a last look at a seemingly unspoiled landscape, the last time I'd be able to see the stern farms of Iowa without seeing the broad economic connections that underlay the patchwork of the fields, without questioning the agricultural practices common throughout the state, without knowing that this was "conventional" agriculture. While writing *Making Hay*, I noticed that the houses and outbuildings on farmstead after farmstead had been pulled down and plowed under to make more room for crops. The small towns I once lived in had dwindled in ways that were confusing, saddening. Those facts were inescapable. But I hadn't figured out how to ask the critical questions that would explain what I was seeing, nor did I conceive that there was an alternative to it. I grew up in farm country but I knew no more about it than most Americans do.

In the early decades of this century, not long after the Midwestern prairie soil was first turned by a plow, the miracle of American farming was a natural miracle, the result of the soil's preposterous depth and fertility, itself the result of centuries of tallgrass prairie being grazed by bison herds and burned by fire. But in the decades after I first came to know my grandfather's farm—the sixties through the eighties—that miracle was beginning to be called by another name, because it had become a different miracle. It was now a technological miracle, an industrial miracle, the result of the wizardry of plant breeders and chemists and engineers and financiers.

The expectations of farming changed. From the USDA all the way down to the local banker, experts advised farmers to tear down their fences, do away with their livestock, and plant from roadside to roadside. Farmers were told to borrow against the speculative value of their land and expand their operations by buying more land and purchasing more products they couldn't make themselves—fertilizer, pesticides, machinery. Production became the sole measure of a progressive farmer. The only way to survive, farmers were told, was to get bigger, and the only way to get bigger was to accrue debt. And buy out your neighbors.

But it hasn't taken long for that kind of agricultural progress to bite the hands that feed us, and not only in harsh years. Bad news has been drifting in from the countryside for the last four or five decades. As remarkable as conventional farming's yields and profits have been, the list of its systemic side effects is tragic: farm foreclosures, rural bank failures, wells tainted by agricultural chemicals leaching into groundwater, pollution of surface water, the steady loss of soil and deterioration of its quality, an undiminishing rate of crop damage to pests despite heavy use of pesticides, a collapse of genetic diversity among agricultural crops and animals, a health crisis among agricultural laborers, the increasing corporate control of all levels of agricultural production, the increasing absentee and corporate ownership of agricultural land, the economic and social marginalizing of farmers and their communities, a burdensome agricultural bureaucracy, a perplexing and often wrongheaded program of federal farm subsidies.

You don't need to be a pessimist to be depressed by the widespread disappearance of small farms or the concentration of agricultural land in the hands of corporations and the demise of farm towns all across the country. Nor is it unpatriotic to ask what the ultimate cost of this kind of agriculture may really be. It's been clear for some time now, in nearly every corner of this country, that the dynamic commercial success of conventional agriculture—a success only for certain sectors of the population and only in certain years—has been brought about by consuming natural resources—topsoil, water, petroleum, people—as if they were purchasable inputs. Sometimes you hear it said, with pride, that it takes just 2 percent of Americans to feed this nation. That's good news only if you believe that having few farmers is better than having many farmers, or that there's something demeaning in farm work or in rural living.

But if what farmers know, as well as what they do, matters, then you can't have too many farmers. And if it's how farmers act that matters, then clearly there can never be enough farmers. Yet the thrust of conventional agriculture has been to drive farmers from the land, to depopulate the countryside, and to turn many of the farmers that remain into nothing more than contract laborers and heavy-equipment operators. The way we farm has divorced farmers utterly from the soil. Society and the soil suffer alike.

As an index to what's possible, it's worth remembering that modern, chemically intensive industrial agriculture has only existed since the end of World War II. But it's also good to keep in mind the words of Allan Savory, creator of an influential decision-making model widely used among ranchers and rangeland managers. "Throughout history," Savory has said, "civilizations have collapsed because they outgrew their environmental resources. There's no reason to believe that our civilization is an exception. We could have sustainable agriculture tomorrow if we abandon the cities. That we will obviously not do. What we need is sustainable civilization."

2001

When I first heard that Vicki Hearne had died, I reread *Adam's Task*, which was published in 1986. I remember how strange the book felt to me when it first appeared, how odd it seemed to talk about dog training and horse training in a language full of allusions to Wittgenstein and Kierkegaard, to Milton and Stanley Cavell. I realize now that I'd read *Adam's Task* backwards. To me, it sounded like the elaborate and unnecessary cloaking of a simple subject— animal training—with the rigorous dialects of poetry and philosophy. It read, in other words, like a serious philosophical discussion of the linguistic acts of naming and command, mingled with strangely hyperbolic assertions about the capacity of animals for moral thought. But at the time the only thing I'd ever studied was language.

Since then, I've been rubbed up hard against the worlds Hearne knew best of all, dog training and horse training. They've changed my life. Some extraordinary animals and some extraordinary trainers have given me a glimpse of the moral universe she was trying to portray. "Dog trainers and horse trainers," she writes, "insist that training—teaching animals the language games of retrieving, say, or *haute école* in dressage—results in ennoblement, in the development of the animal's character and in the development of both the animal's *and the handler's* sense of responsibility and honesty." Those are Hearne's italics. They suggest how serious she was about the reciprocity good training entails.

Hearne was trying to unravel a subject of almost impossible subtlety. To do so she turned to the men and women who had thought most carefully about language, to poets and philosophers. They gave her the tools to express the vigilance she exercised as a trainer, a vigilance that depended not on a mechanistic or behaviorist view of dogs and horses but on a faith, proved by experience, in their moral depth. To her, there was no freedom for those animals apart from their engagement with humans, and no freedom for humans apart from their engagement with those animals.

But Hearne never called it freedom. She called the kinship that develops between trainers and animals a version of the heroic. She called not for mere tolerance or kindness between humans and animals but for a shared nobility. Hearne explained that certain dogs and horses can teach you "whether or not your relationships and your artistries, your grammars, are coherent, whether what you have is a free-floating and truncated bit of the debris of Romanticism or a discipline that can renew the resources of thought." This will only sound hyperbolic if you've never witnessed or experienced the results of that *discipline*, which is a word we fear these days.

Hearne made large claims, but they were always tested by the animals she worked with day in, day out. No one has come close to her ability to articulate what one feels in a working relationship with animals. For her, that relationship—that work—was a human duty, nothing less. It's not a lesson we bestow on animals but a learnable mystery that they impart to us. "Animals matter to us," Hearne wrote, and the "way they matter to us is probably all we can know of how and why we matter."

2004

Beef cattle and dairy cattle are two very different creatures, but their fates are identical. Most Americans don't realize that nearly every dairy cow eventually becomes hamburger when her profitability drops. Holsteins are frequently culled for slaughter when they're between five and six years old. A Holstein first gives milk at about two years old, so that means a productive life of just about three years. In that brief lifespan, everything is done to maximize yield, including the regular use of antibiotics.

After poultry and pigs, the dairy industry has become one of the most concentrated forms of agriculture in America. The old mental picture of a herd of Holsteins standing hock-deep in pasture bears no relation to the way milk is produced in most of America. The herds at some dairies, especially in the West and Southwest, now number in the thousands. The animals spend their lives in barns on cement where they're milked automatically, in some cases on huge rotating platforms that look like something out of science fiction.

Even Holsteins can put up with only a certain amount of this. By the time they mature, at around five years old, many begin to break down from leg and foot problems. Dairy organizations distribute locomotion charts to help workers assess lameness. Other cows begin to fail from the stress of carrying an udder that can weigh as much as a full-grown man. To prepare them for slaughter, the cows must be given time to get any *residue*—the word means traces of drugs—out of their system.

As always, the goals of industrial agriculture create a perverse logic. Instead of adapting the agricultural system to suit the animal, we try to adapt the animal to suit the system in order to eke out every last so-called efficiency. Take it for granted that dairy cows will eventually be slaughtered. But strange as it sounds, it makes greater financial, ethical, and social sense if we subscribe to the cows' notions of efficiency, which don't include living on concrete or eating anything but grass and grain. The animals would be healthier, their milk would be better, and we wouldn't have to worry quite so much what's in our food.

Some day Americans will learn to judge agriculture not by its intentions but by its unintended consequences. The intention in the dairy industry has always been to streamline, modernize, automate, all in the interest of greater profits. But the consequence has been to concentrate power and money in the hands of a few, drive down prices, and create a national surplus of milk that forces small dairy producers out of business. That, in turn, frees former dairy land for development, for suburban sprawl. The consequence has also been to breed an animal that can barely sustain the way she's forced to live.

The river of milk in America brings with it a river of ground beef made from dairy cows, a river that's impossible to inspect adequately in a deregulated industry. The problem isn't just a concentration of meat. It's a concentration of political power that hamstrings any calls for closer inspection. The industry has been quick to point out that far more people die from salmonella and E. coli than from mad cow disease. That's not exactly a reason to stand up and cheer. And that's luck rather than good planning. According to the philosophers at Cow-Calf Weekly, an online journal for the beef industry, "Perception is reality." That's the sort of thing you say when reality is unbearable to look at.

2004

The DNA proves that the Washington State Holstein diagnosed last December with bovine spongiform encephalopathy, or mad cow disease, came from a Canadian herd. You can almost hear the relieved sighs of the American cattle industry, joined by the sighs of grain farmers and exporters and meat packers and the USDA itself. In the world of bureaucratic borders, this fact of origin makes a vital difference.

But in the world of global meat the DNA doesn't make a bit of difference. Moving cattle and meat and meat by-products across borders is one of the things our agricultural system does extremely well. That becomes obvious only when the system stops, and it stops only when a disease looms, whether it's a slow plague like mad cow disease, which takes several years to incubate, or a fast plague like hoof and mouth disease, which ravaged British farming just as it was beginning to recover from the effects of mad cow disease. Industrial agriculture is indeed industrial. It's designed to move parts along a conveyer belt no matter where the parts come from. And if one of the parts proves to be fatally defective—a dairy cow with the staggers, for instance— then shutting down the conveyer nearly always comes far too late.

What's needed to avert a major crisis is real change, from the bottom up. The global meat system is broken, as a machine and as a philosophy. In America meatpacking has gone from being a widely distributed, widely owned web of local, independent businesses into a tightly controlled, savagely concentrated industry whose assumptions are completely industrial. Meatpacking plants are enormous automated factories, as void of humans as possible. The machinery is very expensive. Profitability requires an uninterrupted flow of carcasses. To packers, that means that they, not independent farmers, should own the cattle, hogs, and poultry moving through the line. The federal government agrees. Every effort to outlaw packer-ownership of livestock has failed.

The result is a system in which the average drives out the excellent and the international drives out the local. The structure of global meat creates a forced acquiescence. I know a large-scale rancher in north-central Wyoming who does everything he can to raise beef cattle of the highest quality. That means good genetics, good grass, and as few chemical and pharmaceutical inputs as he can possibly manage. But then the cattle are loaded onto trucks, shipped to feedlots, and hauled to slaughter, where they merge with the great river of American meat, indistinguishable from all the rest. There's no real alternative to the highly concentrated meatpacking and distribution system in this country. Any alternative—grass-fed, organic beef, separately slaughtered, separately marketed—is merely a niche so far.

In science-fiction movies, there's often a moment when space colonists talk about "terra-forming" a suitable planet—giving it a breathable atmosphere and a terrestrial flora and fauna. We're going through a different process on the one planet we have. We are agri-forming it. We've given over vast tracts of rain forest to cattle production. Every distinctive food culture, every island of genetic difference in farm animals, every traditional relationship between humans and the soil is threatened by global meat and its partner, global grain.

The consequences are more far-reaching than we like to think. Last week a USDA spokesman said that a herd of cattle in Washington State was going to be "depopulated" as a preventive measure. Apart from the coarseness of the euphemism, the word is a perfect summary of the effect of agri-forming. Take Iowa, where I was raised. As farms have gotten larger and larger, the number of farmers has plummeted. As a result, the towns have dwindled, and there aren't enough workers for the industrial meatpacking plants in the state, which officially encourages factory farming. A few years ago, the governor launched a program to invite one hundred thousand immigrants to Iowa to fill those empty meatpacking jobs. A depopulated countryside is, in effect, a de-democratized countryside, no matter what the Iowa caucuses may suggest. But so is a town filled with captive workers in a captive industry. We like to pretend that the problem with global meat stops at the borders. But it reaches right down into the heart of our own lives and institutions.

2005

Last month a team of paleontologists announced that it had found several fossilized dinosaur embryos that were 190 million years old—some 90 million years older than any dinosaur embryos found so far. Those kinds of numbers—190 million, even 90 million years —are always daunting. Ever since I was a boy in Iowa, I've been learning to face the eons and eons embedded in the universe around us. I know the numbers as they stand at present, and I know what they mean, in a roughly comparative way. The universe is perhaps 14 billion years old. Earth is some 4.6 billion years old. The oldest hominid fossils are between 6 and 7 million years old. The oldest distinctly human fossils are about 160,000 years old.

The truth of these numbers is like watching the night sky in the high desert. It fills me with a sense of nonspecific immensity. I don't think I'm alone in this. One of the most powerful limits to the human imagination is our inability to grasp intuitively the depths of terrestrial and cosmological time. That's hardly surprising, since our own lives are so short in comparison. It's hard enough to come to terms with the brief scale of human history. But the difficulty of comprehending time on an evolutionary scale is one of the major impediments to understanding evolution itself.

It's been approximately 3.5 billion years since life first originated on this planet. That's not an unimaginable number in itself, if you're thinking of simple, discrete units like dollars or grains of sand. But 3.5 billion years of biological history is different. That's not an abstract lump of time, not a mathematical set or a kind of scientific shorthand. All those years have really passed, moment by moment, one by one. They encompass an actual, already-lived reality, the sum of all the lives of all the organisms that have come and gone in that time. That expanse of time defines the realm of biological possibility in which life in its extraordinary diversity has historically evolved. Time has allowed the making of us.

The idea of such quantities of time, such factual eons, is extremely new. Humans began to understand the true scale of geological time in the early nineteenth century. The probable depth of cosmological time, as well as the historical extent of the human species, has come to light only within our own lifetimes. That's a lot to absorb, and not surprisingly many people refuse to absorb it. Nearly every attack on evolution—whether it's called "intelligent design" or plain "creationism"—radically foreshortens cosmological, geological, and biological time.

Humans feel much more content imagining a world of human proportions, with a shorter time-scale and a simple narrative sense of cause and effect. But what we prefer to believe makes no difference to the facts. We've arrived at a point where it's possible for humans to have beliefs only because the eons have been steadily ticking away, working out the trial and error of natural selection. Evolution is a robust theory that has been tested and confirmed again and again. Intelligent design isn't a theory at all, as scientists understand the word, but a well-funded political and religious campaign to muddy science. Its basic proposition—the intervention of a divine designer—can't be tested. It has no evidence to offer, and its assumptions—that humans were divinely created—are the same as its conclusions. Its objections to evolution are nonserious. They're based on syllogistic reasoning and a highly selective consideration of the physical evidence.

Accepting the fact of evolution doesn't necessarily mean discarding a personal faith in God. But accepting intelligent design means discarding science. Much has been made of a 2004 poll showing that some 45 percent of Americans believe the earth—and humans with it—was created as described in the book of Genesis, and within the past ten thousand years. This isn't a triumph of faith. It's a failure of education. The purpose of the campaign for intelligent design is to deepen that failure. To present the arguments of "intelligent design" as part of a "debate" over evolution is nonsense. From the scientific perspective, there is no debate. But even the illusion of a debate is a sorry victory for antievolutionists, a public relations victory based on ignorance and obfuscation.

Intelligent design keeps God in the history of life on earth in the simplest way possible—by distorting that history. The essential but often well-disguised purpose of intelligent design is to preserve the myth of a separate, divine creation for humans, in the belief that only that can explain who we are. There's a fearful arrogance in that myth. It sets us apart from nature, except to dominate it. It grasps at divinity as the only guarantee of morality. But it misses both the grace and the moral depth of life itself—knowing that humans have only the same stake, the same right, in the earth as every other creature that has ever lived here. There's a righteousness and a responsibility in the deep, ancestral origins we share with all of life.

2007

Recently *Science* magazine published an article called "Domesticated Nature," which noted in passing that by 1995 "only seventeen percent of the world's land area had escaped direct influence by humans." The article was accompanied by one map showing the "human footprint" on Earth and another showing the interlacing of road networks and shipping lanes across the globe. That 17 percent figure is now smaller, and the weave of that interlacing of transport networks gets tighter every day. The article assumes what is obviously true: "There really is no such thing as nature untainted by people." This was a radical thought in 1989, when Bill McKibben's book *The End of Nature* first appeared. Now it's axiomatic.

What does it mean to go from a humanly ancient world in which, say, only 17 percent of nature had been "tainted"—to use the authors' word—to a world in which only 17 percent remains untainted? It's also tempting to wonder where that remaining 17 percent is and how to protect it. It can't be far away—just off a sea lane or a two-track road running into the distance—which makes it all the harder to protect. The authors of this article take the domestication of nature as inevitable—a "natural" part of human behavior—and

100

wonder what the "trade-offs among ecosystem services" might be. You may want to ponder this too the next time you go for a long walk among the ecosystem services.

What I find most worrying here isn't merely the premise of so much loss. It's the emergence of a world in which "nature" means little more than the consequences of human decisions. That world has been emerging for a long time. Humans first arose in a densely articulated natural world, on a globe that had been unaffected by human activity—because there was none—for several billion years. We are who we are, as a species, in part because of the natural intricacy in which we emerged. In a way, we originated in an alien world, alien in the sense that almost nothing we saw around us had been made or shaped or influenced by us. It may sound like folly to talk about the wisdom of nature. But its wisdom is that it will not simply show us ourselves. Wisdom is always a kind of otherness.

I'm oversimplifying. But consider where we are now. The authors of the *Science* article are certainly right when they stress the importance of stewarding "nature in perpetuity for people, as opposed to simply trying to protect nature from people." But they have more faith in people than I do—both in our ability to steward nature and to decide what stewarding it "for people" really means. It's possible to make wiser and wiser choices, but what if the world we make our choices in steadily becomes, in natural terms, poorer and less diverse? More and more, we find ourselves choosing only among the consequences of regrettable choices we made before.

Humans are competent to do many things. But we're not competent to run a global ecosystem. Something has been irretrievably lost by the time we begin to believe that we can manage nature in perpetuity for people. My lack of faith in humans as global managers isn't just a philosophical conclusion. It's based on the sorry, sorry evidence. We've begun to run the global ecosystem already and we're doing a terrible job of it. Our minds are rich, but our purposes are simple, and though our purposes complicate the world around us, socially and culturally, they also simplify the natural environment around us—simplify it to the point of tragedy.

What we'll never be able to provide on our own is feedback from a natural world that's not human. The authors of this article are right in asking the environmental movement to think of its main business now as managing the trade-offs in ecosystem services. The idea is rational, realistic, and human, and it accurately reflects where we've gotten to. But it's not good enough. We love the hidden metaphor in domestication—the idea that we're making the world more homelike for our species. But without alien feedback from the natural world, which enriches and outstrips our imagination, we'll find ourselves less and less at home on this planet.

2008

I won't be eating cloned meat. The reason has nothing to do with my personal health or safety and everything to do with this question, "Who benefits from cloning?" You'll surely hear some people say the consumer does, because we'll get higher quality, more consistent foods from cloned animals. But the only person really arguing for consistency is a meat packer, and since there are only a few meatpacking companies left in this country, that person is a large-scale meat packer, the kind who'd like it best if chickens grew in the shape of McNuggets. Anyone who really cares about food is interested in difference, in diversity.

The same is true for anyone who cares about farmers and their animals. An agricultural system that favors cloned animals has no room for farmers who farm in different ways. Cloning, you'll hear its advocates say, is just another way of making cows. But this isn't entirely true. Every other way of making cows—even using embryo transplants and artificial insemination—allows nature to shuffle the genetic deck. A clone is identical to the animal it was derived from. A clone is produced by asexual reproduction. This doesn't mean it was produced in a test tube. It means it was produced without the extraordinary variability that sexual reproduction fosters.

To me, modern agriculture looks like this. You begin with a wide array of breeds—a truly diverse gene pool. As time passes, you impose stricter and stricter economic constraints upon those breeds—and upon the men and women who raise them. One by one the breeds that don't meet the prevailing economic model are weeded out. By the beginning of the twenty-first century, you've moved from the broad base of a genetic pyramid to its nearly vanishing peak. In other words, the genetic diversity present in the economically acceptable breeds of modern livestock is minuscule. Then comes cloning, and we leave behind any variation and enter the realm of identity.

Cloning itself isn't unnatural. It's natural for humans to experiment—to try anything and everything. Nor is cloning really that different from anything else we've seen in modern agriculture. It's another way of shifting genetic ownership from farmers to corporations. It's another way of creating still greater economic and genetic concentration in an industry that has already pushed concentration past the limits of ethical, environmental, and economic acceptability.

Diversity isn't just good in itself. Genetic diversity is an essential bulwark against disease. And humans are only as rich as the diversity that surrounds them, whether we mean cultural or economic or genetic diversity. That measure of richness helps us understand just how badly we've been impoverished by modern agriculture. There's less and less genetic diversity in the animals found on farms, and farmers themselves become less and less diverse because fewer and fewer of them actually own the animals they raise. They become contract laborers instead.

And one more point. It's possible to preserve plant and crop diversity in seed banks. But there are no animal banks. Breeds of animals that aren't raised die away, and the invaluable genetic archive they represent vanishes. To some, this looks like a basic test of economic efficiency. But it's a colossal waste, of genes and of truly lovely, productive animals that are the result of years of human attention and effort. From one perspective, a cloned animal looks like a miracle of science. But from another, it looks like what it is: a dead end.

2008

Today's vocabulary word is *aerosolization*. As words go, it's cumbersome and unattractive. But it neatly sums up what happens when a solid physical substance is turned into mist. In this case, the substance being aerosolized was pig brains in a giant slaughterhouse in Austin, Minnesota.

Here's how aerosolization happens. A worker slides the tip of a compressed-air gun into the hole at the base of the skull where the spinal cord once entered a pig's head. A few blasts of air, and the pig's liquefied brains are forced out of the same hole that let in the compressed air. This happened nineteen thousand times a day. The workers were protected by plexiglass shields, by hard hats, safety glasses, and lab coats, but they wore no masks or face shields. They worked in a fine mist of brains. When workers at the "head table," as it was called, developed an illness with a strange set of neurological symptoms, the slaughterhouse, to its credit, stopped using compressed air to extract pig brains.

The wonder isn't that some workers suffered from fatigue and numbness. The wonder is that they were able to force themselves to go to work at all. I have just enough experience of pig killing to barely glimpse the psychological dislocation that their everyday jobs must have forced upon these workers. You could build mechanical pigs—nineteen thousand a day, if you like—using robots, who have no feelings in the matter. But you can't disassemble nineteen thousand living, breathing pigs a day without using humans, who do have feelings—and feelings not only about being sprayed with aerosolized pig brains.

The trouble with this picture is that the conventional economic answers do nothing to explain away the trouble with this picture. Pigs can be killed in such huge numbers because the packing industry is overwhelmingly concentrated, and because global consumption of meat is rising. Packers can find workers to fill these jobs because for the immigrants who fill them, these are what pass for good jobs.

Every one of these elements—the scale of concentration, the fact that packers, not farmers, own so many of the animals being slaughtered, the pattern of immigration that fills the jobs, even the fact that reporters aren't allowed into the plants—can be read directly back into the shape of the industrial landscape of what passes for rural America. This is just the way things are, the status quo, and as most of us know, the status quo has a logic all its own. The best explanation of that shady logic comes from George Orwell in *The Road to Wigan Pier*, which was published in 1937.

Orwell describes the brutal conditions in the coal mines in the north of England, conditions that he says were once much worse. "There are still living," Orwell writes, "a very few old women who in their youth have worked underground, with a harness around their waists and a chain that passed between their legs, crawling on all fours and dragging tubs of coal. They used to go on doing this even when they were pregnant. And even now, if coal could not be produced without pregnant women dragging it to and fro, I fancy [Orwell means "imagine" or "suspect"] we should let them do it rather than deprive ourselves of coal. But most of the time, of course, we should prefer to forget that they were doing it."

Health problems associated with harnessing pregnant women to drag tubs of coal along a railway a mile underground would surely cause a medical examiner to wonder, "What's wrong with this picture?" But in the search for the symptomatic picture—the immediate cause of the suffering—it's easy to lose sight of the systemic picture, which is presumed to justify itself. We need coal—or pig brains—and we'd just as soon forget how we get it and what its costs really are.

The mystery in Minnesota isn't the sickness of a few workers. The mystery is the structure of the entire system, the truckloads of hogs arriving at one entrance, the lines of workers arriving at another. It was a good idea to stop using compressed air to blow the brains out of a pig's skull. But at some point it must have seemed like a good idea to give it a try. There will be other good ideas too, most of them equally bad.

2009

For the past dozen years, I've been writing editorials opposing the introduction of genetically modified crops. When I began, genetically modified corn and soybeans were just getting a foothold in American fields. Now, hundreds of millions of acres here and abroad have been planted with these new varieties, which are usually engineered to withstand the application of pesticides—pesticides made by the same companies that engineer the seeds. Even wheat and rice producers, latecomers to the genetically modified table, are feeling the pressure to convert.

There's been a frenzy in the grain markets in the past couple of years—a new volatility in futures and in prices on the ground—that seems to favor genetically modified crops. It makes sense. The cost of conventionally grown grain goes up and up because there's less and less of it. This leaves the world open to the nearly unchecked proliferation of genetically modified varieties.

I still oppose genetically modified crops. This may sound like truculence on my part—a Luddite reluctance to accept the future. It's certainly dispiriting. Like many people, I feel, as I did a decade ago, that genetically modified crops were introduced with bland assurances of safety based on studies from small test plots, a far different thing from the uncontrolled global experiment we now find ourselves in the midst of.

Scientists are still discovering the extent to which genetic fragments from these new crops can drift into other organisms. There's no evidence yet of catastrophic drift, where a genetic shard from a new crop cripples other organisms. But there's plenty of evidence to show that genetically modified fragments are turning up in places they're not wanted. The worry isn't just how widespread the altered versions of familiar crops, like corn and soybeans, are becoming. It's also that many more conventional crops are being modified and that many more landscapes and ecosystems, yet untouched, will be planted with genetically modified varieties.

These crops close the circle on the farmer's knowledge, finally eliminating, after ten thousand years, the farmer's role in the genetics of agriculture. Genetically modified crops are rigorously licensed forms of intellectual property. Every seed is a binding contract with stiff penalties attached.

This represents the final transfer of the collective farming wisdom of the human race into corporate hands. Only the minutest fraction of the DNA in a genetically modified crop has been modified. The rest of the DNA is the result of infinite elaboration by working farmers choosing their own seeds, season after season, over all these thousands of years.

The trouble with genetically modified crops isn't merely the fact that they're genetically modified. It's that they embody so completely the troubling logic of modern agriculture. They demonstrate the tendency of commercial seeds to drive out traditional, locally adapted varieties, a pattern that's been intensifying since the introduction of hybrid corn in the 1930s. They exemplify the bias toward expensive high-tech solutions, when, in much of the world, simple low-tech solutions make much better and much more affordable sense. They foster the spread of commodity crops, grown for cash, in place of subsistence crops.

Genetically modified crops create the illusion of more and better choices when, in fact, they represent a narrowing of genetic ownership and a model of genetic diversity that's unattainable outside the laboratory. Because of that, they may well turn out to decrease food security, especially as new non-food varieties—crops genetically modified to produce pharmaceuticals, for instance—go into production. The risk is enhanced by licensing restrictions on genetically modified seeds that prevent independent research on their environmental impact. In effect, the GM seed industry is able to stifle research, even by agricultural scientists who are sympathetic to the technology.

Above all, genetically modified crops give the illusion of revolutionizing farming without actually changing much of anything. Farmers who plant them do spend less time and less fuel in the field. But trying to pack a revolution into a seed won't do when the entire system needs revolutionizing. Industrial agriculture is antithetical to diversity of every kind—biological, social, cultural, political. To understand its real effects on diversity you have only to look at Brazilian soybeans, a commodity crop, growing where there was once Amazonian forest.

There's no disputing the enormous productivity of industrial agriculture, as long as you measure productivity solely in terms of the relationship between yield and labor and pay no attention to the health of the land or the well-being of the people who live there. But by pursuing the unrelenting logic of industrial agriculture we've left a world of alternatives unexplored.

The human species is still running ahead of the Malthusian prediction that we'll outgrow our ability to feed ourselves. But this is a deeply troubling time for agriculture, as even a quick scan of the headlines reveals. Soaring food prices in the poorest parts of the world, soaring profits in the richest, wholly unnecessary subsidies, growing competition between food and non-food crops, the list goes on and on.

To Americans, the continued resistance to genetically modified crops in other parts of the world may look quixotic, a refusal to accept a done deal. But it's more than resistance to a type of seed. It's resistance to a model of agriculture whose failings are all too plain.

2009

At present there are 6.8 billion people on this planet, more than a billion of whom are hungry. By 2050, there will be an additional 2.3 billion people, most of them living in parts of the world that are already undernourished. According to the Food and Agriculture Organization of the United Nations, feeding humanity in 2050 will require a 70 percent increase in global food production, partly because of population growth but also because of rising incomes. There are hopes that this increase can be brought about mostly by increasing productivity on current agricultural acreage and by greening parts of the world that aren't, at present, arable.

The FAO says it's "cautiously optimistic" about the chances of reaching this goal. It estimates that there's enough land and probably enough water to do so, even though climate change and scarcity will make the distribution of water uncertain.

It's worth looking at this projection in light of another United Nations goal. In 2003, 123 nations committed themselves to "a significant reduction of the current rate of biodiversity loss" by 2010. But the 2010 target won't be met. Biodiversity loss keeps accelerating. Extinctions are occurring at a rate that's 100 times what it was before humans dominated the earth. One by one, species are going out like candles in the dark. They're the candles, and we're the dark.

Under the UN's "cautiously optimistic" scenario, humanity will some-how progress in a more or less orderly fashion toward more and more food production, and in doing so, we'll honor the value of other species, the importance of protecting habitat. We certainly must try. But there's little in the history of the past century that suggests we'll stop degrading and destroying habitat.

It's not a zero-sum game. A 70 percent increase in food production doesn't necessarily mean a 70 percent reduction in habitat—and resulting species loss. But the FAO estimates that agricultural acreage will have to increase by some 297 million acres, a little less than three times the size of California. This is to say nothing about the ongoing rate of habitat destruction—including deforestation—or the growing production of biofuels or other disturbances to natural habitat.

There may be cautious optimism about feeding humans. But there's a profound conflict between what our species will need to survive by 2050 and the needs of nearly every other species on this planet. By default, we seem to be running an experiment to find out just how little biodiversity humans need to exist. We seem to be hoping the answer is almost none. What we're going to find out is whether we can transcend the self-interest natural to every species and act on the principle that our interest includes that of every other species on the planet. There's only one acceptable answer.

The coming 2.3 billion people aren't, in some sense, "extra." They're already in the demographic pipeline—on their way, so to speak. They're a real projection of our near-term reproductive future. And that helps illustrate a point. As things are going now—at current rates of extinction and habitat destruction—the most important difference between humans and almost every other species on this planet is this: we have a reproductive future and they don't. It's really that simple.

The question isn't whether we can feed 9.1 billion people in 2050 or find the energy they'll need. The question is whether we can find a way to make food and energy production sustainable in the broadest possible sense. The only way to do that is to think about habitat—the habitat of all other species—as the frame, the boundary, of our activities. Unless habitat is always a part of the equation, equivalent in weight and importance to our own pressing concerns, we're not talking seriously about the character—much less the future—of our planet.

Our biggest obstacle in doing this isn't our numbers or our needs. It's our imagination. To us, habitat is a loose concept, a metaphor. Because we're able to live all over the planet, in all sorts of physical circumstances, we have trouble understanding the detail and specificity of habitat as it applies to other species. As humans are now—at our current state of technology—we have no meaningful habitat more specific than the entire globe.

But for the tens of millions of other life forms on the planet, habitat isn't a concept or a metaphor. It's ironclad necessity—the individual and defining set of conditions for nearly every species but our own. It is existence itself. Perhaps we'll discover that the real human habitat was the one created by the presence of all other species in their habitats. But we need to act on that principle now. After all, there are no "extra" species, any more than there are "extra" humans.

2012

In its short, shameless history, big agriculture has had only one big idea: uniformity. The obvious example is corn. The Department of Agriculture predicts that American farmers—big farmers—will plant ninety-four million acres of corn this year. That's the equivalent of planting corn on every inch of Montana. To do that you'd have to make sure that every inch of Montana fell within corn-growing parameters. That would mean leveling the high spots, irrigating the dry spots, draining the wet spots, fertilizing the infertile spots, and so on. Corn is usually grown where the terrain is less rigorous than it is in Montana. But even in Iowa that has meant leveling, irrigating, draining, fertilizing, and spraying.

You can argue whether uniformity is the result of efficiency or vice versa. But let's suppose that efficiency is merely the economic expression of uniformity. The point is this: when you see a Midwestern cornfield, you know you're looking at nature with one idea superimposed upon it. This is far less confusing, less tangled in variation than the nature you find even in the roadside ditches beside a cornfield or in a last scrap of native prairie growing in a graveyard or along an abandoned railroad right-of-way. Nature is puzzling. Corn is stupefying.

Humans have spent a lot of time trying to figure out what the big idea behind nature is. It's hard to tell, because we live at nature's pace and within the orb of human abstraction. We barely notice the large-scale differences from year to year, much less the minute ones. But if we could speed up time a little and become a lot more perceptive, we would see that nature's big idea is to try out life wherever and however it can be tried, which means everywhere and anyhow. The result—over time and at this instant—is diversity, complexity, particularity, and inventiveness to an extent our minds are almost unfitted to conceive.

A reasonable agriculture would do its best to emulate nature. Rather than change the Earth to suit a crop—which is what we do with corn and soybeans and a handful of other agricultural commodities—it would diversify its crops to suit the Earth. This isn't going to happen in big agriculture, because big agriculture is irrational. It's where we expose—at unimaginable expense—our failure to grasp how nature works. It's where uniformity is always defeated by diversity and where big agriculture's ideas of diversity are revealed to be as uniform as ever.

To a uniform crop like corn, farmers have been encouraged to apply a uniform herbicide to kill weeds. Modern corn is genetically engineered to not be killed by the herbicide in ubiquitous use. Mostly, that herbicide has been glyphosate, marketed under the Monsanto trade name Roundup. Farmers have sprayed and oversprayed billions of gallons of Roundup, thanks to an economic and moral premise: corn good, weeds bad. And yet you can't help noticing that it's done nothing to stop the endless inventiveness of nature.

To broadleaf weeds and soil microorganisms, Roundup isn't the apocalypse. It's simply a modest, temporal challenge, which is why, fifteen years after genetically engineered, Roundup-tolerant crops were widely introduced, it's no longer working against spontaneous new generations of Roundup-tolerant weeds, especially in cotton fields. This is because research, in nature's laboratory, never stops. It explores every possibility. It never lacks funding. It's never demoralized by failed experiments. It can't be lobbied.

To fix the problem of glyphosate-tolerant weeds, Dow Chemical is hoping to introduce crop varieties that will withstand being sprayed with an herbicide called 2,4-D. When it was first released to farmers in 1946, 2,4-D was a breakthrough—a herbicide that killed only certain kinds of plants instead of killing them all. It's less safe than glyphosate, especially because it's sometimes contaminated with dioxin. But it's not an indiscriminate, lethal killer, despite the fact that it was one of the chemicals in Agent Orange, the notorious defoliant used during the Vietnam War. (The dioxin in Agent Orange came from another component chemical called 2,4,5-T.)

Still, this is backward-engineering of a sort, like trying to breed birds that will tolerate DDT. And while the USDA hasn't decided whether to approve Dow's 2,4-D-tolerant soybeans yet, it's decided to speed up the process of reviewing genetically engineered crops, mainly to help deal with the spread of so-called superweeds caused by the nearly universal application of glyphosate for the last decade and a half. According to Dow's numbers, superweeds affected some sixty million acres of crops last year. If things go right, bureaucratically, that's just so much cash in Dow's pocket.

"Farmers needs technology right now to help them with issues such as weed resistance," a Dow official said. Translation? Farmers need technology right now to help them with issues created by right-now technology introduced fifteen years ago. Instead of urging farmers away from uniformity and toward greater diversity, the USDA is helping them do the same old wrong thing faster. When an idea goes bad, the USDA seems to think, the way to fix it is to speed up the introduction of ideas that will go bad *for exactly the same reason*. And it's always, somehow, the same bad idea: the uniform application of an antibiological agent, whether it's a pesticide in crops or an antibiotic on factory farms. The result is always the same. Nature finds a way around it, and quickly.

This is the irrationality of agriculture as it's practiced in the United States and now all over the world. It has one big idea, and it will never give it up, because it has invested everything in that one big idea. Against uniformity and abstraction—embodied in millions of acres of genetically modified crops— nature will always win. Whether it can ever win against the uniformity and abstraction embodied in the human brain is very much in doubt.

2012

Like many people, I've spent a lot of time thinking about and mourning the cascading extinction of species caused by human activity. But only recently has it occurred to me to frame it this way: humans have lived past the peak of biological diversity on this planet. There may well be other, higher peaks of biodiversity after we're gone, but the best I can imagine as long as we're around is a slight decline in the calamitous rate of extinction.

As it happens, we've also lived past the peak of linguistic diversity—the number of different human languages spoken on this planet. The loss would be more evident if each of this planet's nearly seven thousand human languages was spoken by a separate species—one species per language. But losing language is as human as using language. After all, we live in a country where, for the past two and a half centuries, people have come to abandon their ancestral tongues in the second generation after arrival—a country where most of the aboriginal languages had long since been destroyed.

According to a recent study, there's a close correlation between biological diversity and linguistic diversity. A biological hot spot is likely to be a linguistic hot spot. Put simply, there are more human languages where there are more species. "Of the 6,900 languages currently spoken on Earth," the authors write, "more than 4,800 occur in regions containing high biodiversity." The corollary? Most of those languages are threatened. Nearly 60 percent of the languages in high biodiversity regions, like Amazonia, are spoken by fewer than ten thousand people. More than 1,200 of them are spoken by fewer than a thousand people. Every language is a species, but most languages are also habitats, linked closely to the physical habitats in which they occur.

Human languages evolve far more quickly than the single species—
Homo sapiens—that speaks them. And languages speciate for some of the
same reasons that organisms do—topographic separation, for instance.
A good example is New Guinea, which is as rich in linguistic species (972
endemic languages) as it is in biological species. Topographically speaking,
New Guinea is famously difficult, a torturous landscape that isolates humans.

It's tempting to assume that the correlation between biological and linguistic diversity is functionally negative. In other words, high linguistic diversity occurs where the conditions of biological diversity—dense forests, harsh
terrain, and other barriers, like disease—force small human societies to
remain separate. But there's another way to think of it. What if the correlation
is functionally positive? Instead of merely *forcing* linguistic diversity, high biological diversity also *affords* linguistic diversity. The richness of one sustains
the richness of the other.

There's something curious and unsettling in all of this. It seems odd
to think that such a pure extension of human-ness as language itself (apart
from mere vocabulary) is so niched, so profusely and divergently rooted in
the natural world. A universally shared language seems like a universal good.
But most languages spoken by small numbers of humans in regions of high
biodiversity do not and will not survive extended contact with widely spoken
languages like English, Spanish, Portuguese, and French. No matter how
desirable it may seem, a universal language is a bulldozer with measles.

I think we inevitably underestimate the bond between biological complexity and cultural complexity. So let me turn to a landscape I know far better than the jungles and mountain ridges of New Guinea: northwestern Iowa.
Within my lifetime, the cultural and biological complexity of rural Iowa has
declined precipitously. What underlies both kinds of loss is the decline in the
number of farms. Modern farming is a way of spreading vacancy. The farms
grow bigger and bigger—declining in number—and fewer and fewer people
live on them. This has been accompanied, in Iowa, by a decline in the biological diversity of the farm itself. In most of the state, there are now only soybeans,
corn, chickens, and hogs, a huge change from even fifty years ago.

This much is easy to see. But so is the loss of cultural complexity. The
way to measure that is to ask as many good questions about the components
of social and cultural texture as you can. What kinds of questions would you
ask to get at the diversity, the complexity of a small town? Some are fairly obvious. How many independent banks are there? How many independent grain
elevators? How many independent slaughter houses? Creameries? Grocery

stores? How many farm implement and auto dealerships? How many butchers and livestock breeders? How many farmers sold milk and eggs in town? How many entries were there in the county fairs?

But these are really technical and economic questions. So let's consider some others. What percentage of the children learned how to play a musical instrument? How many unconsolidated school districts were there? What about amateur theatrical societies and singing clubs—even small-town opera houses? How many softball teams? What about sewing circles and baling rings and card clubs? How many people in town had grown up on the farm or had friends on the farm or went out in the country to do part-time work? How much barter was there?

All these questions point in one direction. With the decrease in biological complexity—the regression to corn and soybeans—came a decrease in social and cultural complexity. The farmscape emptied and the towns became ghosts of themselves. You might argue that the one didn't directly and necessarily cause the other: in other words, if most of the 203,000 farms that existed in Iowa when I was born (1952) suddenly switched to growing only corn and soybeans, that wouldn't necessarily have reduced the population and complexity of the countryside. But the fact is that Iowa did switch to corn and soybeans and when it was done, fewer than ninety thousand farms remained. Not many people live on ninety thousand farms.

It may seem far-fetched to compare social and agricultural change in Iowa with linguistic and biological correlation in some of Earth's biodiversity hot spots. But the underlying premise is the same. Biological diversity and cultural diversity go hand in hand. This is a hard idea to absorb for the simple reason that humans, in our pride, have always assumed that cultural diversity and complexity is the result of who we are, not what nature has made of us and we've made of nature. We still believe fiercely, against all the evidence, that we're independent of most other species. And we still believe fiercely that the habitat that matters most is the one we create. We couldn't be more mistaken.

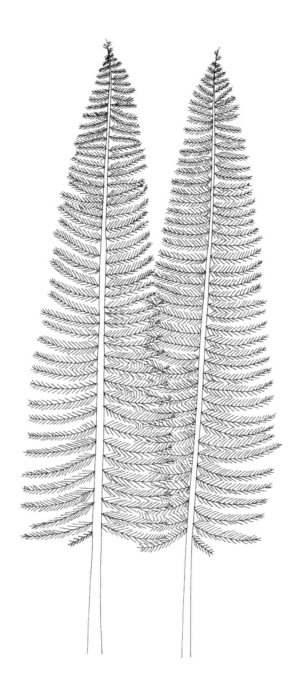

Year

SIX

⁊●

January 1

Sooner or later the pickup will be packed and the dogs loaded. We'll roll down the driveway and around the corner and onto the highway. With any luck it will still be early in the morning. The horses will be standing over a bale of hay, and the chickens and geese and ducks will be wondering why they weren't let out of the poultry yard. The dogs, too, will have some questions, especially as the day of driving grows longer and longer and we don't seem to be getting to the vet or the dog sitter's house. By next week this time, we'll be well down the road to Southern California again, angling across country however winter lets us.

I don't know how it came to seem so natural to load up and set out. My parents certainly had the habit. My dad has always liked the thought of being packed and ready to go—and then going at first light. In the early nineties, Lindy and I hauled the dogs and horses west every summer, and when we got there we found ourselves among people who made a living hauling horses all across the country, people for whom five days in any one spot was a good long time.

I try to imagine what it would have been like driving across country about the time I was born, but I can't. Once, when I was seven or eight, I rode a hundred miles home from my grandparents' house in their car with my grandfather behind the wheel. His top speed was thirty-five miles an hour. It nearly killed me. I wanted to be anywhere but the backseat of that old Dodge plodding down the highway. Now I'd love to see all over again what I must have seen on that trip, the hogs in the fields, the creek-bottom pastures, the windmills and farmhouses. Iowa wasn't yet a tyranny of soybeans and corn.

I'm struck this time by the change in how I imagine the trip across country. It's become so easy to look down the road. The last time we made this trip I spent weeks staring at the road atlas, pondering the mysteries of the American highway system. Now, instead of the road atlas, I contemplate the National Weather Service website—the page displaying a map, updated every five minutes, of all the weather warnings, watches, alerts, and advisories across the country. Right now, the only good weather slot for crossing west is somewhere near El Paso.

This morning I ran through the whole trip on the GPS, mile by mile, turn by turn. I plotted out some driving distances on Google Maps, wondering how long we'll want to drive each day. I scouted a couple of websites that list dog-friendly lodgings along the way. I've already downloaded the audio books we'll listen to. We're driving west this time in a cloud of information—the exact opposite, I suppose, of that trip with my grandparents, when all the information worth gleaning would have come in conversation with the two old people in the front seat and with the world that lay beyond the highway ditches.

January 16

It was a fitting end to the trip—a fifteen-mile traffic jam snaking over Cajon Pass and down into the refrigerated depths of Southern California, where avocadoes were freezing on the bough and sprinkler-soaked lawns iced over by morning. The day before we left it was seventy degrees at home. The route across country was snowless nearly till Santa Fe. But we drove through flurries in the Mojave Desert, and more snow fell on the San Bernardino side of the pass than we'd seen at home in all of November and December. The jam was a place to put impatience aside, to never mind the twenty nine thousand miles we'd driven and hope that somewhere in the last thirty miles the traffic would break up, like pack ice in a turbulent sea.

In 2005, it felt as though the trip we were making was continuous with all the long-distance drives my family took when I was a kid. Those trips embodied the modesty of our expectations. We were camping then, not staying in motels, and we were driving, not flying or taking the train. Driving across the country wasn't only normal. It was a sign of frugality. But this time I felt the excess in the trip. It was like traveling along the edge of one's historical epoch and knowing the judgment that would be made upon it in the future. The scale of the road system—the volume and velocity of its traffic—seemed grievous. And so did the painful, nagging awareness that there's nothing sustainable in this way of life. As easy as the drive was, it felt wholly untenable.

If you get up morning after morning and drive all day you eventually get to California. That still surprises me. The miles came and went, the soybean fields of Illinois, where water stood in place of snowdrifts, the hills of Missouri, the broad sweep of Oklahoma shoaling off into Texas. We headed out of Tulsa an hour before any sign of dawn, its refineries glistening in the dark. No matter where we stopped, it seemed hard to believe that we were really there, because the only there was the pickup cab and the two sleepy dogs in the backseat and the sound of our audiobook.

"Last spring, 1846, was a busy season in the City of St. Louis." So begins Francis Parkman's *The Oregon Trail*, which recounts his adventures along the Platte and Arkansas Rivers in what are now Kansas, Nebraska, Wyoming, and Colorado in the summer of 1846. Nothing defines the moment you travel in like listening to the moment of someone else's travels. We began the book as we crossed the Mississippi into St. Louis, and whenever Parkman mentioned the trail to Santa Fe I felt a kind of historical serendipity, as if we had more in common with him than the fact that we were pointed west.

From a distance of 160 years, it's easy to see the boundaries of Parkman's historical epoch, except where it overlaps with ours. Every buffalo he comes across is "stupid," and of the bulls he writes, "Thousands of them might be slaughtered without causing any detriment to the species, for their numbers greatly exceed those of the cows." He feels a profound ambivalence toward the emigrants who are just beginning to crowd the trails west. He can praise the Indians he meets only by comparing their bodies to the works of ancient Greek sculptors. Otherwise, "So alien to himself do they appear that… he begins to look upon them as a troublesome and dangerous species of wild beast."

Parkman was not yet twenty-three, and he carried with him a large quiver of judgments, all of them sharp edged and many utterly wrong. Most of them he eventually set aside, becoming in time one of America's greatest historians. We listened to him not for his prejudices but for his powers of observation, his ability to translate the freshness of the prairie in language that still sounds newly felt. I looked beyond the fence lines crowded with tumbleweed and thought about a sentence of Parkman's, something he says after an unnamed Indian looks at a vacated campsite and names the men who stopped there. "By what instinct he had arrived at such accurate conclusions," Parkman writes, "I am utterly at a loss to divine."

The real question is why Parkman chalked up the careful observations of a different mind to instinct. It was a way of asserting primacy, of assuming that that Indian knew what he knew without knowing how. That passage marks a seam between two cultures, a profound gulf between Parkman and his Native American compatriot. The more I thought about Parkman's words and our trip west, the more I began to feel as though we were driving along a seam of our own, across a landscape of vanished knowledge, secure in a cultural instinct that was coming, year by year, to seem more and more insecure. Around Victorville, we were brought to a dead halt by the snows of San Bernardino county.

February 15

The other night there was thunder along the lower flanks of the San Gabriel mountains. It began just before dark, and at first I didn't recognize what I was hearing. I thought it was the sound of Thursday night—the rumble of heavy plastic trash dumpsters, a whole street of them, being wheeled out to the curb. The rain came and went and came again, throwing the scent of eucalyptus and dust into the twilight, the scent of this dry California winter. We watched the lightning—quick as a lizard's tongue—from a plastic picnic table at Juanita's, a taqueria near the San Bernardino Freeway. If you were driving past Juanita's in a hurry, you might almost mistake it for a bail-bond shop, except that bondsmen are partial to neon and don't wear hairnets at work.

We're living farther down the alluvial skirts of the San Gabriels than we did when we were here two years ago. In fact, we live in what tract housing looked like half a century ago—uniform houses, stucco-clad, whose only homage to their location is small windows on the south side, where the desert sun lives. Across the street, a perfectly graceless little two-bedroom, one bath has been marked down to $465,000. This was jackrabbit country once, and now it's full of jackrabbit houses. At 7:50 A.M., all the cars back out of all the driveways at once. You can feel the haste—see someone dash from the house to the passenger door even as the car begins to roll backwards out of the garage. I'm sure the same thing goes on in the ochre mansions higher up the mountain, where every now and then a cougar steals a Doberman from its own backyard. Everyone can feel the freeway beckoning.

What I find myself looking for here in Los Angeles is a sense of dislocation. And what I've come to realize is how closely dislocation and a sense of the ordinary are linked. I find myself watching instead for the pattern of ordinary life, which is all the more moving to me here because I don't understand its rhythms. I listen to band practice in the neighborhood park. I admire the profusion of baseball gloves in the local sporting goods store, a reminder that the amateur season is well under way here. I watch a young father in scrubs and his soccer-playing daughter waiting in line at the local burrito place, and I wonder what it's like to grow up taking good *carne asada* for granted. I try to see how people's lives are shaped, how they construct what seems normal to them, and whenever I get a glimpse of it, I find all the dislocation I could ever want. It's like standing on a strange lawn in the dark watching the glow of a television on the living-room ceiling.

We go exploring along the boulevards, up La Brea, down Pico, over on Wilshire. All the business is on the boulevards and so are all the landmarks. But what always catches my eye is the side streets, which yawn open for an instant left and right and then close again, like gaps between the rows in a field of corn. A glimpse is all we allow ourselves—a double row of trees shading a quiet street, houses moated by lawn and landscaping. And yet looking into the crevice of each side street is like looking into a separate decade. I wonder what I'd know if I lived there, and what I'd take for granted.

We, in turn, have cobbled together a temporary life here, so different from life in the country at home. I bicycle up the alluvial grade to teach, and when office hours are over, I coast all the way back, across the Metrolink tracks and down onto the jackrabbit flats. The dogs, who are used to a pasture, stare transfixed at the squirrels on the power lines overhead, and they woof mournfully through the chain-link at a cat standing two houses away. The morning we arrived, I brushed against a glossy shrub at the edge of the driveway. A tart oily scent clung to my hands. It took me half a day to place the smell. It was rosemary—not a sprig of it but whole, in the bush and about to bloom. It's not as if I'd forgotten the smell of rosemary—lost the memory of it somewhere on the trip west. What I'd forgotten is the difference between familiar and unfamiliar, expected and unexpected, out here where the herbs grow wild and thunder sounds like solid citizens taking the trash out to the curb.

March 12

I'm sitting on the front porch of my father's house in a small town in the heart of California's almond country. It will be eighty degrees today. I've been watching the park across the street for hours. I can hear the delayed irregular heartbeat of a basketball game on the far side, all the slap gone out of the ball at this distance. A young boy pedals his bicycle across the lawn, and I suddenly remember how reluctant a bicycle feels on grass, how hard it is to urge it forward. A girl—just barely a teenager—walks to the diamond to practice softball with her father. On the way, she walks a dozen feet behind him. On the way home, she walks half a block ahead. He's a terrible pitcher.

The horizon across the park is a line of cement tile rooftops. Beyond them, the almond groves begin, invisible from here but discernible nonetheless. Everything would feel different if those almond groves weren't there, if the houses went on and on, as they tend to do in this state. The houses across the park, now a decade old, would be nearly identical if they weren't so intently un-uniform, gables here, a mansard roof there, and front doors in every degree of involution. This is a quiet neighborhood in a quiet town. Every now and then a car passes—nearly always an suv roaring like a jet—and a garage door opens automatically and the suv is ingested after spilling the children onto the driveway: a boy with a bat, a girl with a jump rope, a younger sister with a pink baseball glove.

Toward sunset, my dad and I go for a drive west of town, into the glare of the sun, which is lying just above the tops of the evenly pruned orchards. On the way to the country, we pass through the new part of town, the rich part, where the houses are nearly new, monuments of encrustation. They look like fortresses facing each other across the street or like something you might find on the turquoise gravel of a starter aquarium next to a treasure chest sending up a stream of bubbles. The front yard has vanished in this neighborhood. Instead there's a paved forecourt for automobiles and a hangar-size garage. It's as if the vehicles that occupy these driveways had decided to build very nice living quarters for the people who operate them.

Where the houses stop, the orchards begin. The almonds are just past full blossom and beginning to drop their petals. I always drive through these orchards with a sense of wonder. The whole world has been ruled into lines of perspective. These aren't tall trees, and the almond branches converge well before they reach the horizon, which creates the illusion that the orchards are endless. I never drive past them without wanting to stop the car and walk down the long swaths of grass that lie between the trees, into an infinite checkerboard of light and shade and blossom. The trees have been planted with industrial precision but the effect is completely aesthetic, as if these were groves in a pleasure garden.

A Cooper's Hawk detaches himself on the wing from a high bough and drifts into the orchard a few feet above the ground. He stays with us, gliding through row after row of trees, eclipsing himself until he vanishes from sight. At crossroads, we come upon old farmhouses—and sometimes a very new one—almost hidden in the orchards, broken shade all the way up to the back porch. We pass a family playing baseball in a pasture. It's a treacherous game there, every grounder a bad hop.

And then the orchards end in piles of boughs and overturned stumps. The trees have been toppled and the good firewood cut out and hauled away. It's hard to say whether the trees had lived out their productive lives or whether the land had been sold for houses. We pass mountains of almond hulls and a paper mill and a steel-fabricating plant and a processing plant for eggs. We turn back into the old heart of town and cross over the spine of the Central Valley—Highway 99—and drive back to my dad's house.

All day long there has been only one question on my mind. The day seems almost perfectly still, but it's a stillness against the backdrop of steady, intensifying change. What's it like to grow up—to live—in the midst of such constant, radical alteration? What effect does it have on how you think of the future? It is, I suppose, all part of a succession. The native grassland gives way to orchards, and the orchards give way to houses, and I can't stop myself wondering what the houses will give way to.

April 9

Last week I read with my students an essay by Lewis Thomas called "On Medicine and the Bomb," which was first published in 1981. It's been a long time since I taught that essay, and a lot has changed since Thomas wrote it, including the structure of global politics and most of the numbers he uses. It's a simple essay. Thomas surveys the state of research and practice in several medical fields, including bone marrow transplants, burn therapy, and the treatment of what he calls "overwhelming trauma." And then he considers the good of all these resources against the prospect of a nuclear missile falling on New York City or Moscow. Which is to say no good at all.

This is a useful essay for young writers. It reminds them of the importance of dwelling wholly in each sentence they make. It teaches them to trust the reader. Thomas never peers around the corner of the next paragraph. He never hints where he's going. His prose is plain. He never exaggerates. He presents facts, one by one, about medical research and technology. But reading the essay is like watching a great magician perform a simple card trick. One card, two cards, three cards, four cards, none of them out of the ordinary. Then he lays down the last card, and it's the one you've been having nightmares about your entire life.

My entire life, I should say. I asked my students, mostly freshmen and sophomores, whether they'd grown up with any fear of nuclear holocaust. The answer was no. My students are so very old that I forget how young they are. The youngest were born in 1988. If they came to some embryonic political awareness about the same age I did—I was eleven when Kennedy was killed—then it happened about 1999. We finished with Thomas and moved on to other things. But I went home in the California night feeling as though I were carrying a precious relic of memory inside me.

The answer my students gave—that unhesitating "no"—brought to mind a few of the landmarks of my own nuclear fears. They include Pat Frank's *Alas, Babylon*, Peter Watkins's *The War Game*, John Hersey's *Hiroshima*, Stanley Kubrick's *Dr. Strangelove*, Jonathan Schell's *The Fate of the Earth*, to which you might now add Cormac McCarthy's *The Road*. I remember—and it seems very strange to have to "remember"—the way these books and films seemed to stimulate and desolate me, the way they led me to a point I always had to turn away from, and sooner rather than later. The problem wasn't trying to imagine the unimaginable. The problem was trying to realize that the unimaginable had been carefully planned, as Thomas says, by "so many people with the outward appearance of steadiness and authority."

It occurred to us that night that Lewis's essay could be rewritten about global warming. You could show the extent to which we're prepared to make the drastic changes needed to mitigate the worst effects of climate change, survey the technology that would allow us to hold back the rising oceans or cope with increasingly violent storms or provide us with alternative sources of energy. And you would conclude that we haven't even begun to prepare for the forthcoming changes. You could argue, as Thomas does, that "we need, in a hurry, some professionals who can tell us what has gone wrong in the minds of statesmen in this generation."

Except that climate change isn't just about statesmen, about the men with secret access codes and red telephones on their desks. It's about all of us, in every choice we make every day. I had the unspeakable luxury to grow up in the 1950s and 1960s, when it was possible to believe in the otherness of the nuclear insanity that threatened the world. I look at my students and realize that they're in the first generation to grow up knowing that there is no otherness to the insanity that threatens us now. The insanity is what we call normal, and it's all our own. There's a good chance that my students are better prepared for this than I am, because they've never been allowed to believe that the problem of climate change is only a matter of politics at the highest level. They know it's their problem, too.

We got this far in our seminar that night, possessed by the quiet outrage that Thomas expresses and a little puzzled by the different burdens our generations seem to have assumed. And what I added is that the nuclear arsenal Thomas was talking about still exists. The numbers have changed and so has the global politics, but the weapons still stand, waiting. The capacity to handle radiation sickness and burns and trauma has grown since 1981, but so has the number and concentration of potential victims. What it comes down to, in Thomas's words, is this. "Get a computer running somewhere in a cave, to estimate the likely number of the lucky dead." This is a fear my students will have to grow into.

May 18

I'm writing from a mile high in a small Wyoming town on the edge of the Wind River range. The snow on the nearby buttes has finally melted, and the creek-bottoms and pastures and hayground are an unhoped-for green. The drift of cotton from the cottonwoods is almost over, but the lilacs are still in high bloom. The town is nearly damp with their scent. It's two scents really, a floral dissonance, a sweet astringency. There's a dark, grating baritone of sorts, which is veiled by a lighter, more liquid perfume, a second soprano I suppose. I find myself wondering how a scent so strangely unsettled can also feel so homely.

We're driving across country, heading home from Southern California. It didn't occur to me until this drive how segregated the botanical scents of Southern California really are. You come upon them in pockets—a planting of this, a gathering of that, upwellings of sage and jasmine and orange blossom and rosemary. But half a block down the street the fragrance has faded or been overlaid, or it's simply surrendered to the ozone. By late afternoon our first day on the road, we were a little short of Cedar City, Utah. We stopped to switch drivers, and when I stepped out of the truck the breeze was suddenly full of the fragrance of unhardened grasses, an entire landscape of gramineous scent. The desert was long behind us—the Joshua trees and flowering yucca—and so was everything that Southern California calls to mind. But it took that smell on the wind to make me know it.

We had to climb higher still before we came upon the lilacs. We caught up to them in Coalville, Utah, up near the southwest corner of Wyoming. They were growing in every yard along the gravel street on the edge of town, just as they do in the town I'm writing from. By the time we get home the lilacs will have long since gone by. When we first bought our small farm, now nearly ten years ago, I spent part of one summer trying to grub them out. They seemed so ordinary, so deeply familiar. It says almost enough about where I was raised to say that I was raised among lilacs.

Here, in the scent of them, I can smell the spareness of a cold climate, the beautiful austerity of a short growing season. In its own way, a lilac is as pushing, as immodest as anything that grows in Southern California. Just ask the person who has tried to grub one out. But when I smell lilacs, I see a nearly bare yard in a small town and children playing in the weight of their scent not knowing what it will come to mean to them in time.

May 25

The tires whine and sometimes they moan. Sometimes they send up a whistle I don't even hear until it stops. Now and then the asphalt runs smooth and true. But mostly the interstate is a series of unpredictable discontinuities—a sharp thump at a shallow overpass, a few miles partly paved with recycled rubber, a long sequence in western Nebraska where the tires make the sound of the special effects in Walter Mitty's mind. And then there's Omaha, a dozen heavily corrugated miles that must drive truckers insane.

In imagination, Interstate 80 is a single line, the shortest practical distance between San Francisco and New York. To be at any one point on that line is to feel the length of the whole, as if the only here that matters is the here you come upon when you're finally there. I watch the landscape zoom past and forget that we're the ones zooming along while the landscape stays perfectly still. We come to the Nebraska grasslands. A windmill is pumping water into a stock tank surrounded by cattle. The grass is bent low.

These are reminders that the wind is more than just the breeze of our passing, the bucking windstorm that follows a semi. This is a native wind, quartering down stiffly out of the northwest. This is the wind that everyone who lives here learns to live with.

Whenever I drive across country, I carry a single question with me, and I ask it over and over again: Could I live here? It's natural enough, I suppose—a central question for a species whose habitat is so broad, defined as much by imagination and emotion as it is by strict biological constraints. It's a question that raises the matter of time as much as place. Cutting across central Wyoming, I look up a draw and see a sheltered spot under the hills where the sagebrush breaks into grass, and I think, "I could live there." And I could, now, because living anywhere has been made so easy in our time. It's no longer a problem of physical limits—how far you have to haul water and salt and flour, how long you can go without company.

But what I'm really asking when I wonder "Could I live here?" is "Who would I be if I lived here?" To that question I never know the answer. Some places seem obviously unlivable, like Jeffrey City, a nearly abandoned Wyoming town that sprang up during a uranium boom and died a couple of decades later. The answer is no along the southern fringe of Cheyenne, where a new Jeffrey City is being built, thanks to the petroleum boom that has turned the state upside down.

But when I ask, "Could I live here?" I usually get a more equivocal answer, and it's the uncertainty that sets me thinking. I see an abandoned farmhouse on the high plains, a broken-down corral, the ruins of a few old cottonwoods, and I can imagine hearing the notes of a meadowlark being carried on the wind as I go to work on the place. This is an experiment in relativity. I'm the observer traveling along the interstate at 75 mph, and I can't allow myself to imagine living anywhere I can see from my current position. But what if it were a place just like this and over the horizon?

Perhaps this is a mental game everyone plays—a way to test the life you're actually living. You drive through a small town at night and wonder what it would be like to feel at home in one of those houses where only the bedroom lamp is still shining. You wonder what your own life would look like if you could stand outside it as a stranger. But what this question always confirms in me is something I must have understood when my wife and I decided to settle on a small farm in the country. Driving across America, I see place after place I can happily imagine living. And what I notice is that they're mostly uninhabited places.

So Nebraska comes to an end, and the next day we drive into Iowa, where I've already lived a good part of my life. It's been raining since dawn, and now the wind is pounding down from the north. There's water standing in every row on the hillside fields, and it's begun to cut across the rows and run down to the creeks and rivers, carrying Iowa away to the Gulf of Mexico. Two more days on the road, and we'll be back in the place where I no longer wonder if I could live there because it's the place I live.

June 1

Seven years ago, I planted a pair of white spruces—*Picea glauca*. They came by mail in slender tubes from a nursery in Oregon, mere wisps of vegetation. I wasn't sure where I wanted to put them, so I stuck them in the ground in an improvised nursery bed, beside the sweet corn and the pole beans. A year later I planted them just inside the fence along the gravel road that runs past the house. It has been to their liking. By late summer, the new growth hardens off to an immortal green, but this time of year it's still soft and drooping and pale. Those trees are now well over ten feet tall—lone emissaries, in a sense, from the great forest of white spruces that reaches across Canada.

There's always an assumption of selflessness in planting a tree. You're supposed to think, while digging the hole, how far into the future the tree will grow and what shallow, unconvincing weeds we humans are in comparison. Standing by the young sprout, you're supposed to wonder who will see this tree when it's full-grown, and you're bound in duty to consider the serenity of your own grave. It's true that I'd like to see these spruces in another eighty years. But I can take in the whole tree now. I can watch the growing tip—so wan in early June—gradually turn into trunk. I can still remember that I planted these spruces myself. When they're fully mature, they'll seem to have planted themselves, as mature trees nearly always do.

The rest of the garden grows much faster, of course. The peas and beans shoot up and so will the tomatoes and corn. But every year the vegetables get to be just so tall, just so ripe, and then down they come with the harvest, the frost. I know their limits as well as they do. I'm not going to be staggered by a patch of corn that turns out to be thirty feet tall. The garden will tell me soon enough where the summer went.

But I'm staggered by these spruces nearly every day. I see a great deal of their growing time, because they're growing in full view of my office window. Again and again I go out to stand beside them, to measure their height against my own. It shouldn't be possible for them to sneak up on me, and yet every year they do. I began asking, "How did they get so tall?" when they were only waist-high. I'm still asking now that they're beginning to dwarf me. I'd like to say that slow has turned sudden in these spruces, because we imagine a stoicism in the way trees grow. But I've been a close witness of their vegetative life, and in my mind I can't keep up with it.

July 2

The barn will never be clean. It has a dirt floor, and hay is always sifting down from the loft. Swallows have nested over the light fixtures and the chipmunks are everywhere and someone has dug a proud hole under the wall near the horse tank. Clean I cannot make it, but I can recover some territory. I'm not a real farmer, but I have a real farmer's hoarding instinct—the sure belief that the thing I'm about to throw out will be just the thing I need down the road. Right now I'm trying to keep myself from throwing out a rubber feed pan one of the horses has pawed a hole through. I have no idea what I'd ever use it for, but that isn't really the point. It isn't a matter of knowing, looking forward. It's a matter of not regretting, looking back.

What I regret right now is all this junk, and so I'm cleaning the barn. In practice, this means allowing myself to feel a sudden hatred for objects I've been moving around for years. I spend the day muttering. I tear apart an old tool bench I've loathed all this time. I throw out the last of the previous owner's electric waterers and the eight-foot yard hydrant with the bend in the middle and the plastic tarps full of holes. I see the limits of my character and, in a sense, the limits of my life. I love the gratification of fixing what's broken, but it takes a certain kind of breaking for me to be able to do any good. I'm never going to be able to weld in a hay barn.

I stop sometimes to watch the swallows fly through the barn or to admire the fact that all the wrenches are now in one place. I pretend that I'll know in a week where I put everything today. I admire the dried up litter of immature mice I found in a drawer. And I finally admit to myself that a half-decomposed box of books that has lived in the barn for a decade has lost its place in civilization. So I load the books one by one—Derrida's *Of Grammatology*, Frye's *The Great Code*, even my old copy of Heidegger's *Being and Time*—into the tractor bucket along with a great wad of used baling twine. The burn pile or the dumpster? That's an easy question. The books flutter down from the bucket onto an old hayrack on the floor of the dumpster. I wonder if I'll have to answer for this someday.

127

July 26

Here's how things stand at midsummer. One of the Tamworth pigs is tame enough to be scratched behind the ears. The other isn't. They're going through a hundred pounds of feed every three or four days. Two of the white geese have clubbed together and banished the third white goose from their society. The lame Ancona duck has taken refuge under the old chicken house. We'd put her out of her misery, except that her misery is her life. The old Dominique rooster seems to be in a vertiginous state, always leaning and nearly always dozing. During the listless heat of the day, the chickens lie in the dust beneath the pickup truck. The horses stand in the hickory shade, incognito in fly masks, tails flicking.

The vegetable garden has gone feral. The walking onions, the chives and the blueberries are the only signs of cultivation there. The less said about that the better. Hopes are high for next year. The crop of chipmunks is incredible. There have never been fatter woodchucks. The pasture is filled with the trial cawing of young crows. The swallows nearly clip me with their wings as I throw hay down from the loft. The bees are populous. The pasture at dawn is covered with spiderwebs that look like the footprints of ethereal elephants. The scarlet bee balm is in bloom down by the mailbox, and the thistles have purpled. The hollyhocks are coming into blossom and also rotting in the leaf, as they always do. The black barn cat pauses to decide just where his blackness will be most welcome, and in pausing chooses.

The days still come in order. Gray light collects in the bedroom long before dawn. Then comes a bleached noon and nearly always the threat of a late-afternoon thunderstorm. When rain falls, it's a relief. The darkness is annotated by fireflies, who have been unusually numerous—or is it unusually bright?—this year. The crickets are whining away, as if they were somehow reeling in August. Moths beat against the windows, and now and then I feel the presence of a bat feeding among them. I'm laying in all the thinking I can against a time when summer is in short supply.

August 3

At the moment, I'm sitting in my office watching someone else mow the lawn. He's just caught the mower blades on some weed-barrier cloth at the edge of the hostas. He'll probably clip the hidden rocks just down the hill from the paperbark maple. And I wouldn't be surprised if he got stuck in one of the holes I dug for a tree that never got planted. I never think about these things when I mow the lawn. I miss them instinctively. They've grown

128

into my bones like everything else about this place—the bedrock submarines surfacing in the middle pasture, monarchs drifting over the milkweed, bumblebees drinking at the edge of the spot we keep wet for the pigs.

I came here thinking about the impression I might leave on this place. It was a foolish thing to think. It has worked the other way around. Some days I feel like a grave rubbing, as if the record of this place, the terrain, had been traced onto me. Not that there haven't been plenty of changes here. But none of them begin to add up to the changes in me. The tractor is the same as it ever was, only dustier. The first time I drove it I barely recognized myself. I felt like I was acting a part, lifting and lowering the bucket with an almost painful self-consciousness. Now it's simply an extension of who I am. Or perhaps I've become an extension of what it can do. So it goes with every tool on this place—the chainsaw, the pry-bar, the mower.

The farmers brought hay from Massachusetts this morning and that meant lowering the hay elevator from the loft. I do it once a year, always the same way. I pretend I know what I'm doing, but I'm doing only what the barn and the elevator and the horses and the hay wagons require me to do. And now the bales come jerking up the elevator, and I swing into an easy rhythm, arms heavy, using the bale's weight against itself. It may look as though I've tossed that bale in a long arc, back to the darkness where the stack is rising. But I know now that that bale has used me to fling itself. I stand in the barn opening, trying to feel a breeze and pretending to have thoughts. But I know, too, that the thoughts are having me.

August 16

I've been thinking of a line by A. J. Liebling quoting the man he called his literary advisor, Whitey Bimstein, who also trained prizefighters. "I once asked him how he liked the country," Liebling writes. "He said, 'It is a nice spot.'" I love that line. It reduces the nonurban land surface of the planet to a single, homogeneous vanishing point. Mr. Bimstein, without knowing it, was perpetuating an ancient poetic habit, singling out an idealized setting— a *locus amoenus*, or pleasing place—from among the chiggers and ticks, the pokeweed and the poison ivy, in the actual countryside. I know some of Mr. Bimstein's rural counterparts. They've lived in the country their whole lives and never once been to the city.

Our house isn't far from the highway, and every day is filled with traffic passing by, some of it clearly heading for a nice spot somewhere. Most of the time I ignore it, but every now and then a car slows down and I can see the

129

occupants looking up the hill at the horses or the geese or at me on the tractor mowing the lower pasture.

I wonder what it is they see. I begin to feel a little allegorical, like a peasant shearing sheep in a medieval book of hours. I begin to wonder what I stand for in the eyes of those passersby, whether there's a moral to me or whether I simply illuminate a month in the calendar. This place is a nice spot in itself, and so I'm happy to pretend to impersonate one of the merry rustics even as I go about teaching the pigs to like scratching.

These days I'm a little dizzy with that doubleness. The city has come to seem like a place of nearly perfect sincerity. The country, it turns out, is a place of pervasive irony. This is exactly the opposite of what I always expected, the opposite of what the pastoral poets taught me to expect. To understand rural irony, all you have to do is watch a woodchuck in among the cabbages. It makes a perfect mockery of my intent in planting those cabbages. The woodchuck, sitting erect and nibbling, seems to imply that if I'd been just a little more sincere, this would never have happened. There's no laughter more hilarious, or more cutting, than the laughter of farmers.

So I stand in the pasture watching the heads turning in that slowing car, and I wonder do they see the man who pines for the city and inwardly blames the pastoral poets? Do my T-shirt and jeans look like overalls to them? Am I wearing a straw hat and chewing a blade of grass in their eyes? But then I look a little closer and notice that they're fighting over the map, lost on the way to some pleasant spot further north.

September 28

On Wednesday last week, I made a quick trip to Washington, D.C.—down on the dawn express, back on the dusk. And because I was riding in business class on the Acela I was surrounded by the sounds of business—the young women whose voices ring out like high heels on marble, the false laughter of a young executive talking to a headhunter on his cell phone. (He makes 175, going up to 200 in December, and is happy to relocate.) Everyone around me was speaking managese, that strange dialect used among the shepherds of other humans to communicate an enthusiasm for communication. It sounded as though the English language had been seeded with advertisements advocating the use of the English language.

The full moon was rising on the ride home. At first there was just the suggestion of a disk low on the horizon. It might have been a moon painted on old red brick, faded and soot-stained over the eons, the remnant of an ad for some forgotten nocturnal medicine. I'd been watching the way Baltimore backs blindly onto the tracks—the toothless old houses beyond despair, leaking their privacy into the night. And then we were passing the water's edge, and there was the moon just beginning to glow, though the night was too muggy for the water to catch the moon's reflection.

There was an ancient notion that the moon's orbit marks the boundary between the immutable heavens and the mutability of the sublunary sphere. Against the backdrop of urban demise and development, this moon seemed impossibly constant. Even along the shore, where the flat waves seemed to abandon the land over and over again, the moon persisted. To really understand the metaphor of the moon's mutability—the inconstancy of its path through the sky, its time of rising and setting, and especially its phases—you would have to live in a much darker world, where you could feel the steadiness of the night sky. The byword for mutability these days is the planet Earth.

Something about the moon brings to life one metaphor after another. Long ago, I described a full moon rising in far northern California as "a fat man climbing a ladder," which was accurate at the time. But this moon wasn't a fat man climbing. It seemed to hang over the horizon, though the word *hang* is an injustice to the forces that governed the moon's appearance. Slowly it slid up the sky, and its color deepened. I tried to name its colors as it ascended and in doing so remembered how steadily and surprisingly life supplies us with the right analogies.

Just as darkness was really taking hold, I let myself say—and it was a cliche—that this moon was as ripe as a tropical fruit. It really was exactly the color of the flesh of a tropical fruit I'd bought the night before. The fruit was called a mamey sapote, which comes from Central and South America. Unpeeled, it looks like an oversized, oval potato. But under the rind is a deep mahogany seed and the mildly sweet flesh of a ripe September moon, which is slightly aphrodisiacal, they say. Not only was the moon that night the color of the pulp of a softening mamey. It wore the same open-mouthed expression as the woman behind the cash register when she realized that the mamey she was ringing up on Broadway cost some five hundred times more than it did in the markets at home in Ecuador.

So the train hammered and rocked along, and the business of our rail car went quiet while the world outside receded. For another few minutes the moon was still the pulp of a singular, arousing fruit imported at great cost to be purchased as a curiosity from a woman who knew exactly how ordinary it was and how little it was worth. But soon the moon rose into some new analogy, and by then I'd fallen asleep.

October 24

Soon a farmer and his son will come to the farm to kill our two pigs. If that sentence bothers you, you should probably stop reading now—but you should also stop eating pork. The pigs weigh nearly three hundred pounds apiece, and killing them is the reality of eating meat. I talk to the pigs whenever I'm in their pen, and ever since June I've been slowly taming them, getting them used to being scratched. I truly love being with the pigs. And taming them means it will be that much easier for the farmer and his son to kill them swiftly, immediately. If I have no more foreknowledge of my death than these two pigs will have of theirs, I'd consider myself very lucky.

The questions people usually ask make it sound as though I should be in a state of moral outrage against myself. They imply that it's impossible, or indecent, to scratch the pigs behind the ears and still intend to kill them. Saying that it's quite possible isn't much comfort to anyone. People assume I'm either confessing a terrible defect of character or declaring that I prefer bacon to living pigs. If I belonged to a more coherent rural community— one that comes together as a unit for pig-butchering in the fall—I would get to see the greater comedy in it all, the sudden abundance, the culinary wealth a well-fed pig represents. But it's hard to act out a social comedy of that kind when the cast is a gruff farmer, his gruff son, and my wife and me, who have been silenced by the solemnity of what we're watching.

Because we do watch. That's part of the job. It's how we come to understand what the meat means. The word *meat* is at the root of the contradictory feelings the pig-killing raises. You can add all the extra value you want—raising heritage breed pigs on pasture with organic grain, all of which we do—and yet we're doing this for meat, some of which we keep, most of which we trade or sell. It makes the whole thing sound like a bad bargain. And yet compared to the bargain most Americans make when they buy pork in the supermarket, this is beauty itself.

Knowing that you're doing something for the last time is a uniquely human fear. I thought that would be the hardest thing about having pigs. In fact, it's not so hard, though it reminds me that humans have trouble thinking carefully about who knows what. One day soon I'll step into the pen and give the pigs a thorough scratching, behind the ears, between the eyes, down the spine. Their tails will straighten with pleasure. It will be the last time. I'll know it, and they won't.

October 30

Suddenly, in the absence of a general, killing frost, people have become expert in the subtleties of what the season hasn't delivered. The other day I heard a farmer refer to the "high" frost that hit his farm in upstate New York. It coated the windows on his pickup but didn't touch the fields. Down in the valleys, people know that the frost on their lawns doesn't count, because the hillsides above them haven't been hit. A killing frost to a pot of basil is a pleasant evening to a stalk of Brussels sprouts. Until the past few days, even the basil hasn't been bothered.

But I think the first frost has finally come. It wasn't a deep black frost, the kind that makes the unprepared gardener weep. Two mornings in a row the pasture has turned white, and the thick stands of goldenrod have given up the golden for silver instead. Even the fields of corn stubble have been glazed with anticipation, a readiness for snow if snow ever comes again. A thin line of woodsmoke hangs just above the trees, and where the hillsides rise above the highway, the woodsmoke lies in tendrils, the way water vapor does on a wet summer day.

Everyone up here has noticed how late the frost is and how deep into October some of the trees have kept their leaves. Pastures that were going brown in the drought of summer have greened up again. There has barely been skim ice on the stock tanks. But if things seem awry and you want to talk about it here in the country, you talk about what it costs when the fuel truck comes, and you feel uneasily grateful that it's come so few times yet this fall. Winter usually arrives on a tight schedule, and it's hard to regret a little slack, even if it feels worrisome.

I'm still waiting for the hard frost, the one makes the steel gates bitter to the touch and drives the bees deep into the core of their hive. That frost puts away any thoughts of last-minute regeneration. It makes it clear that time is going to have to pass—and it's going to have to get a lot colder—before there's any hint of rebirth. When that frost will come is anyone's guess. Right now, the frost we're having still seems ornamental, a last-minute embellishment for Halloween.

November 19

I'm sitting at the northwest corner of my grandmother's table in a house on the edge of a small Iowa town. I'm young enough to feel that my presence at the table is a promotion. There's something bewildering in the passing of plates, the coming and going of serving dishes, and I can see—looking into this memory from a long ways away—that the adults at the table find my presence a little comical. It makes them speak to each other in asides and to me in a language that seems both ironic and slightly formal, as if I were an ambassador from the everyday planet of children to the special planet of Thanksgiving, where dinner is eaten at three.

With the turkey comes teasing. Here come the mashed potatoes, and teasing. Cranberry sauce, more teasing. It's the condiment of choice at this Thanksgiving table, and I'm very fond of it, in part because the adults are so busy teasing each other, too. I really have no idea what they're saying, but I can sense the pleasure in how they're saying it. I don't understand the way they make each other laugh, but I end up laughing with them. Even now I can almost taste that laughter, the way I can still smell an overcooked under-tone in the turkey gravy.

The women orbit the table, never sitting for long. Their responsibilities are clearly superior to the men's and more immediate. Back and forth to the kitchen they go, always with an air of preoccupation, as though some secret is hidden there, in the oven, behind the sink, out on the porch. This is fuss-ing, which isn't entirely unrelated to teasing. It, too, is a kind of attention, a language that, in one aunt, is puzzling and anxiously self-referential while in another it's the soul of generosity.

Soon we're all so busy eating that my presence at this table of adults is no longer something separate or special. It's as though they all forget at once that I'm here. Somehow, that makes them specially visible to me. I can watch them without being watched myself. And what I notice isn't one adult or another. It isn't the place settings or the table decorations or the hands and elbows and napkins and mouths. It's the way it all comes together, the clearing created by sitting round a table and facing each other over a feast.

I was young enough then to be getting down from the table after pumpkin pie rather than getting up, the way the grownups did. And I'm sur-prised to realize that I remember the feeling of doing so. It seemed to me that something was missing, and thinking back, I know what it was. Grace was said at the start of the meal—a pause before eating—but we should have paused at the end of the meal, for a second grace, before we all left the table. All these years later, I haven't turned out to be a grace-saying man. But I'm grateful for the people around me and for their coming together. The thanks we say as we sit down together is also the thanks we should say before we separate, before we're hurried away into life.

November 21

A couple of days ago we had what the forecasts call a "wintry mix," which sounds to me like something you set out in bowls at a cocktail party this time of year. It was, in fact, rain, snow, and sleet mixed with sand and salt and the sludge that gets thrown from the tread of tires. One minute the snow was falling in clumps, and the next it was raining. The sky was the color of duct tape and it let about that much light through. A "wintry mix" makes you want to stay home—or perhaps go into the world foraging for provisions simply for the pleasure of getting home again.

This is the kind of weather—true November weather—in which I learn to admire the stoicism of the animals all over again. *Stoicism* is the wrong word if only because it implies an awareness of being stoic—a sense of putting up with what you have to put up with. I know the horses are aware, but I understand it as an awareness that isn't busy comparing states of being. They stand over their hay in the wintry mix, and they seem to take it as it comes. I imagine them thinking, "No flies!" as a way of enjoying this grim weather. Even that implies a differential state of mind.

Till now, this has been a bright oaken autumn. The most vivid fall colors came and went—the sugar maples garish as always—leaving behind the oaks, which hold their leaves far longer. The last few weeks have been dusted with a dry, wooden light, and the oaks have shown just how various and pungent their colors can be, while behind them the beeches hold out their leaves more stiffly. It was as if the oaks had all stepped forward a couple of weeks ago to reveal their pendulous, lobed leaves, to remind us of a spectrum of color that goes undisplayed most years.

But everything changes on a wintry day. The woods seem to withdraw, though the snow on the ground creates the illusion that you can see deeper into them. The brightness vanishes, and that gives all the subtler colors a heightened presence. It doesn't take the oxblood of an oak's leaves to impress you. It takes only the variations of gray on the bark of a maple tree.

As voluminous as the woods seem in summer, when they're full of shadow, now is the time they seem most corporeal, most alive. I don't mean the fact that you can trace a squirrel's route along the maple high line or watch the woodpeckers in a hickory queuing for suet. I mean that the trees seem to be making a gesture of a kind they never do when the leaves are green, as though they can only really be themselves when the light is low and the air is damp and the year is drawing in.

December 3

For the past few days I've been writing in rural Wyoming, not far from one of the main routes to one of the major coalbed methane developments in the state. Morning and evening, there's a rush of four-wheel-drive diesel pick-ups with flatbeds and heavy steel grill guards—deer catchers. I sometimes think it will take the energy equivalent of all the methane coming out of the ground near Gillette just to run the pickups going back and forth from the well sites. Highway 16 may look like a modest rural two-lane, but it's the local equivalent of what some Wyoming residents have come to call the Jonah 500—the stretch of highway leading from Rock Springs to the Jonah natural gas fields near Pinedale.

But the weekend makes a break in the high-speed traffic, especially when snow is falling, as it was last Saturday. The sky was lying as low as it ever does in Wyoming, and the wind was nearly still, which made the snow-fall seem oddly static, as if the sky were full of charged particles never destined to reach the ground. It was enough, though, to cut the traffic to almost nothing—here and there an SUV or a ranch pickup pulling a stock trailer. I followed a late seventies Lincoln Continental, vinyl peeling from its roof, into Buffalo, where it pulled up to the drive-through window at a liquor store. I kept going and made the turn for Ten Sleep, Highway 16 over the Big Horn Mountains.

A couple of miles up the grade, the bare asphalt gave way to a black two-track through packed snow. The storm was heavy enough to blur the world around me, to create the sense that I was driving at the center of a bubble of visibility sliding along with me, while all around the forest seemed to be closing in. The temperature dropped into the low teens, then to nine and seven, and though there was nothing particularly dangerous in the driv-ing, there was every good reason to slow all the way down, including the best reason of all: no one else was on the road.

Long before I got to the pass—9,666 feet—I realized I was actu-ally enjoying the slowness. And I realized that I'd long ago thrown out the notion of a "scenic drive," a drive just for the pleasure of seeing what you can see and at a pace that allows you to see it. Partly, that's the fault of my own sense of urgency, but it's also an acute instinct for sticking with the pace of traffic, an instinct refined by driving in New York and Los Angeles.

That was the beauty of this drive. I was the traffic. I was free to exaggerate the severity of the weather if I liked. It gave me an excuse to peer into the stands of lodgepole pine along the road, to look down into the willows along the creeks, to ponder again the signs pointing out rock formations—and stating their age in hundreds of millions of years—on a highway that is often driven by people who believe this Earth is only a few thousand years old.

I came down Ten Sleep Canyon at a crawl, the cliffs above hidden in the clouds. After a few more miles, I drove into Worland. The safe driving lay well out of town, where the north wind had picked up and was blowing the asphalt nearly clear. In town, even the modest comings and goings of a bad-weather Saturday had churned the snow into an icy muck, turning Worland into a place where straight ahead was the only safe direction, if you could figure out how to get where you wanted to go by going only straight ahead.

Even in Shoshoni—a town spread-eagled on the high plateau—the falling snow and the falling light created a sense of enclosure. And in Lander—my destination—there was an oddly investigative feel to the way people were driving, as if they were trying to read the numbers on the houses they passed in a vain search for their own. Fluent drivers were hunting and pecking their way across town, never quite sure whether turning the wheel would produce the desired effect. On one of the side streets, a father on a four-wheeler pulled a child on a sled. A mule deer grazed on one of the lawns. The only question was whether the streets were snowy enough for a horse-drawn sleigh.

December 11

It's barely midafternoon, and the light outside is dropping fast. By 6 P.M. it will feel like midnight, and by midnight it will feel as though we've slipped into a temporal crevasse. Two nights ago, a storm passed through. It began with the chattering of sleet on the skylights and then it turned silent. The next morning, the farm was covered in ice. The wind has barely stirred since then, or perhaps I'm deceived by the new rigidity in my surroundings. Perhaps the world has frozen the way a fox does when it knows I'm watching it.

I spent some time yesterday chipping ice off the pickup. The ice fractured in thin sheets and slid down the windshield. If the wind does begin to blow, I thought, tubular fragments of ice will come raining down from all the trees. But on my trip out to the mailbox this morning—crossing the toboggan chute the road has become—I fingered the small branches on a pear tree and saw that the ice had bonded with the bark of the tree. It was tenacious, as if clinging to the tree for support. Meanwhile in the poultry yard, the geese had given up trying to get around. The chickens flapped their wings in vain, able to hover but unable to propel themselves forward. In flight, they looked like feathered asterisks.

The sun came out for a few minutes this afternoon, and, honestly, it seemed a little garish. It imposed a concentricity on the ice glare in the tree-tops, shaping partial orbits everywhere, as if the trees had nothing better to do than bow to the sun when at last it decided to appear. Then the light faded, and the world resumed its old organization. It was like watching the scene in some extraordinary pop-up book fade back into the pages. I walked down to the barn to feed the horses. The flattening light was as gratifying as the crunching of ice underfoot, a token of mid-December's grim seasonality.

It's now little more than a week to the bottom of the trough, where daylight is concerned. I'm always surprised when we get to this time of year, always sure that winter is darker than this. It's a false artifact of childhood. I remember winters being colder and snowier when I was young—surely they were more opaque as well? Apparently not. As the solar system is constructed now, you can only drain so much light out of the year at this latitude.

December 31

At midnight tonight, the horses on this farm will age a year. That's the custom—every horse has the same birthday, January 1. Like all things calendrical, this is a human convention. When it comes to genuinely equine conventions, I know enough only to notice the simpler forms of precedence—who goes first through a gate, who gets to the grain feeder ahead of the others. But I can report that the horses make no fuss about their common birthday or the coming of the new year. At midnight tonight, they'll be standing in the dark, dozing on their feet, ears tipping back and forth at the slightest of sounds. It's a night like any other.

I join the horses in the dark a few minutes before the clock strikes twelve on New Year's Eve. What makes the night exceptional, in their eyes and mine, is my presence among them, not the lapsing of an old year. It's worth standing out in the snow just to savor the anticlimax of midnight, to acknowledge that out of the tens of millions of species on this planet, only one bothers to celebrate the way it chooses to mark the passing of time.

I remember the resolutions I made when I was younger. One way to describe nature is a realm where resolutions have no meaning. It would be nearly as shocking to find horses who want to make resolutions as it would be to find humans who needn't.

It's not that time isn't passing or that the night doesn't show it. The stars are wheeling around Polaris, and the sugar maples that frame the pasture are laying down another cellular increment in their annual rings. The geese stir in the poultry yard. A hemlock sheds its snow. No two nights are ever the same.

I always wonder what it would be like to belong to a species—just for a while—that isn't so busy indexing its life, that lives wholly within the single long strand of its being. I'll never have even an idea of what that's like. I know because when I stand among the horses on New Year's Eve, I'll feel a change once midnight has come. Some need will have vanished, and I'll walk back down to the house—lights burning in the kitchen, smoke coming from the woodstove—as if something had been accomplished, some episode closed.

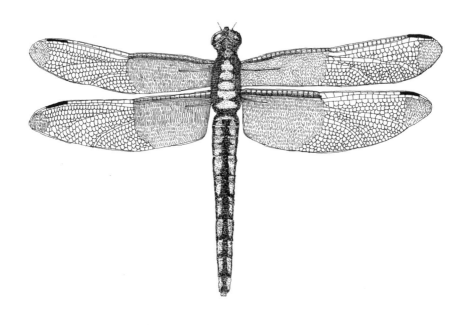

Year

SEVEN

January 3

The other day I knocked the mailbox off its post with the tractor. The mail doesn't come unless the approach to the mailbox is carefully plowed. The town road crew leaves a moraine of snow and gravel in front of it when the big blade comes by. So after every storm I sculpt a sort of drive-through lane to the mailbox. I won't tell you how I fixed the mailbox. The temperature was dropping fast, and the wind was howling. That's all you need to know. Except that winter is full of this kind of self-defeat.

The New Year's Eve storm dropped a lot of wet snow. Enough clung to the satellite dish to knock out my internet connection. The next storm added a layer on top of that. The dish is on the peak of the house, far too high for any of my ladders. So I stood in the yard at twilight on New Year's Day, throwing snowball after snowball at the dish. Twice I hit it, and both times the snowball stuck to the dish. As I write, the sun is shining. It's also zero outside. I'm waiting for a warm rain so I can rejoin the global mob.

The snow turns blue in the late afternoon, and it's hard to remember how stealthy this beauty is and how violent the cold can be in the galactic night, when the stars are brooding right overhead. I find myself double-checking even my oldest habits—making sure the barn doors are latched and the gates closed, watching my footing, being doubly sure of myself around the horses. Only a little has to go wrong for a lot to go wrong in this weather.

A hard winter is a season of attrition and clumsiness. The pleasant monotony of plowing—pushing back the drifts, keeping claustrophobia at bay—leads to daydreaming, and the next thing you know the mailbox is dangling by a single screw. I find myself clinging to a rigid routine because any variation leads to trouble. I usually gather eggs in the afternoon. The other morning, I found one lying beside the chicken feeder and stuck it without thinking in the pocket of my chore coat. When I went out again at three, I shoved a hand into my pocket and crushed the egg. I thought I'd thoroughly drained the hose to the horse tank the last time I used it, but no. I dragged it up to the house and let it thaw in the mudroom.

At first a day near zero doesn't feel very different from a day in the teens. The degrees seem to be squeezed together, as if there were less difference between zero and fifteen than sixty and seventy-five. That's how it feels until it starts to warm up. The next morning, at three degrees, my eyelashes no longer stuck together. And as the day warmed, the sounds that had rung out so clearly in the freeze—the clinking of the gate-chain, the stiff squeal of my boots on the snow—grew more and more humid. I won't need a balaclava to fix the mailbox. Only the sun can fix the satellite dish.

January 18

Every now and then I meet someone in Manhattan who has never driven a car. Some New Yorkers confess it sheepishly, and some announce it proudly. For some it's just a practical matter of fact, the equivalent of not keeping a horse on West 87th Street or Avenue A. I used to wonder at such people with a frank cultural prejudice, as if they were members of an outlandish tribe that adhered to the old ways. But more and more I wonder at myself.

I've been driving for some forty years, right through what will come to be thought of as the heart of the Internal Combustion era. No learnable skill—aside perhaps from reading and writing—is more a part of me than driving. Even calling driving a part of me makes it seem too separate. It would be more accurate to say that my senses have completely engulfed the automobile, like a vining plant. Or perhaps it's the other way around, and the automobile has completely encased my senses.

That first time behind the wheel, probably 1965, I could feel myself manipulating the machine through an unimaginable series of linkages with a clumsy device called the steering wheel. The car—a Dodge, I think, from the late 1950s, without power steering—felt more like a fallout shelter than something mobile. I had very little sense of where it began or ended. I was keenly aware of what it prevented me from seeing. A highway was just a linear succession of blind spots. As for backing up, how could you really trust what the mirrors told you unless you got out and checked? The transmission—manual, of course—was an instrument of betrayal. To drive down the road, those first few times, was to lurch through a series of unrelated states of being.

And now? I understand the richness of the phrase "second nature." The car's mirrors are no longer a cubist experiment in perception. They've joined together in a panoramic view of the past, of where I've just been. I feel the road through the tires' treads as though they were my fingerprints. When I learned to drive, I was taught to prize continuity above everything—to feel the drift of the car, to understand inertia, to ease into and out of a stop, to emulate, in a way, the smooth orbital passage of the planet itself. Speed itself has turned into an extension of my consciousness.

How "natural" all this is becomes apparent when you realize how few people—how miraculously few—are killed in accidents every year. If there weren't some profound intuitive fit between us and these machines, we'd be dying by the millions. Our behavior in them reveals our innate orderliness, our willingness to get along with each other while completely distrusting the drivers around us. Imagine a time-lapse film of the roads and streets that were built on this continent in the past century, and what you would see is the growth of a nervous system—without a brain, it's true, but a nervous system nonetheless.

Driving is the cultural anomaly of our moment. Someone from the past would marvel more, I think, at our speed of travel and the resulting expansion of our geographic consciousness than at anything else in our extravagant culture. Someone from the future—a future that's already embedded in the present—will marvel at our blindness and the hole we've driven ourselves into, for we're completely committed to an unsustainable technology.

And it's all come to pass in just a couple of generations. My dad was born in the mid-1920s, just as the automotive moment was becoming inevitable. And now here I am, always wondering how much longer we'll be driving, aware that every time I start the engine in my diesel pickup I'm firing up a dinosaur technology. America is full of people like me, who remember when gas was twenty-one cents a gallon, which is the price of admission to climate change.

The irony is that, in the long view, my life has been defined not only by the things I've chosen—to read and write and teach—but by things it never occurred to me I was choosing. To be a driver—to have owned cars and trucks and trailers and driven again and again across the country—is obviously a choice. But try explaining that to me when I was thirteen and learning to drive on the back roads of Iowa.

February 15

One afternoon last week, Ida was stepping slowly as she came into the corral. A horse's mobility is everything, and I began wondering about a hoof abscess or a muscle strain. But when I walked over to Ida I saw a gaping wound on her neck. I could look through the muscle wall and into an anatomical cavern. There was blood, but not the disastrous stream there would have been if the wound had been a couple of inches lower. I could barely watch Ida while we waited for the vet. I was afraid I'd see her slide to the ground.

I don't quite understand how we got from that terrible place to where we were half an hour later. A young vet only a few months out of school was standing beside Ida in a stall with me. It took a few tries to find the vein, but the sedative was working. Ida's head sagged into my arms, and I could feel the sedative working on me, too, as if I were the one who had gotten the shot. The vet slid most of her gloved hand into the wound. She shaved around the opening and flushed the cavity again and again. Then came the antibiotic and the local antiseptic and then two layers of stitches, one to pull the muscle together, the other to gather the skin.

Through all of this, Ida seemed to have surrendered herself. A couple of months ago, I shooed her up the pasture, and she threw a kick at me that barely clipped my chest. I knew it was coming as she turned away from me. She has never lived in a stall. But we stood there for an hour and more under the lights while the vet worked, and Ida never flinched or stirred. The other horses came by, one at a time, to look into the stall and see what was happening. It was a bitter afternoon and they were waiting for their hay. I searched the pasture again and again for the place where the injury occurred and never found it. A mystery wound, said the vet—all too common.

I could do nothing for Ida. I held her head in my arms, but it made no real difference. My arms trembled from the weight the rest of the night. Somehow she kept her legs under her. I know that what I took as trust was mostly drugs. But it was also trust. If she got even half the comfort from me that I got from her, then she was fine. And she's fine now—trotting across this prison house of ice with the other horses. It was horrifying at first to see that wound. Now that it's healing it's merely disgusting.

March 19

For some reason, the look of the woods and pastures now, just at the turning point of spring, make me think of the Civil War. Perhaps it's the matted leaves and the flattened grass or the hoof-torn earth where the horses make a habit of standing. Perhaps it's because the woods look winter-beaten, skeletal, though they're really the same as they were in November. The snow withdraws and leaves behind the feeling of something that shouldn't be seen, not yet. I don't know why I imagine a ghostly landscape—the fields overhung with the smoke of campfires and the weary presence of Union and Confederate soldiers—but I do.

This is a deeply contentious time of year. The rains have torn out the road without fully melting the soil. What the calendar promises, the day itself retracts. Unless you knew better, you'd hardly believe the readiness of spring was anywhere to be found. The witch hazel is blossoming, but undemonstratively, not in a way that really means anything. The only sign of spring I trust is the sound of the birds singing. It's too early to call it ebullience, but it's pointed in that direction. They're gathering to court and breed.

That sense of contention belongs only to a human witness. The robins mob across the half-frozen pasture in the sleet, and yet they appear as dry and dusty as they always do. For all its disarray, nothing in nature looks discomfited. I pretend to see patience in the sugar maples and the hickories, but any patience I find is mine, and there's little enough of that. I'm ready for a headlong season.

There will be time to fix the fence rails that winter knocked down, time to scrape out the barnyard and make a pleasing mound of muck. This will have to be the year the old chicken yard is seeded to grass and all its occupants moved to new quarters. There's nothing like mud season to persuade you that a fixed habitation is a bad idea. This would be a good year to let the land recover, except that the recovery I have in mind, like the wear we put on the land, isn't the work of a single year.

What cheers me is the thought that spring isn't a human season—not like the seasons we create for ourselves. It comes without caring what you make of it. It may find you unprepared, ill at ease, in a state of erosion. It makes no difference. It will stir your blood anyway, once the freezing rain goes away at last.

April 8

Lately I've been thinking about the word *vang*. If you look it up in the glossary of *Royce's Sailing Illustrated*, you find that it means a line to prevent "the peak of a gaff from falling off leeward." That's how it goes when you're learning a new technical vocabulary. The language seems self-enclosed at first, each new definition an opaque cluster of words that themselves need defining. During vocabulary lessons in grade school, I was taught to try using a new word in a sentence. "There is a vang." "Can someone show me the vang?" "How much does a vang cost?" Those are my best efforts so far.

Part of the trouble is that I've never seen a "vang." But it's also that *vang* doesn't sound like a noun to me. It sounds like the past tense of *ving*, which sounds like something you might do to a *vong*, and those are words with no meaning, nautical or otherwise. It all brings me back to that childhood feeling of being happily encumbered with new words and trying them out tentatively, watching to see, on the faces around me, whether I'd misused them. At present, I trust myself to employ only a few easy sailing terms, like *mast* and *anchor*. I worry about the rest. I imagine myself standing at the tiller and shouting out nonsensical commands: "Vang the leach!" "Steeve the bumkin!" "Harden the Quangle-Wangle!" At sea, I'm fit only to crank a winch, unless, of course, one "winds" a winch.

Being lost in all this terminology—struggling, for instance, with the nautical meaning of *scandalize*—is an old, familiar feeling. I've spent most of my life happily sailing into fogbanks of specialized language. Some, like the vocabularies of philosophy and literary theory, never lost their slightly foggy quality, thanks to their inherent abstraction. But others, like the languages of fly-fishing and hog raising and horse riding, cleared up just as soon as I laid hands on the objects they named. I wondered what a *pulaski* was until I used one. There's something endlessly appealing about the care with which the contents of the world, especially the tools of the working world, have been named. Those words—like *fid*, to choose another nautical term—seem to have been smoothed by the friction of so many hands over the years. This is the elemental poetry of the human mind.

And yet it's all just vocabulary until it comes alive. I'm a longtime reader of sailing narratives, and when I come to the technical bits—where the bumkin is being steeved and the leach vanged under gale force winds—I let my mind glaze over the way I do when I come to the math in books about cosmology. Something important is happening, and I'll wait till the plain English tells me what it is. But there's no glazing over when you actually begin sailing, as I did under tutelage for the first time only a few weeks ago. You find yourself at sea, awash in the natural world, and yet at the same time you find yourself immured in a vigilant properness—a clear sense of how things should be. It's not just a matter of proper names. It's a matter of proper actions, proper responses, without which there's a world of trouble. There's something deeply ethical about it all, as there always is in the command of language.

Sailing is just one more thing I've taken up as an adult but wish I'd begun doing as a child. It isn't just the experience that would have accrued by now. It's the innateness you feel for things you've been doing a long, long time, the lack of self-consciousness with which you inhabit a language that seems outlandish to newcomers. I look back and wonder what I've been doing innately since childhood, and I can think only of this. I've been picking up words one by one, feeling their heft, wondering who's used them before, and slowly adding them to my permanent collection.

May 1

I've been stopping by a local swamp where the peepers live. It's hard to believe that the high-pitched chorus of such small frogs could amount to a roar, but it does. It rises into the night sky and swallows the listener. My mental compass seems to go awry in the midst of such an outcry, as if the peepers were jamming my sense of direction. In the darkness there's no horizon except a silence somewhere on the far edge of that cacophony. If a peeper has a sense of identity, it must dissolve completely in that night-song, because I certainly feel myself dissolving when I hear it.

Somehow the question of identity is always emerging on this farm. I found the body of a barn swallow lying just inside the barn the other day. It must have died just after it returned to the farm. I noticed the particularity of its body, how sharply cut its wings were, the way the darkness of its iridescent plumage seemed to glow with some residual heat. But it was the particularity of death, not the identity of life, a body in stillness while all around me its kin were twittering and swooping in and out of the hayloft. What's a swallow without its flight?

And then I consider myself and my species. If it were audible, I wonder what the roar of human consciousness rising over our swamp would sound like. I watch the same thoughts swooping in and out of my brain, over and over again, as if they had young to feed in the hollow loft of my skull. I find myself stunned by the human ability to think of one's life as a thing apart with its own particularity, like a swallow held in the hand. I end up admiring the thoughtless animate persistence of every creature around me—the wood-chuck without doubts in the goldenrod stubble, the horses certain in the pasture, the arrogant geese whose footprints melted the frost this morning.

I keep a dead hummingbird in a bag in the freezer, a downy woodpecker, too. Down at the barn, the dead swallow lies beside a wren I found this winter, its tail as impertinent as it was when alive. I don't know why I keep them except to notice, as I often do, that death among small birds isn't corrupting. Flight vanishes, and so does song. But the feathers live on as if that swallow might wake at any moment, surprised to find itself perched in my hand.

July 2

The last couple of nights I've stood at the edge of the pasture watching the fireflies. They rise from the grass, flickering higher and higher until one of them turns into the blinking lights of a jet flying eastward far above the horizon. I can feel rather than see the bats working around the house and in the coves between the trees. They're feeding on insects invisible to me, and I'm watching insects invisible, though not inaudible, to the bats.

What the insects are noticing—the bats too—is beyond me. Our perceptions overlap without ever converging in the night. There's a solipsism in each species, a preoccupation with its own narrow concerns, that's disarming when you first begin to think about it. All the entangled lives on this farm seem to run on separate tracks, except where they collide as predators and prey. Push this thought far enough and nature seems to fray into a disunity that's gathered up only by our human perceptions. And yet that gathering up is just our own kind of solipsism. I don't know whether the horses have ever made a general proposition about nature, but then they don't know whether I've made one either.

The best part of the season is that long twilight moment when the swallows are making their last excursions, just before the bats and the fireflies begin. The swallows work in the column of bugs that rises halfway up the hickories. They arc up out of the barnyard pasture and fold their wings back near the peak of the house, coasting and diving. Compared to the swallows, the early bats—fluttering between the trees—look at first like origami contraptions capable only of struggling flight. It seems unlikely that a firefly can fly at all.

The overgrown edges of the garden darken. All the luminousness is starting to fall out of the sky, and yet I can still see the bright spots of ripening color on the cherry tree at the back of the garden. To tell whether those cherries are ripe, I pick a couple every day and eat them. So far, I wince when I eat them. And yet every bird on the place, except for the insectivores, carries a secret knowledge of the ripeness of cherries. I'll know when the cherries are ripe by their absence.

July 3

When I was in graduate school, I dug a small garden, just room for some tomatoes, sweet corn, lettuce, and a few other things. I intended to sit by the garden and watch it grow and do the heavy reading I needed to do for my graduate work. I'd grown used to the kind of books—literary criticism mostly—from which one looks up a lot and sees the weeds infesting the carrots and feels the need to do something about them. The books would drive me to the garden and the sun would drive me back to a chair in the shade with the books. That was the plan.

It was ruined by Dorothy Sayers. Her mysteries are books from which one does not look up. The weeds take over the tomato cages, pages and pages of scholarship go unread, and still one does not look up from Sayers. It isn't the suspense. These are mild adventures. It isn't the wit or the powers of observation or the whimsical hero, Lord Peter Wimsey, or his less whimsical foils—Bunter, his man, and Harriet Vane, his eventual woman. All of these pieces play a part, of course. But there was enough world in those attractive books—an entertainment complete enough in itself—to keep me from bothering about the world around me. I was never tempted to take a note or pull a weed or do anything but turn the pages and move my reading chair out of the sun.

From Sayers I moved on that summer to Raymond Chandler and I forget who else. It was a summer of pure detection—murders genteel, murders grisly, but always a murder being solved. I noted that my garden had begun to resemble a couple of overgrown graves. As for my mind, it would be hard to say whether it was dulled or whetted by the task of following one detective after another through the chain of evidence and coincidence that finally bags the culprit. I began to think of writing my own mystery, about a detective for whom none of the clues ever come right and who never gets his man. It was too sadly like a dissertation.

These days I scatter my summer reading throughout the year. But I know there will come a week in July or August when I ignore the beauty of the season for the ink on the page in front of me. It may be another week of mysteries or perhaps I'll finally embark on Patrick O'Brian. All that matters is not looking up.

July 9

For the past few hours the wind has been rising and falling, the start of a storm coming in from the west. When the wind climbs, a kind of elation blows through the house—it's the hushing sound of the leaves outside and the way the breeze sweeps the floors and lifts the curtains and slams the doors. The dogs snap to and look around when a gust whistles through the screens. And when the wind drops, it seems to drop us—the dogs and me—into the trough of an ordinary summer afternoon, the kind of afternoon when a breeze changes everything.

I spent a humid morning recently in the barnyard with the farrier, who was shoeing Remedy. Remedy was dozing over the work being done on his feet the way a customer dozes in a barber chair. First one hoof, then another, heel and toe trimmed and rasped and the shoe nailed home, followed by more rasping. The other horses stood in the corral, lower lips drooping in the heat. A twist of wind came across the pasture, up from the highway, stirring the sumac along the fence line. The farrier stopped and stretched his back. Remedy shifted his feet and looked intently at the mares. I turned my face into the wind and re-coiled the lead-rope.

There have been times here, mostly in winter, when the sound of the gale outside has made me want to go down to the basement and sit by the roar of the furnace. But the breeze this afternoon is more like respiration, in and out with a prolonged sigh now and then. When the wind is still, I can feel the expectation of a storm building. This isn't simply the quiet of an afternoon. It's the quiet in which something is about to happen.

I hope it's a good storm, a high wind, rain slanting across the pastures, geese splashing in the sudden puddles, chickens huddled inside their house trying to keep the wind from getting under their feathers. For a moment, the house seems to fill with air that was just outside, just over the hill a few seconds ago. For a moment it feels like a sail filling, lifting, as though this cranky old farmhouse might loose its mooring and reach toward the sea.

The power will go out and the house will go dark. And for at least one of these summer nights, I won't hear the sound of insects tapping at the windows and screens, hoping to come into this lighted room while the bats make havoc among them.

July 25

Early most evenings, the dogs and I walk across the pasture in front of the house. It's a piece of ground I think I know well. I've fenced it twice, kept chickens and pigs in it, ridden horses over it, and watched the weather come across it for a decade now. I mow it a couple of times every year, and when the snow is good I ski around it. And yet every time I walk across that acre and a half, its topography surprises me—its lifts and hollows, the points of rock, the long slope down to the eastern fence line. I keep wanting to believe the pasture is flat.

It may be the memory of the first time I saw it. It was late August and the pasture was overgrown, its bones invisible under tall drying weeds and grasses. It's hard to explain how mysterious it was to me, how far away the western tree line seemed, how tawny the rank growth looked, as if it were a stand of wheat ready for cutting. It was only an overgrown field, badly fenced and cross-fenced, getting ready to reforest itself. It was a season away from an upspringing of poplars. But I felt at the time as though I were standing at the edge of a limitless prairie.

Since then the horses have kept the grasses closely trimmed, short enough to make a woodchuck nervous. There's a spring to the turf now and here and there a small clump of the bird's-foot trefoil I seeded a decade ago. I never go into the pasture without thinking about lying on my back and staring up at the stars. Once a cool fall night comes—long after the mosquitoes are gone—that's what I'll do.

Looking at the pasture now is like looking at the face of a friend who has grown gaunt over the years. Cheekbone, jaw, the orbit of the eyes, they all stand out in high relief. And when the shadows lengthen—just about the time the dogs and I go out—I can see clearly how the pasture tumbles downhill from the west. If the earth under our feet were water, this would be a roaring rapid. Winter heaves stones to the surface, and the other seasons reabsorb them. But nothing has changed the underlying topography of this pasture in the decade I've lived here. There's nothing flat about it. I came here seeing what I expected to see, and it's taken me all this time to see what the pasture had to show me.

August 15

Ten years ago, I planted a row of fruit trees on either side of the driveway— a couple of pear trees and four apple trees. One of the apples died a few years ago, and when I wrapped a chain around the trunk and inched the tractor forward, the tree seemed to leap from the ground as if its roots had never held fast. I've pruned the apples a few times since, but one of the pears got away from me. To harvest the fruit at the top, I'd have to chop the tree down. The apples are now full of fruit, and I'm grateful to them for needing so little urging on my part. They've known their business and gone about it.

I've written from time to time about the trouble that overcomes me here on this farm, the way the land outwits me, the way my sense of time— conditioned by nonagrarian life—causes trouble again and again. I act as if mine were the only will that matters on the place, forgetting that everything that grows here has a will of its own. You have to be humble to live properly on the land. That's one truth. Another is that you have to be able to accept humiliation. Some days that's easy enough, just a matter of acknowledging the limits of my time and ability. Other days, it leads me into serious trouble with myself. The land doesn't have a conscience, but I do, and the land—and what I've done to it or not done—is reflected in it.

This may just be a way of saying that fall is plainly coming, even though the farmers here are just finishing the first cutting of hay. The conifers have done well this summer for the same reason the farmers are grumbling— plenty of rain. I've scarcely ever seen a rabbit on this place before, and yet here they are this summer, as if the rain had brought them. They huddle on the lawn, in the pasture, along the drive, as if someone had placed them there or they'd grown up like mushrooms. They don't seem to move. They appear and vanish without locomotion. It's a good trick.

August 26

It's 6 A.M., a dark gray morning in late August—the dim light a reminder that it's two months downhill from the start of summer. Ethel the Border terrier and I are behind the house investigating a woodchuck scent. There's a dark smudge in the mist above us, and then another. The bats are returning to their bat house high up under the eaves. Each bat comes in over the roof, makes a dive for the ground, and then swoops upward toward the narrow entrance of the bat house. Some slip inside on the first try, some fall back and try again. After a few minutes, the air is still, the last bat home. Ethel and I turn toward breakfast.

I've watched the bats come out at evening again and again. It's one of the joys of living here, seeing them drop one by one into the night. But I've seen them coming home only a few times. The bats of evening are the last flutter in a world that's growing still. The bats of morning have already been engulfed by birdsong, rooster crow, the stirring of nearly every creature on this place. Their flight is less erratic just before roosting, no longer distracted by insects in the air. It's as though each bat brings a scrap of night's darkness home with it, leaving the sky pale and brightening. It's as though night itself were being stored in the bat house till dusk.

When the last bat vanished, I felt almost absurdly alone, strangely vacant in that thin slice of morning. It reminded me of a feeling from long ago—that moment, after staying up all night, when you can feel the world gathering pace and energy just as you're beginning to fade, the city stirring, streets coming to life, a crescendo that grows and grows. You can almost pinpoint the moment when the city reaches full throttle. You glimpse what a powerful movement morning really is. There's no coaxing about it. It marches you right into the day, right through life.

Watching those dawn bats, I imagined them punching out of their night work as they settled, and I felt as if I'd somehow clocked into their schedule. The best use of a dark gray morning with mist in the air is to go back to bed, only a few feet—and a couple of walls—away from where the bats are sleeping.

September 4

Horse people I know all speak with great respect of a horse's memory for place. For a long time, I imagined they meant that horses carried around in their minds remarkably detailed maps of their experience of the world. But that's just a human way of thinking of it. There are no horse maps. To a horse, how things are is how things are until they change. Then they're that way. The only map of the world is the world itself. Riding through country your horse already knows is a reminder of how abstractly humans take in their surroundings, how we generalize our place in the world. A horse's attention is particular. It shows in the cant of its ears, the flicker of its eyes, the fluidity or hesitation of its gait.

I sometimes wondered about these things while my wife and I were hauling the horses to Wyoming, as we often did more than a decade ago. They stood quietly in the trailer, side by side, flanks rubbing as Ohio or Iowa or South Dakota went past. Sometimes a head drooped and a lower lip fell square and quivering. Mostly the horses watched the countryside, not quite as rapt as a dog sniffing the breeze through an open window, but attentive enough. Thinking of those things made it clear that the signs along the freeway—flashing neon, enormous billboards—were designed for a highly inattentive species. And it's true. Every time I've gotten in trouble on horseback, it was because my attention had wandered.

Last week I drove past the farm I lived on when I first moved to the country. I hadn't really expected to go that way. I hadn't been paying attention. But there I was suddenly, in a little hollow along a river, and there was a run-in shed I'd built and the tiny creek that trickled down off the mountain to the east. I thought of a Border terrier named Tonic—now long gone—who lived there too, and it all seemed impossibly distant. I wondered if the human ability to map the world around us is connected to how separate the past sometimes seems.

It's a question I'd like to be able to ask my horses. Are the past and the present the same for you? Do you remember those trips west and the herd you came from? Or would you have to relive it all for the memories to come alive?

September 13

For the past week, I've been in northern Finland, just south of the Arctic Circle and a few kilometers shy of the restricted zone that marks the Russian border. This is the boreal forest, a place of almost surreal silence this time of year, when most of the birds have already migrated. The first night I was here, I stood in the middle of the road on a bridge over the Oulanka, a broad, slow-moving river that flows into Russia. It was dusk, a clear night, and I had come out to listen to nothing. There was no wind in the trees, not even the slightest breeze. The river below me was silent, and for the half hour I stood there I heard not a sound.

In fact, I found myself checking, again and again, to see whether I'd gone deaf. I popped my ears. I scuffed a shoe on the road. I tossed a rock into an eddy along the river's edge. I tapped the guardrail with a knuckle. There was nothing wrong with my hearing. I listened to the Finnish night and realized that I was listening actively, trying to hear something. The human ear isn't really meant for straining, and yet I was straining to hear. The silence felt more like an unnatural muffling of my senses than the porous stillness of the natural world.

The next week I spent in and out of the forest, listening with my eyes, so to speak, and not my ears. It's been a cold, wet summer in Finland, a season filled with the sound of rain falling through the spruces and pines. All the Finns I met grimaced when they talked about it, as if the summer had tasted like cold, weak coffee. But the past week has been dry, and every night there has been frost. The leaves are turning fast. A fog hangs above the river in the mornings, which only deepens the illusion of silence.

On my last night here, I went back to the bridge, again under a clear sky. There are long shadows even at mid-day this time of year, and dusk is still reluctant to give way to real darkness. I was waiting for stars to appear in the clearing overhead, but they were apparently busy elsewhere.

As I stood there, I heard the faint but quite audible roar of the rapids a half mile downstream and around a great bend. Why had I not heard it that first night? The answer, I suppose, is that I was too busy not hearing the things I'm used to hearing, including the great roar that underlies the city's quietest moments. It had taken a week to empty my ears, to expect to hear nothing and to find in that nothing something to hear after all.

October 7

On a still day—rain threatening—a tall stem bobs back and forth in the garden. A goldfinch has landed just below the flower head and is eating seeds from it while the stem sways like a pendulum. The rain begins, and above its steady, even rhythm, there's a clatter in the leaves and a sudden pop on the woodshed roof—a hickory nut falling. Soon the clouds tear apart overhead, and the sun spills through. Steam rises from the horses' backs. Maple leaves are coming down in ones and twos, and the ones and twos are beginning to add up in drifts along the pasture edges.

Most of the time, nature is simply there—when I do chores, when I walk down to the mailbox, when I look up from writing. I don't expect solace from it, nor do I theologize it with my own desires. It simply persists in sublime indifference, a quality that's inherently unsurprising. And yet from time to time I find myself surprised by it, and I know that what I'm really noticing is the volatility of the human world.

That feeling first struck me after 9/11—a sense of shock, as I wrote then, at discovering the "old news" of nature after living amid the new news that had erupted in the city. I have the same feeling again now. Nothing in the natural world upbraids me. It offers no commentary. It has nothing to say about financial meltdowns and dirty politics or, for that matter, personal grief. But the other lives on this farm do remind me how captive I've become—like all of us—to the tensions of this incredible human season. I can feel the pricking of shame in that sense of horrified captivation, a feeling of having forgotten something fundamental.

That's the trick in nature. There's no escaping to it. It throws you back upon yourself again and again. The geese shriek when they see me coming and then drop into their bassoon tones. The chipmunks freeze on the stone wall, waiting to see what direction I'll go. Remedy makes the sound that's usually called nickering but is really a slow, deep equine purring. I'm carrying the grain bucket, which is why. I'm also lost in my thoughts, and when I slip out of them, walking beside the horses up the hill to their grain buckets, I can feel for a moment how insubstantial those thoughts really are before they engulf me again.

November 3

Every now and then I feel as though I've woken up in a Rembrandt etching—a low, tangled thicket of pen-strokes from which a landscape emerges. It's not that the sky has taken on the tint of seventeenth-century drawing paper or that the world has lost its color. It has more to do with the balance of time. I wake up and nature seems to have paused in expectation. There's a numb overcast overhead, with little drift to it. Woodsmoke slides down the roof and onto the road. The wild apples are waiting to fall. We're all inked in, caught in the moment.

It's an appealing illusion. I imagine being the human in one of Rembrandt's landscapes—that small figure standing in front of what looks like a cross between a house and a haystack. He's resting from something. Perhaps he's even looking out from his garden at the artist working in the distance. It took no more ink to draw that figure than it would to write out a simple equation. And yet there's no mistaking his posture or the moment he's given himself to rest, though that moment has now lasted since 1645.

That's how it felt this morning—as if time had simply stopped. A crow—an extremely precise inkblot—had paused in the pasture. I counted fifteen immobile mourning doves resting on a power line. The leaves that were going to fall had fallen, and the oaks were not about to relinquish theirs. The weather seemed to be waiting somewhere off to the west. A flight of birds stirred from the branches and then settled back almost immediately. I heard what sounded like a small dog barking in the distance and realized it was a flock of geese beyond the tree line. They never came into view.

Before long the breeze will stir, and rain will begin to fall. The silent anticipation hidden in such a quiet morning will be forgotten. The cry of a red-tailed hawk will unsettle the mourning doves, and one by one those wild apples will become windfall. And as the weather changes and the clock resumes its ticking, I'll have to consider freeing myself from the artist's ink before it dries completely, stepping outside and walking over the hill toward the sound of those distant geese.

November 22

I'm in central California, finishing up some family business, the kind that means lawyers, taxes, the Department of Motor Vehicles in Manteca, and staying in a chain motel at a freeway exit. My room is just a few feet from a Starbucks drive-through lane. I'm only a few car lengths away from several fast-food joints, all with drive-through lanes, not to mention several gas stations and two truck stops, which, by their very nature, are nothing but drive-thru. This is a place where you realize that what Americans like to feel is full, quick.

Highway 99—the commercial spine of the Great Valley—bristles along behind me, a vulcanized mist rising from it in the rain. There's also the faint, puckering odor of a distant industrial dairy. Where there's new construction, the mud is light brown. Where meadows once cycled the rain, there are now parking lots beading up with an oily sheen. Main Street is still moving to this off-ramp. But this is also a place where businesses are busy going out of business. Hawaiian barbecue sounds like a good idea until you put it in a faceless box beside an on-ramp.

In the motel last night, I found myself listening to the roar of an ice-vending machine rising above the rumble of the soda-vending machine beside it and the whine of the fluorescents in the ceiling. I began to think about the sheer number of roaring machines in the immediate vicinity of this freeway interchange—machines for heating and cooling, compressing and expanding, blowing and sucking.

Some are easy to notice, like the diesel semis gearing down with a thump as they come off 99. Some, like the ice machine, seem at first almost as quiet and familiar as the sound of blood through the veins until you notice them. And then, suddenly, it's hard to stop hearing them. At this perfectly ordinary freeway exit, the mechanical and electrical shrieking never stops.

Choose the right direction, and you don't have to go far from this exit before you find yourself in nature—I almost said "back" in nature. Choose the wrong direction and you find yourself in the housing wasteland of San Joaquin county, where everything is changing quickly. House sales are way up—even though prices are way down—and the number of rentals is also rising quickly. Some of the commuters who moved here from the Bay Area have moved back—giving up on the idea of home ownership and a torturous daily commute.

But these are local concerns, no more the business of Exit 237B in a drive-through state than the egrets standing in an irrigation ditch a few miles away. The true business of this wayfarers' station is to hum and whine and shriek and roar in its own glare without ceasing.

November 26

Last week in Sheridan, Wyoming, I saw a family loading groceries into the nose of a gooseneck horse trailer, while in the back the horses watched the shoppers coming and going in the parking lot. It was one of those glimpses you sometimes get—the kind that draws your mind down whatever road that truck and horse trailer might end up taking. For all I knew, the horses had been to the grocery store many times. What struck me wasn't the oddity of doing some shopping while hauling horses—I've done that myself. It was the way the scene pulled me out of my own life and into theirs.

In the spareness of Wyoming, those kinds of mental detours happen all the time. The landscape tends to isolate the humans in it, and there aren't that many humans to begin with, which increases the imaginative pull of almost every scene. I drove through Buffalo, Wyoming, while the municipal Christmas decorations were going up. Two teams of men unloaded them from flatbed trailers. Then a phone-company truck with a cherry picker mounted them high on the street lamps. I wondered what it would be like to drive under the Christmas decorations in town and know exactly how it felt to have put them up, and to have been taught how to put them up by some old-timer who had been doing this back when they were still using the old decorations, and there was no phone-company truck to borrow.

Let your mind wander far enough, as mine tends to do in Wyoming, and just about everything in the landscape draws you out after it. Driving to Casper the other morning, I began to wonder how many highway fence posts there were along a hundred miles of the two-lane road I was on. My guess was between fifty and sixty thousand, which led of course to pondering the lives of the crews that had drilled or driven all those posts and strung all that wire. For a while I counted the ravens on the fence posts, until there were simply too many. But I can report that on that morning on that stretch of road, there were seven golden eagles and one black cat sunning themselves on the tops of the fence posts, just above the frostbitten grasses.

There was also a burning car, which had crashed through the fence and set the range on fire. The firemen were just putting it out—car and grass—and the driver was stretched out on the shoulder, wondering what had happened to the simple story of his drive to somewhere. But the drama was over, and you could see it leaking out of the faces of the young firemen standing near their trucks in the road. They looked as though they could now allow themselves to enjoy the outing and the way the breeze carried the thick smoke over the ridge line and out of sight.

December 29

Last Sunday, almost all the snow melted away up here. Along the edge of the road there's still a steep mound covered with gravel, a snowplow moraine. But the yard and pastures are suddenly bare. To the dogs, I think, this snowy farm was a relatively scentless place—all those odors trapped under snow and ice. The dogs stood on the drifts snuffing the air around them, sometimes digging at a vole track under the surface. Now they walk in the old way, noses down, questioning the soil.

The melt came swiftly, temperatures pushing sixty degrees. Before long the dry stream west of the barn—a staircase of bare rock most of the year—was running hard. Even the bees came out that afternoon, and that evening I saw a bat swooping low under the porch lights. And yet this didn't feel like a false start, a disheartening, premature spring. It felt like getting back to the bare foundation so winter can begin all over again.

The new year is always a kind of chronological trope, an imaginary point of debarkation. After all, come January first, we're hardly shoving off for parts unknown. We're so deeply knotted to time past and time future that the presumption of change implicit in the new year seems like nothing more than what it is—a mental leap forward, a recasting of the imagination.

Somehow it's fitting to come into the new year on bare ground, even as the snow is gathering again. It makes it so much easier to assess the work to be done, the decisions to be made and unmade. Some years the new year is just a gray transition from one calendar to the next, the resumption of a postponed meeting and an old agenda. But that's not how this year feels. Time for the rotting fence posts to be replaced, the sagging gates to be rehung.

The freeze will come again and the stream at the back of the property will recede into dryness. Snow will fall, and as it accumulates it will capture in intricate detail the topography of the ground beneath it. But as it keeps falling, the detail will fade. And when the wind picks up, as it nearly always does, the snow will drift into a whole new landscape, bearing only an oblique relation to the past.

December 30

Sometimes on the train north from the city, I catch a glimpse of a heron rookery in a swamp by the tracks. To call it a *rookery*, now a general term for a breeding colony, is to catch a linguistic glimpse of the great colonies of rooks' nests—raucous, brawling places—that once dotted the English countryside. What I see from the train is really a heronry, a village of broad, well-built heron nests high in the trees. In winter, they stand out against the sky like dense, concentric clouds or congealed puffs of dark smoke caught in the uppermost branches.

The ice storm last month left a lot of shattered trees behind, including many in the swamp. But as far as I could tell, none of the nest trees had broken. Nor had the high winds pitched any of the heron nests to the ground. I began to wonder about all the intersecting decisions that go into a heronry. It starts with the presence of water, which is where great blue herons feed. It requires a certain height in the trees, which means trees of a certain age and branch structure. But do those qualities also give resistance to wind and severe ice storms? Or do the birds prefer certain species of tall, well-branched trees over others? No respectable heron would nest in a birch.

I'm used to thinking of evolution doing the selecting—blind, impassive adaptation over millions of years. That's a dispassionate way of understanding behavior, of contextualizing tree selection among nesting herons. And yet evolution is like other forms of history: it explains the present, all but the inexplicable parts. To me the inexplicable part is this. A heronry embodies a system of knowledge present in the herons themselves, a complete, successful, and highly inventive understanding of the world around them. Grasping how it came to be doesn't make it any less marvelous.

The train rumbles past that swamp a couple of dozen times a day. Who knows how many humans have looked up at that heronry? The train exaggerates the way we usually see nature—flattened against a window, moving at speed, a pattern of impressions. The hard part is learning to see nature as a dense web of interconnected knowledges. We see, in our flattened way, the dimensions of the landscape, but we miss seeing the fullness of the understandings that inhabit it. I look up at the heronry and the question that stays in my mind is this: what do herons learn from living together?

Year EIGH T

January 15

When the thermometer bottoms out, I remember that winter isn't a season, it's a place. Just over the hill is the nineteenth century and somewhere beyond the river lies the eighteenth. Why winter should seem so much more continuous with the past than summer is never clear to me. But this morning it's three degrees, and I can hear Melville, a few miles north of where I am, writing to his sister, "The weather here has been as cold as ever. Other than the weather I know not what to write about from Pittsfield."

That's how it feels in the neighborhood of zero. There is no "other than the weather." I feed the woodstove, keep the diesel pickup plugged in, and admire the fortitude of the crows, who look at me as if to say, "It beats freezing rain." On the reservoirs, the waterfowl crowd into the open water. A couple of Canada geese walk along the edge of the ice as though they were lifeguards. The rivers, all but the Hudson, dwindle to a narrow sluice of dark water. It takes an effort to remember that the water—which looks so bitterly cold—is the warmest element in the landscape.

As dusk comes, the snowmobile tracks that cross the fields fade in the growing darkness, and I imagine a huddled figure coming through the trees and down the hill, stumping through the snow as if he had walked right out

163

of the distant past and was making his way toward the lights of this house. The smoke spilling from the chimney smells completely familiar to him, whatever century he comes from. And about then in my private storytelling, I remember that I'm living in the warmer, brighter future that nearly everyone in the country of winter has always aspired to.

A couple of nights ago, dusk brought a different illusion. The clouds had been hammered flat—a cast-iron sky almost all the way to the west. But in the last few moments of afternoon, the sun slid below the overcast, diffusely at first but then coming out strong and red along the rim of the horizon. I couldn't help feeling that this was the sun of summer shining all the way back into the heart of winter, just a glimpse to see how we were all doing huddled together here. The only warmth the last light brought was chromatic, but that was enough to turn my thoughts to soil and seeds and new shoots rising.

February 2

Up here, the world gets a used-up look a day or two after a February snowfall. Dust drifts over the fields from the dry roads, the corn stubble begins to poke through, and the plows have left a margin of gritty slush and knocked down a mailbox or two. The stern snowpiles from the January storms have slumped in on themselves, looking more and more animate as the days begin to warm.

All the more reason to look for those moments just after a snowfall, when the snow isn't public yet, when it's only been tracked by an animal or two out on the ice and in the fields. I never see a straight track. There's always a bend in it, as if curiosity were a kind of lateral gravity, always pulling the creature off course. But then I remember that "off course" is a human conceit. Judging by the tracks I see, there's no going so hard that one has to go straight. I can't begin to guess why fox prints meander along the river ice. The fox knows, and that's enough.

Minus the human footprint, this is still a world of animal trails. An animal track is the trace of an animal mind, working things out in a nonhuman way. I see two tracks cross in a field, and I can't help thinking that perhaps those two animals stopped to confer. And yet both tracks may have been made by the same creature, coming and going. Perhaps it stopped to sniff the scent of its former intention.

Over the fields, the hawks are laboring in an absence of updrafts. Is that how the year divides for them?—a season of thermals rising over the dark earth, and a season when snow captures the wind and holds it down? Out on the lake ice, anglers are sitting on upturned buckets, the bold ones having snowmobiled to their holes. And yet they tested the ice with no more sophistication than the deer I saw walking across Piney Creek in Wyoming a week ago. You ease out onto the surface and see what gives.

I've grown used to the sullen light at last, and I find myself hoping for another storm, another chapter in a private winter. But the south-facing slopes are melting quickly, and the skunks are almost certainly starting to think about breeding. Soon the male skunks will be out on the roads, and February will have come in earnest.

February 25

"You must walk like a camel," Thoreau writes, and I can feel my lower lip drooping and a hunch coming into my back. This isn't what he means, of course. He means that I must ruminate while walking. The temperature is in the midthirties, the wind has settled at last, and the snow has withdrawn from the corn stubble. I set my thoughts aside for a few minutes on the uphill leg of this walk. But now they're back, and they bring Thoreau with them.

By his standards, I'm walking all wrong. But then Thoreau is a prig. He's often right, about almost anything. What makes him priggish is the self-rejoicing in his rightness. What saves him is the spirit of self-contradiction rampaging through his work. If I were to walk like Thoreau, I'd walk elliptically, stepping into a different dimension with every stride. I can't manage his daily four hours of scrambling through swamps. "If you have paid your debts, and made your will, and settled all your affairs...then you are ready for a walk," he writes. And yet I've come out walking anyway.

The river is slapping at the underside of the ice along its edges. A man sits sharpening a chainsaw, cutting firewood from the debris that has piled up on the banks. I saw a pair of bluebirds in that spot a week ago. Sometimes the cedars crowd close to the ditch, and sometimes I find myself walking under the lip of a high bank where a cornfield meets the road. Not long ago, there was a wind-driven cornice of snow on that bank. Now, I can smell the earth again, not the upsprung smell of full spring, but a scent that has Lazarus in it.

And still Thoreau is with me, like a border collie nipping at my heels. He's terribly hard on any self-satisfaction but his own. We're all one of his townsmen, a little puzzled by his orientalism, a little mystified that such a stern, practical woodsman has been overlaid with so much philosophical marquetry. "I believe in the forest," he writes, "and in the meadow, and in the night in which the corn grows." This is a kind of ecumenicism, at least among townsmen who believe mainly in day-corn.

Thoreau goads me uphill, and he chivvies me along the heights, and yet he repents at the turning homeward. For he has just remembered that "a truly good book is something as natural...as a wildflower discovered on the prairies of the West." After this long winter walk, I'm going to sate my camel-like thirst, lie back on the couch, and read a wildflower. I wonder what Thoreau has to say about February naps.

March 17

A couple of weeks ago, when the snow was at its deepest, I walked up the hill in the middle pasture after evening chores. By then, I'm often trudging through my thoughts, barely noticing anything around me. Part of the pleasure of chores is that they happen in the same light every day, though the hour changes as the days lengthen and contract. No matter what I'm doing or feeling or thinking, I find myself propelled outside by the falling light, which means I'm often doing chores midparagraph. I imagine that the animals are midparagraph too, for we're all just going about our business together.

Coming back down the hill, plunging knee-deep through the snow, I stopped. There was the print of a bird's wings spread in the snow. The snow was too dense to have taken the subtle trace of the bird's feathering, but the shafts of the wing feathers had left their mark. From their angle and size, I guessed it was a goshawk. I looked across the pasture and saw a squirrel's track, which ended at the wingprint—no sign of a struggle, just an abrupt vanishing. Going up the hill, I'd walked right past these marks without noticing them.

A week later, all the snow had melted, which has left me thinking about a question I don't know how to ask, a question about ephemerality. That wingprint in the snow was a solid fact, the remains of a bone-jarring collision between two animals. One life ended there, and another was extended. But now that the snow has gone, the only trace of that wingprint is in my mind. And if I'd come down the hill in the fog of thought that surrounded me while I was doing chores, I'd never have seen the print of those powerful wings and they would have left no mark in me.

Nearly everything that happens around me in nature happens unobserved and unrecorded. A snowy winter sometimes retains a transcript of hidden events, but even those transcripts are rare. The bills of animal

166

mortality are almost completely invisible otherwise. Who thrives, who dies—there's no accounting at all, only the fact of thriving and dying.

That wingprint allowed me to glimpse the uncompromising discipline of nature. But it will stand in my mind as the model of an almost perfect ephemerality, a vision of life itself. The snow has melted away, taking with it the squirrel's track and the arc of those wings and my own track up the hill and the burnished spots where the horses rolled in the snow. It continues to exist only in a memory, which will melt away itself one day.

March 20

When I heard that Ray Hunt had died, I found myself wondering how many times he'd saddled a horse in his life. The number must be in the hundreds of thousands. Most of us can't put the second arm in the second sleeve of a coat as easily as Ray saddled a horse. I first saw him do it at a clinic in Wheatland, Wyoming, in the fall of 1992. I was new to saddling horses. I knew enough to know that I knew nothing about it. What I didn't know until a long time later was just how much nothing that was. Ray was one of the people who pointed that out, without saying a word.

What I thought I saw in Wheatland was a man saddling a horse, a man who might have been saying to that horse, "Whatever you think of this is fine with me." He meant it, but he'd also prepared the horse to be readier for the saddle than the horse could know. Gentle, but not too gentle, ready, but not too ready—that was how it went. I've often wondered how Ray found the balance between those things. But I realized recently that it was never that fine a calculation. Ray was ready for the consequences, whatever they happened to be. It was genuinely okay, whatever the horse did. It was all a step in the right direction. Me, I had a mental list of things I didn't want to see happen while saddling the horse I was starting. It was a long list. That changes everything.

I didn't get to know Ray well, which is something nearly everyone who rode with him can say. I suppose that Wheatland clinic must have looked to Ray like a bunch of worried, frightened mammals trying to saddle worried, frightened mammals. No matter what you thought of being human, you would think a little less of it after spending time with Ray. I try to understand who he was, and the best guess I'm ever going to get will come from looking at the horse he's sitting on. She's the purest horse in the string, the one listening and watching and feeling, with eyes as bright as we've ever imagined the human soul to be.

March 24

The last time I stayed at this house—up the hill and around the corner from Point Reyes Station, California—there were Holsteins grazing on the tidal flats below me. But now the tidal flats have been restored, the cows are gone, and all day long the equilibrium shifts before my eyes. On one tide Tomales Bay runs up into Lagunitas Creek. On the next tide, Lagunitas Creek runs out into Tomales Bay. No matter what time of day it is, the wind tends to confuse the appearance of the tides, depending on how it's blowing.

I suppose those old Holsteins were tidal creatures in some sense—eating salt grass, their udders filling and emptying like the flats themselves. But now the creek channel spills out across the mud and the grass twice a day, and birds rise and settle without ceasing. Now, it's possible to feel the bay respiring. The water is constantly catching me by surprise. I look, and there's a bright, wind-tugged sheet of it from here to Inverness. I look again, and the light adheres strictly to the creek channel, eeling its way across the darkness.

Vultures flare above my head, and quail start across the lawn. An osprey dangles in the stiff wind, then folds and drops on its prey. Great egrets practice their stillness. Looking out across the flats, I find myself thinking of all the chronologies in which I live, all the ways a life gets measured out. The least familiar of them is the one right before me—the coming and going of the tides. There's a suspense in it, a constant sense of expectation. I consult a tide chart and note that the tide is ebbing, but I'm not experienced enough to feel it. The best I can do is see where the water is now, and then where it is an hour from now. It's like having to look repeatedly at the sun to guess its direction across the sky.

I always tell my writing students to avoid chronology, because we live in the thick of it. We need no reminding how it works. And that's what I love about watching these flats. They undermine my landlocked sense of chronology. The day comes to an end, but the tide may be ebbing or flooding. Morning breaks, but the tide may be ebbing or flooding. The perfectly cyclical nature of the tides feels countercyclical to my understanding of the flow of time. If time were like the tides, we would surge into the future and rush back toward the past, twice daily, while the narrow balance point we call the present steadily worked its way forward.

Surely the egrets and ospreys and plovers understand all of this intuitively. So do the flocks of waterfowl that rise like a rippling on the water and beat their way out over the bay. I suspect those long-gone Holsteins would think of the tides pretty much the way I do, as a wonderment in this otherwise sensible world.

April 2

The other morning, I watched a starling make a long curving descent over a farm-field that was just coming up green. There was a breeze from the southwest, and as the starling turned into it the bird suddenly seemed to be floating—a far more aerodynamic creature than I usually imagine starlings to be. I seemed to see the true shape of the bird as I saw it then—wings extended and still—not as I usually see it, wings folded and quarreling over the bird-feeder.

Seeing a bird in a soaring descent like that—suspended from itself—always sets me wondering. What does it feel like to have wings and be able to ride them across the wind? The same thought occurs when a pair of Canada geese pass overhead, moving sharply away from me. The word *flap* is no more use describing the flight of geese than describing the swimming of penguins. Goose wings quiver in flight, deflecting only slightly, and if you watch closely, you can see the goose's fuselage moving up and down against the stiffness of the wings.

At moments like those, I'm uneasily conscious of my arms and shoulders, the way I'm conscious of my legs when I see the horses standing asleep in the pasture. It's as though I'm really detecting how little repose there is in the human body. Surely a red-tailed hawk is resting when it soars across the horizon on a thermal. There must be a sufficiency of rest even in the flight of a goose. How else could it fly so steadily and so far? To see a bird with wings outstretched is to imagine the hopeless outstretching of my own arms, which is a backwards way of realizing what it must mean to be native to flight, to feel the air beneath you as substantial as the earth itself.

To me, birds in their element always seem to be offering a comment on the human species. I see a vulture looking side to side as it slides by overhead, and it looks to me as though it's artfully not noticing the skill of its flight as it hunts—not noticing it for my benefit, that is. I saw the same thing in the Chilean fjords a year ago. We sailed past dozens of black-browed albatrosses while we were there, and every one of them—serenely afloat—looked up at me from the waves with the supreme unconsciousness of an athlete, unaware of its grace, just effortlessly drifting on the tide and wondering what element humans are native to.

April 16

The sun went down half an hour ago, and in its absence there's a nearly perfect stillness in the evening. I stand outside and wonder how such a night is possible, how—in the great cycle of air masses thrusting and obtruding their way across the planet, boiling up from the oceans and scattering over the plains—this small-valley quiet comes to be. The sky is red-ribbed behind the unleaved trees on the horizon. The grass in the field is as thick as a woodchuck's fur and just now giving up its green to darkness, which is settling like a cold dew.

If there were leaves on the trees, they would show where the wind lies. Instead, there are stiff blossoms, the aching buds of a spring that's just about to happen. Every twig seems to end in a red knot. In the uplands, people are still dragging winter to the roadside—tangled hedgerows of ice-broken limbs. Along the even ground, an old man scrapes the plow-duff into a wheelbarrow from the edge of his lawn. I got a glimpse today of the last snow slowly rotting high on a ski slope. There's a stillness in winter too, but it's nothing like the stillness of a spring evening, when it feels as though every living thing has stopped quivering with expectation just for the moment.

I passed a clump of deer on the roadside the other afternoon, and they looked as though they'd been carved out of decaying wood. It was a trick of the light. A much more solid deer is crossing the horizon, walking along the ridge line that borders the farm. The deer pauses and looks down over this house and its lights, or perhaps it's looking to the sound of the river, which is nearly as quiet now as it will be at midsummer. The sound of the river takes over for the sound of the missing wind, which has been rattling the windows for the past few months.

I know what grows in the warmth and the expanding light of spring. But I wonder tonight what grows in this stillness. Perhaps it's only the mosquitoes hunting for the first time this year, or the diptera that will be rising and falling along the river's edge tomorrow morning. But I think something human grows in the stillness of a night like this—fulfillment, if you like, or an untroubled hope. Soon the stars and a late-rising moon will add what they can to the calm outside.

May 5

A couple of months ago, I was asked in a public forum what language the land uses when it speaks to me. It was a serious question, and a startling one. Several glib answers drifted through my brain, but it wasn't a setting for glib answers. So I said what I really believe—that I value the land for its silence, its freedom from language.

Not that I always experience the farm this way. There are days when I feel pestered by nomenclature, when words like *Robinia pseudoacacia*—the black locust, which is blooming profusely now—chime in my brain like a simple-minded rhyme. Those are the days when I get tired of words and start whistling back at the woodchuck that lives in the middle pasture. I'm getting good at a woodchuck whistle. I think that if the land starts speaking to me in a human language I'll have to move to a boat on the sea.

One of the other panelists remarked that he thought of the land as a text, a place inscribed with profound historical meaning. This is obviously true. But the word *text* makes me uneasy. It's the same old metaphor, the overlay of human consciousness upon the natural world, and it makes me realize that I'm trying to push through language toward some other way of being in nature. I know people whose most precise word for *black locust* is *tree.* And I know people who can tell you the pattern of its blooming, the uses for its wood, who can look down my fence line and say, without hesitation, which of my fence posts are locust. As for me, I can still feel the weight of those posts when I reset them. They were here when I moved to this place a dozen years ago, and I expect they'll still be here when I'm gone.

There's no escaping language. But perhaps it's possible to live between the sentences. In my experience, being a writer means putting up with an inner voice—a maker of sentences—that's always clamoring to be heard. More and more, I find myself listening for the moments when that voice lapses, when all I hear is the sound of my breathing on a steep upward trail or—not often enough—the wordless sound of a canoe slipping forward across a lake while the paddlers pause.

After a dozen years, I can name many of the species that inhabit this farm, most of the plants, and nearly all the birds. But what's the word for the wake the pileated woodpecker leaves as it dips, flying, across the pasture? How can I imagine that language is how the land speaks when I'm surrounded by animals whose wordless attention is at least as great as mine? All I can do is put a period to this sentence and hope I can live, for a while this morning, in the pause that follows it.

May 21

The other night, my neighbor called, in tears. Her mule had foundered—that is, the inner tissue of its feet had swollen, a sometimes fatal condition that causes intense pain and immobility. The vet was coming, and there was a real chance the mule would have to be put down. My neighbor wanted me to listen to what the vet said and help her make the hard decision. By the time we got up to the barn, it was nearly dark. The mule had spent two and a half days on its side, unable to stand, but now it was standing, frozen in place and shivering with pain. The fact that it was standing at all was an improvement.

The mule had a name once, but for years it's been "the mule," a small, dark beast with long ears, a wicked imagination, and a genius for gates and getting through them. As I got ready to meet the vet, that was how I pictured it, an impish creature, more Puck than Bottom. But to see it transfixed by pain—caught in the beams of two flashlights—was to see only its beauty. I couldn't help thinking of the burros that appear in Nativity scenes, wide-eyed everyday animals caught in a celestial event. The mule's coat was sleek and dark, the densest blacks giving a glossy relief to its dark brown flanks and neck. To see a mule or a horse in pain, unable to move, is to see an animal trapped within itself, fallen back upon the dignity of its conformation, the bottomless surface of its moist eyes.

The vet was hopeful. Trimming the hooves would help, and, right now, something for the pain. And as it became clear that we wouldn't be killing the mule that night, I caught a glimpse of something I almost never see, except in the implicit presence of death. Let me call it the unabashed vigor of life itself, the way the living force—whatever that is—filled the being of that pain-chastened mule and made death seem almost extinct. I imagined where the needle would go, and how the tremors would cease, and then the settling onto the hay and the rolling inward of the awareness in those eyes. I thought of the deaths that I've witnessed—human and animal—and I knew that the life in this mule wouldn't be denied.

Afterward, I walked homeward down the road in the dark. I hope that in another few weeks, the mule will rush the fence when I pass, as it always does, catching me unaware, as it always does, making me jump midstride. I'd like to think that I'll look at it differently when that happens. But there's a good chance I won't.

May 27

I've always admired my friends who are wide readers. One or two even pride themselves on never reading a book a second time. I've been a wide reader at times as well, foraging outward, working my way through a long string of books by leaping from allusion to allusion. But at heart I'm a rereader.

The point of reading outward, widely, has always been to find the books I want to reread—and then to reread them.

In part, that's an admission of defeat, an acknowledgement that no matter how long and how widely I read, I'll only ever make my way through a tiny portion of the world's literature. And in part, it's a concession to the limits of my memory, which is overtaxed by the simple job of remembering which books I've actually read, never mind what's in them. My memory is like a beach in which the sand that washes out to sea is replaced, grain for grain, by the sand the sea washes in. I forget a lot, in other words, which makes the pleasure of rereading all the greater.

The love of repetition seems to be ingrained in children, as every parent knows. And it's certainly ingrained in the way children learn to read—witness the maddening, bedtime love of hearing that same book read aloud all over again, word for word, inflection for inflection. Childhood is an oasis of repetitive acts, so much so that there's something shocking about the first time a young reader reads a book only once and then moves on to the next. There's a hunger in that act but also a kind of forsaking, a glimpse of adulthood to come.

The work I chose to do in adulthood contained, by definition, the childish pleasure of rereading. To be a literature student in graduate school meant being a close reader—i.e., a close rereader. Once through Pope's *The Dunciad* or Berryman's *The Dream Songs* wasn't going to cut it. A grasp of the poem was presumed to lie on the far side of many rereadings, none of which were really repetitions. And the same is true of being a writer. The work of writing is partly the work of obsessive rereading, to an extent that most non-writers would never believe.

But the real rereading I mean is savory rereading, the books I have to be careful not to reread too often so I can read them again with pleasure. It's a miscellaneous library, always shifting. It's included a book of the north woods—John J. Rowlands's *Cache Lake Country*, which I reread annually for many years. It may still include Raymond Chandler, though I won't know for sure till the next time I reread him. It includes Michael Herr's *Dispatches* and lots of A. J. Liebling and a surprising amount of George Eliot. It once included nearly all of Dickens, but that has since been boiled down to two: *The Pickwick Papers* and *Great Expectations*. There are many more titles, of course. This isn't a canon. This is a refuge.

Part of the fun of rereading is that you're no longer bothered by the business of finding out what happens. Rereading *Middlemarch* or *The Great*

Gatsby, I no longer have to pay attention to the motion of the train. I'm able to look out the window and contemplate the scenery as the sentences go by. While the plot is busily taking place, I'm able to pay attention to what's really happening in the thicket of the language itself—a pleasure as great as discovering who marries whom, who dies and who does not.

The real secret of rereading is simply this: it's impossible. The characters remain the same, and the words never change, but the reader always does. Pip is there to be revisited, but you, the reader, are a little like the convict who surprises him in the graveyard—always a stranger. I look at the books on my library shelves. They certainly seem dormant. But what if the characters are quietly rearranging themselves while shelved? What if Emma Woodhouse doesn't learn from her mistakes? What if Tom Jones descends into a sodden life of poaching and outlawry? What if Eve resists Satan, remembering God's injunction and Adam's loving advice?

I imagine all the characters rushing to get back into place as they feel me taking the book down from the shelf. "Hurry," they say, "he'll expect to find us exactly where he left us, never mind how much his life has changed in the meantime."

June 28

For the past month, late-afternoon thunderstorms have coasted across the farm. After three or four storms in as many afternoons, they seem almost domesticated—an aunt or uncle stopping in for a surly, savage tea but leaving the air surprisingly refreshed in the aftermath. While the storm was building one day, I found myself imagining words we might use to capture the sound of lightning and thunder, but don't. As the skies darkened around tea time once again, I could have sworn I heard crumpeting in the distance.

It's late afternoon as I write. There is blundering just beyond the tree line. Soon the tuberous blunderheads trundle over the horizon, and as they approach they begin to wampum, wampum, wampum until at last they're vrooming nearby, just down the valley. Or perhaps they're harrumphing and oomphing, from the omphalos of the storm. Onomatopoeia is such a delicate thing.

But as the clouds tumble into position directly overhead, the sound changes, as does the color of the day. Suddenly the air is grackling, dark and furious in its plumage. The lightning and thunder begin to come as one— ZEBU! ZEBU!—drowning out the wishing of the rain and the concurring of the wind, which turns the maple leaves white-side up. Hail begins to adder on the skylights, and soon the only light left in the world is the sickly green of the storm's hunkering belly. The roar in my ear is the sound of the gravel road toshing away, worsing downhill and forming a lake on the highway. Water runs in revels and midriffs through the pasture, where the horses stand indifferent to the caucus around them.

And then it's over, just like that, only a bumbling far to the east of me, a last faint snicker of lightning. The sun gloats in the sky, casting a gleam on the pasture where there was so much umbering and ochreing only moments before. Steam begins to rise from the horses' backs, and the extravagance begins to leak out of the evening. The grass in the pasture lies in scallops, as if a great scaled beast had recently slumbered there. The static electricity of the day has been discharged. The storm has left me ravenous, hungry as a raven.

July 17

Day after day, night after night, life on a farm is an exercise in comparative living. This is how humans go about their lives, and that's how other creatures manage. The big difference, I can say after twelve years of watching, is sleep. What a lot of shut-eye all the other species get, and how sleep deprived humans seem in comparison! I have to wake the dogs to take a nap with me. Out in the pasture, two of the horses stand in the posture that says they're sleeping, one heel raised, one hip dropped, lower lip slowly giving in to gravity. The third horse is lying down, doing her impersonation of Napoleon's retreat from Moscow while the white line on her belly gleams in the sun. The entire farm is comatose in the heat of the day.

I can only wonder what it's like to be so well-rested, to know that the deep pool of sleep within you—the somnifer, I suppose it's called—is filled to the brim. It's not just a matter of how much sleep the animals get. It's how abrupt the border between sleeping and waking is. I carry sleep inside me too, and I'm a good sleeper. But not compared to the creatures around me. For me, sleep is a kind of orderly embarking. For them, it's a sudden plunge—a nod, a shudder, and the instantaneous snoring of those that snore—the dogs—and the silent dozing of the rest. They live in a mirror universe of sleep and waking, and all day long they pass effortlessly back and forth.

What I most admire is the animals' attitude toward daytime sleeping. It is without prejudice because, unlike humans, they know there's no propriety in sleep. It steals upon you when it steals upon you. It rises up and claims you, no matter how hard you try to confine it to the ghetto of night.

You're not a worse chicken for snoozing in the early morning, not an inferior pig for napping the afternoon away in the shade beneath your house. To grasp the force of human culture, all you have to do is consider how hard we try to organize our sleeping.

And that's the nub of it. I conform to an artificial pattern of sleep, trying to get a mythic eight hours in the course of the night. But all around me are natural sleepers, sleeping in rhythms established only by their bodies and the flight of the sun and moon overhead. Almost none of us have ever experienced that, not since infancy at least. It must feel wonderful.

July 30

I don't detest slugs. They're a perfectly valid life form, as successful in their own terms as *Homo sapiens*. I discover them in the garden. I find them on the stone walk in the early morning. I step around them, respectfully. But now I find them on the walls of the house, climbing the door jamb, climbing the door itself as if they were going to pick the lock and come in out of the rain. In their form, their liquid, droplike appearance, they distill the essence of this appalling summer. It's as if the thunderheads—rising fungally above us—were now raining slugs.

The summer so far is a reminder that water isn't the neutral substance we imagine it to be. It's a powerful solvent. Up here, the world is dissolving before our eyes. During a heavy storm—the kind we've had day after day—you also begin to understand that water has a purpose of its own. It's always pressing its mechanical advantage. The merest tongue of a rivulet slips under a stone, and the gravel road washes away. The run off catches an edge of asphalt, and there goes a section of highway, great slabs of tarred road cantilevered downstream.

In the downpour the other night, just at dusk, I came to a temporary bridge at a construction site on the highway north of here. The bridge crosses a meek little stream called Kinderhook Creek. But it had risen and risen through the day and now it had sluiced over its banks and was on the verge of shouldering the bridge aside. People stood outside watching in the rain, hands to their mouths in concern. From the look in their eyes, you could tell that what they were seeing wasn't a flood. It was a metamorphosis, a transfiguration, some slumbering protean god rising out of the streambed and walking the Earth, treading not too carefully among the prefab houses.

As the storm began that afternoon, the horses moved out into the open from under the maples along the fence line, shaking their heads up and down.

They came to the place they always stand, square in the middle of the pasture, and settled into immobility. The hiss of the rain rose into a drumming roar, and I thought about the shelter the horses had found in their own stasis. There's nothing like a good storm for washing away mental debris. I stood there, looking out the window, while the kitchen door swelled in its jamb and the slugs began fingering their way upward toward the knob.

August 28

My internal timekeeper went out of order this summer—broken down by the sodden month of June. Time passed as usual, and all the biological events that happen on the farm happened in their usual order. But somehow I made no connection between the two. Every blossom, every sunset and sunrise, is a temporal sign, and yet I failed to recognize them as such, like a person who has forgotten how a calendar works.

A couple of weeks ago, I noticed the goldenrod beginning to come into bloom. It seemed like an oddly detached fact, almost anomalous, as if it really had nothing to do with me. And yet the goldenrod ripens over the landscape of this farm with nearly the same power as the leaves turning in the fall. It's one of the strongest temporal clues I know, and I usually respond to it the way I respond to most signs of a shifting season, with an inward emotional tug. But not this year. I seem to be absent, somehow, or perhaps I'm resting in the lull of late summer. Or perhaps I've truly become just another of the creatures on this farm.

I don't suppose the bees answer the blooming goldenrod with a rush of emotion. I don't suppose they contemplate time at all. They're acutely aware of the sun's position in the sky. They're connoisseurs of ripeness, the moment of nectareous perfection in each blooming species. And yet I imagine that time for them is simply the aggregate of those moments. They aren't cues to something else—to an abstract sense of temporality, an awareness of one's life-arc. In the life-sequence of the hive, bees certainly know what comes next, the order in which things are done. But it isn't—or so it seems to me—a next-ness that reaches beyond the task at hand. And yet what could all that honey mean except an awareness of the future?

What I needed, besides the goldenrod, was a couple of cool nights. And now that they've come, I can feel my clock restarting. The goldenrod is pointing headlong into September, as it always does, and soon the world around me will be turning copper, deepening the blue overhead. I moved to the country, long ago, in order to live with time. I believed then that it was something happening in the world around me. Now I know that it's really passing in me.

October 12

If you drive up the Pinedale way from Lander to Jackson, you get the full brunt of it—Wyoming on the move. The town of Farson, sixty miles south of Pinedale, is a good place to take it all in. It used to be little more than a dusty crossroads. Now it's a staging and storage depot for equipment used in the Jonah Field—a gas field that boomed in the last decade and is now the economic heart of Sublette County and the western half of the state. The highway ripples with gas traffic—pickup trucks with jib cranes for lifting pipe and gear, bigger trucks towing crane-fitted pickups, the biggest trucks hauling machinery and rigging of every kind.

But it's October, so everyone is on the move. Ranchers on horses are moving cattle down off the leases well upslope, and a state-wide convoy of aluminum cattle trucks is moving to meet them at the corrals and chutes. The cattle trucks travel in a hailstorm of grit, which rattles over my car as they shudder past in the opposite direction. With the wind blowing stiff out of the west and snow kicking up from the tires of the trucks coming at me, I can hardly tell which ones are loaded with steers and which are empty.

As the cattle move down from the high country, the elk hunters move up. Most of the pickups without jib cranes have four-wheelers in the back—all-terrain vehicles with rifle-scabbards on the sides. Horse trailers stand parked at nearly every access point along the road. Three or more trailers means elk hunters. One or two means ranchers on horseback gathering cattle. Every trailered horse I pass on the highway is already saddled, ready to step down and ride out.

Early snow plummets from the clouds, bringing down limbs on the cottonwoods, which still have their leaves. It isn't a drifting snow—it isn't cold enough for that—but it swoops down on the school buses, slowing their daily exodus onto the gravel roads, over a sagebrush horizon and a wheezing stop at a long ranch drive. I see a band of antelope standing in a hollow under the wind. Just up the road, three riders make their way back to the horse trailer and home. It's a good direction to be going.

November 9

The grass has stopped growing, and so has the wild mint and spotted-touch-me-knot. The snow hasn't begun to fall. Most of the firewood is stacked and all of the hay. The thistledown has blown, milkweed ditto. The leaves are down. That's about as organized as it gets around here.

For a few weeks in midautumn, I feel as though I can see the farm plain. I get a clear picture of what needs doing, and I rediscover the pleasure of doing those things one at a time. A rubber feed pan needs moving from the chicken yard to the barn. I walk it down, leave it there, and it stays put. In summer, every object on this place gravitates freely from place to place. Every morning I get up, and everything is everywhere else. That feeling goes away when fall comes. Fall is the season of staying put, everything but the leaves.

There was a wet, sloppy dousing of snow the other night, heavy as a deep depression. The dogs and I looked at it regretfully, as if the darkness were growing even thicker as the snow fell. But that, too, is the beauty of this time of year. Darkness can only get so dark, so deep. What it does get is longer, and yet even that's good news. We've been here before—in the long dark of December, the deep chill of January. This isn't some galaxy we've never visited.

As the snow melted the next morning, I found myself wondering how it all feels to the striped-bark maple I planted a decade ago. Its leaves were among the first to fall, but now its twigs are stark with dull ruby buds. They're poised for a season I can't imagine yet. It's tempting to believe that all of that maple's strength has swollen precariously in those buds, but it hasn't. It's deep underground, rooted in the equilibrium of Earth itself. Horticulturists say that a good wind firms up a young tree's roothold, and that's how I'll think of this season. Here in the clarity of fall—before the weather gathers and snow climbs up and down the storm—I look for ways of increasing the order in life, firming a roothold I too seldom feel.

December 2

This farm lies on an eastward-facing slope, which rises gradually to a thickly wooded ridge in the west. I can feel the mass of that hill whenever the sun goes down, and yet when the wind is blowing, there's very little lee to it. Last week, the wind came ripping over the crest like breaking surf, scurrying leaves out of the pasture, knocking down sections of post and rail fence, gnawing at the trees with a suctioning, siphoning sound. All day long, the air outside boomed and roared.

By evening, even the horses were weary of it. They'd been blown about all day long as though they weighed a few ounces instead of a thousand pounds apiece. A tree cracks in the distance and they trot, alarmed, across the pasture. A whirlwind of leaves twists past, and they race away from it. The corner of a tarp gets loose and off they go. They transmit this emotional energy directly to me, undiluted. This is why I like pigs and chickens. In a high wind, the pigs lie close together at the back of their house, snoozing, straw pulled over their heads. The chickens sit on their perches, knitting and doing their accounts.

The day was abraded by the wind and then the night. But sometime during the dark, the wind dropped, a phrase that makes it sound as though it got tired of running and fell to the ground rapt in slumber. The next morning was still, smoke rising straight up from my chimney and those down the valley. There was a strange sense of propriety, a primness in the way every tree had come back to attention. The day before, I could see the horses trying to shrug off the wind, which pressed them closely. But in this new silence, there seemed to be an aura of stillness around them. They were no longer bracing themselves. Their bones and sinews had relaxed.

And I relaxed too. Like them, I stood in the sun feeling the strength of its rays now that the wind wasn't scattering them. When the wind blows, the horses always stand with their heads facing away from it. In the morning quiet, they were no longer magnetized. Without a wind, they were free to face in any direction they chose. Without a wind, the day could go any way it wanted.

December 8

Not quite fifteen years ago, my wife adopted a mixed-breed puppy she found tied to a storage tank behind a gas station in Great Barrington, Massachusetts. I say she adopted it, because I wasn't sold on the idea. We had a new pup already—a Border terrier named Tavish—and this gangly new addition looked, in comparison, like a badly made dog. Darcy's feet were too small for her body, her hind knees were weak, and her coat, someone once said, made her look like a wire-haired golden retriever. But who ever loved a dog less because it was ugly?

And now it's all these years later. Darcy still makes it up and down the stairs, hind feet splayed, knees no longer flexible. She lies on the lawn, basking like a lioness, and barks at the pickups going up the road. Much of the day she has the look in her eyes she has always had, the look of a gratified mutt. But there are hours now when her eyes, misty with cataracts, seem worried, hollow. And she has stopped eating, or rather, she eats with deliberation and reluctance, a spoonful of this, a forkful of that, a good day at the dinner bowl followed by not so good ones.

Which means that now is the hard time, because the decision to be made must be made on its own merits. According to the vet, there are no signs of disease, other than the disease of age—nothing to force our hand. When Tavish died four years ago, his liver was failing, and there was no choice but to sit on the floor with him and hold him while the vet inserted the final needle. Darcy raises the matter of an owner's responsibility in its purest form.

I've known too many people who waited far too long to put their dogs to sleep, and I've always hated the sentimentality and selfishness in their hesitation. Last week, watching Darcy out in the sun, it felt as though I was trying to decide exactly when most of the good life inside her has been used up. Is it conscionable to wait until it's plainly gone? Or is it better to err on the side of saying good-bye while she's still discernibly Darcy, when there are a few good days, maybe weeks left, while she seems, as she nearly always does, to be without pain? There's no way of knowing how much time she really has, no looking for a request from her.

It comes down in the end to the pleasure she shows, the interest she takes in the world around her—and not to anything her humans feel. Even now, as the days get colder, she likes to spend more and more time outside, her nose lifted so she can take in the perfume of the world. She's waiting, I'd like to believe, to catch a scent on the wind that will tell her what she needs to know about her own mortality. She has not had the life she might once have expected. She's had a far better one instead. My hope is that she gets exactly the death she deserves, in her humans' arms, at the proper time. The world will be a poorer place without her.

December 24

The school buses have left, and now the teachers are heading for their cars and trucks, the day over, the afternoon thick with relief. The bitter cold of the weekend has lifted. Out on the ice, just past the school, there's a precise rectangle of banked snow, the outline of a skating rink that was carefully shoveled and swept clear when the snow was deep. But now, after a few warm days, the entire pond is clear of snow, all but the boundary of the rink, where a solitary man is lacing his hockey skates.

He skates away from his shoes, stick in hand, puck before him on the ice. He isn't thinking about speed or a slap shot. He skates just bent enough to clap the blade on the ice, urging the puck forward and boxing it in. He gathers almost enough momentum from the shifting of his weight, a little more when he straightens his legs, one after the other. The whole pond is his. He's holding himself in, making the ice last, measuring his possession of it by the slowness and grace of his movements. Behind him the snow peaks rise, for this is Livingston, Montana.

He worries the puck a little—chivvying it from side to side like a fox toying with a vole. Or perhaps it's a gentler motion than that, as though he were domesticating the puck, showing it the limits of its freedom. Imagine the slow sweep of his legs, the clacking of the stick, the deep-night blackness of the puck on the dull gray ice, which is soundless except for the gnashing of his blades. Now he skates down the pond, dwindling and dwindling, and now he rounds back, as if to revisit the spot where he left his shoes.

I think of Wordsworth's midnight ecstasy on the ice. This is a spot in time every bit as moving. The light is tumbling out of the sky like a snow-fall of dusk. Out on their routes, the school buses are turning homeward again. Before long, the houses along this pond will spill an amber glow into the night. But for now there's more than enough light to keep skating. There's nothing prepossessing about the man out there except the grace of his movement and the way he keeps house with his hockey stick.

To walk past a pond while a man skates across the afternoon is to feel suddenly stiff gaited and woefully destination-bound, even though this is just a leisurely walk. The best I can hope for out here on the pavement is a stone to kick ahead of me. But inside I'm skating through the fading light too, feeling the depth of the ice under me, the poise of my blades. Like the man on skates, I know that now is the precious time. Out on the ice, he's guarding the moment, keeping it close with his stick.

December 30

Last week felt like a last chance before winter. The snow melted, dying back until the vole trails became visible, sinuous green paths through the remains of whiteness. The ice unbound itself from the rim of the horse tanks. In the ditch along the gravel road, the runoff slid downhill over a still-frozen streambed, the water as agile and globular as mercury. A bat fluttered past my head one warm morning, resting on the clapboards for a moment and then arcing around to the east side of the house, where the bats live in the eaves. Despite the sense of relenting, the ground was still frozen solid.

And then it began to snow again, light, voluminous snow, swelling in the air and muffling every detail in the landscape. Watching it snow, I felt an unexpected sense of intention in the weather—as if those mild days, which had felt like spring, were just a way of clearing the canvas, scraping away the old paint, the old knife marks, before laying down a fresh and even ground of white. It was less a fall of snow than a fog of snow, the flakes suspended in air, never seeming to reach the earth, darkening the day and brightening it at the same time.

At the bird-feeders, it was traffic as usual. Opposite the feeders, the birds line up on the boughs of a pignut hickory and swoop in by twos and threes, titmice and juncos, a crowd of chickadees, a demure pair of cardinals. Woodpeckers cling to the suet feeders, and squirrels, red and gray, rummage among the shells on the porch. Everyone eats in a kind of mutual disturbance, which the falling snow intensifies.

The weather maps say that the edge of the storm is only a few miles west and that the storm will be shutting down soon. It will end in a last bank of dark gray clouds—so dark that the blue sky shining through their gaps will be the color of diluted turquoise. And then the sun will beam through the cold air and the sense of urgency will dissipate.

I'm reluctant to see the storm finish, reluctant, for once, to see the sun emerge. At this time of year, winter only begun, I feel the way I did when I was a child. I want the snow to keep falling and falling, soft and deep into the night and the next day and the week after, until I wake up in a world completely unknown. In that world, there will be no melting back to the vole trails over bare ground, no going back to spring. There will be only an unknown track into the dark, snowbound woods.

Year

NINE

February 4

For the spring semester, I'm renting a small house in Claremont, California, a modest ranch in a modest neighborhood. Like most of the houses on the block, its facade pays a dutiful, glib homage to the street. The house's real attention—its gaze—is directed toward the carefully fenced backyard, where an orange tree grows and there's shelter from the sun under the long, wide roof of the porch.

For wildlife, there are cats. I seem to be living in a feline observatory. The back porch seems to be used as a kind of theater by the cats of the neighborhood, a place to work on their soliloquies. One by one, they come across the yard and up onto the boards, where they rehearse a repertory of poses. Then they make their exit, stage left, departing through a small gap between the gate and the fence. To say that each cat acts as though it carries the key to the city is merely to say that they're cats.

I see these cats—I've counted nearly a dozen so far—and can't help thinking of a sentence by Guy Davenport: "My cat does not know me when we meet a block away from home, and I gather from his expression that I'm not supposed to know him, either." Perhaps that's the value of my backyard as feline habitat. It's a college-owned house, and it sat empty for the past few months. I'm unknown to these cats, and therefore they put on no pretense. Perhaps some of them are feral—street cats. I suspect that most of them have perfectly good homes with owners unwise enough to let their pets out. My yard is where they come to be themselves.

I especially admire one nimbus-gray cat who comes walking across the yard looking like a feline bull. I'm fond of the longhair that spends a good part of the day sitting on top of the van parked across the street but takes a tour of my backyard around dusk. I stand back from the windows, hoping to remain undetected, but at least one of the cats—a gray and white—has found me out. It watches me as though it had never seen a writer in its habitat before. Then it walks away, jaded.

I'd trade all these cats for birds but the one precludes the other. I've seen a flicker and a scrub jay since I got here, also a hummingbird and several doves along the power lines behind the house. The rest of the birds have been turned into cats over the years, just as the desert has been turned into houses with cats in them. Meanwhile, the neighborhood dogs stand behind their fences and bark at what they think is going on.

March 9

I've been considering the four-way stop—the smallest and most successful unit of government in California. It may be the perfect model of participatory democracy, a fusion of "first come, first served" and the Golden Rule. There are four-way stops elsewhere in the country. But they're ubiquitous in California, and they bring out a surprising civility in drivers, here in a state where so much has gone wrong so recently.

What a four-way stop expresses is the equality of the streets that meet at its intersection—and, by inference, the equality of the drivers who meet there. For the four-way stop to work, no deference is required, no self-abnegation. It doesn't matter what you drive. Precedence is all that matters, like a water right in Wyoming, except that at a four-way stop everyone gets to take a turn being first.

Sometimes two cars—even four cars—arrive at the stop simultaneously. At moments like that, I find myself lengthening my own braking, giving an unambiguous time signal to the other driver, as if to say, "After you." Is this because I'm from the East? Or do California drivers do this, too? I don't know the answer. What I do know is that I almost never see two cars lurching into the middle of the intersection, both determined to assert their right of way.

I'm strangely reassured by the four-way stops I pass through here in Southern California. At each one, a social contract is renewed, and I pull away from the intersection feeling better about my fellow humans, which some days takes some doing. We arrive as strangers and leave as strangers, but somewhere between stopping and going, we must acknowledge each other. California is full of drivers everywhere acknowledging each other by winks and nods, by glances in the mirrors, as they catapult down the freeways. But at a four-way stop there's an almost Junior League politeness about it.

And if the stoplights go out at the big intersections, everyone reverts to the etiquette of the four-way stop. But it's a caution to us all. We can only gauge precedence within a certain distance and among a small number of cars. And self-policing—the essence of the four-way stop—soon breaks down. We need help in numbers. But when we come one by one to the quadrille at the four-way corner, we're who we are at our best, bowing, nodding, and moving on as by right.

March 15

When the sun finally rises, this will be a gray day, a great slab of flint laid across the plains. But the sun is still an hour off, and the snow is salting down just east of Riverton, Wyoming. My eyes are straining for sight in the void out there, looking to see what emerges first from the darkness. The answer is the blackest objects—old tires that ranchers sometimes place beside their cattleguards and the cattle themselves, black Angus stirring in a creek bottom. The cattle look as though they were bred black just so humans could find them in the gloom.

But mostly there are ravens, moving in singles and mated pairs, fighting off the stiff north wind. They know the lights of this highway well, and I see them hopping into the ditches or flaring upward on the wind just out of my path as I hurtle by. I can just discern the seam between earth and sky, and in that seam—farther down the highway—I can see ravens sitting on the telephone poles as if they'd been planted just for the convenience of ravens.

Slowly color begins to emerge, gray greens and bloodless tans. Up in the mountains the river willows would look like a tartan now. Out here on the plains, they seem to be blushing furiously but only by contrast with the immense drabness that surrounds them. It's only a mood, I know, only a wan hour of morning that makes their beauty feel so hidden, so lost.

And then there's the question of what emerges last. One answer is the pronghorn. I pass a small band standing right by the fence line—the sun well up now behind the overcast—and they're barely discernible, almost without dimension, as though they'd been camouflaged for just this light. But the last thing to emerge in the dawn is a red heeler dog trotting toward me in the brush along the ditch. He looks up at my headlights as if I were lost and he was the way home. I hope he isn't lost and keep myself from turning back. The day is now up in central Wyoming, and I feel suddenly as if I'm merely microscopic, driving across the fawn-colored hide of a great beast.

March 23

Lately, I've been studying celestial navigation, the seafaring kind that requires a sextant, a chronometer, and a nautical almanac. It's a way of adding a little trigonometry to a life that's mostly addition and subtraction. I began this project just as spring arrived and quickly noticed that spring, to navigators, isn't so much a season as a point. Spring occurs, in the nautical sense, between two lines of numbers in a large book that's crowded with lines of numbers.

There's more to it than that, which is one of the basic rules of celestial navigation. Spring is the vernal equinox—one of the two points of intersection between the ecliptic and the celestial equator. (The other is the autumnal equinox.) It's also the moment when the sun reaches what's called the First Point of Aries, a fictional line of demarcation that happens now to be in Pisces. I'm not going to try to explain these things, since I'm just beginning to grasp them myself. This much seems to be true. Spring is many things, most of them mathematical when you're on a boat looking up at the sky, wondering where you are.

In the nautical almanac, spring comes like clockwork, whether the snow has withdrawn or is falling fast. The table of hour angles and declinations that pinpoints celestial spring seems to say, "Here it is, just where it always was. Make what you will of it." And then there's terrestrial spring, which is a matter of hints and wishes, promise and hope, a season only vaguely calendrical. On the first day of spring, I was driving along the Shields River in Montana looking out at a season called "calving." It was nearly over. Most of the new calves—Angus nearly all of them—wore ear tags and moved with confidence. Some chased each other across the fields and around their sober dams, as though they could never grow up to be that stolid. A few seemed already businesslike, thuggish, looking across the fence line at a wider world.

But along the edge of one creek bottom ranch, a cow had just given birth, the umbilical still trailing from her as she tried to lick her calf to its feet. It rose and stumbled. The cow seemed both agitated and patient, eager

188

to have her calf on its feet beside her but somehow certain it would be soon. I moved down the road, because there were other things for her to think about besides me. On a tree in the next pasture there were six bald eagles, waiting. There were ravens on the fence and magpies in the ditch. Their young were yet to come.

April 25

Nine Angus bulls are moving down the fence line in a pasture along Clear Creek, north central Wyoming. I can see only their backs, black and as powerfully angled as the mounded coal in the hopper cars running north to Montana. There's a man on horseback ahead of the bulls and another behind them. They turn the bulls out onto the asphalt just at the highway crossroads.

To use an old word, it's a viridescent day. The cottonwoods stopped moaning in the rain overnight. Every creature is suddenly addled with the season. A pair of sandhill cranes stand motionless against the hills. A bald eagle circles higher and higher. A tom turkey works the fence line, making Kabuki moves, his eye on some invisible hen. The deer are trapped in their winter coats, looking disreputable. The air is full of the ticking of red-winged blackbirds, full of the soft spring sun.

But what I hear myself thinking is, "The bulls are out." They make for Clearmont then change their minds. They head toward me, the Sheridan way, before the riders veer them off, whooping and swinging stiff team-roping loops. The bulls are not belligerent, only confused. They don't know the question they're being asked, much less the answer. The correct direction is toward Buffalo, and soon the nine are strung out in an amiable line along the ditch, snatching mouthfuls of grass as they make their way down the road.

My worst dreams are the ones in which the horses or pigs get out. I like tight fences and good working gates. I like to see animals with deep grass and their heads down in it, grazing contentedly. I think I share my sense of order with those nine Angus bulls, who are being driven from home with too many choices. They go the right way at last just to calm the men on horseback.

The road stretches for miles into the low hills in every direction. The fences are tight, all the gates closed but two: the one the bulls came from and the one where they're heading. There's nothing but pasture and creek bottom, nothing but green grass and highway and the sound of birdsong. There was no getting out for those bulls. They crest a hill to the west, and I can feel the whooping and hollering inside me dying down.

May 16

Nearby, I can hear the sound of the 10, a waterfall of asphalt and rubber. A helicopter putters past overhead, and there's the sudden, tubular flare of a motorcycle—a big one—climbing the on-ramp just a few blocks away. Mockingbirds swoop from fence to wire down the long line of backyards in this part of town, and the small, gray bird nesting in an angle of my porch-roof has bedded down with her eggs for the night. The twilight sky has reached the moment when, if I could, I'd break a shard from it and keep it in my pocket to light my way in the darkness.

Meanwhile, up in the village, every restaurant is full, every corner crowded. Claremont, California, is a college town, and the parents have arrived for graduation. They've put their simulacra through college, and now they're all dining out in a haze of anticipatory nostalgia. I know the feeling. I graduated from this place—Pomona College—a long time ago, and I remember seeing so many adults who looked eerily like their younger selves. I remember the nostalgia too.

I've never had children, and so for me there's something a little extra in coming to semester's end with the students I've taught. Week by week, I watch their thoughts get clearer and clearer until suddenly my students are able to say things we can no longer quite account for. One by one, they come into focus, to me and to each other, in their writing. Just why this should be such a beautiful thing I've never figured out, unless perhaps it's this. Even at their age, they carry such a weight of life. They're such experts in the particulars of their circumstances. They have the strange and impermanent gift of not knowing how much they know.

One by one, I've talked to my students about what comes next. There are plans, places. Beijing, France, Woods Hole, London. Schools of every kind, and every kind of service, as well. One by one, my students express their longing and their sense of loss as they get ready to leave this place. I tell them to keep in touch, to write and send me what they're writing. I'm the constant one. I'm now a voice in their heads, a voice that will sound surprisingly familiar to them the next time we talk. Yet only a few of them will keep up the uneven acquaintance of professor and student, which is just as it should be.

What I get in return is the knowledge of who they are at this very moment. I get to see, through the writing they've done for me, how life appears to them just now. And looking at my students, I can only wonder who I was all those years ago, on this same night, this one final evening.

But I'm long forgotten, even to myself. Tomorrow, I leave this place like everyone else, and what I'll think of is that nest in the porch-roof and how the last light shone through the orange leaves before I sat down to write.

June 5

The birds begin. Ethel the Border terrier stretches and yawns beside me. I listen for a while, then consult the time. It's so much earlier than I thought—5:11 and nothing to do about it except listen for a little longer, then get up. I have the brief, puritanical thought that I should know all these birds by their songs. Perhaps they're the same birds I hear at twilight, some of whose names I know.

I've been away from the farm for longer than I care to think, away from the work and the mental habit of it. And yet on this first morning home, I find myself stepping out the door at 5:30. Ethel comes first, her walk and breakfast, and then it's down to the barn to let the horses out of the night corral. They pause in the barnyard, always—I like to think—with a sense of delinquency. I come out of the barn with a screen door that needs rescreening and startle the horses up the drive and into the pasture, where they settle to grazing.

I have an endless list of tasks. I begin by lopping a pair of hickory saplings that are crowding a *Parrotia persica*, which has sprung into adolescence since I last saw it. I'll have to do something about a worn-out piston shaft on the mower. The bees are spilling out of the hive, but before I can inspect it, I have to fix the fence post that's leaning against it.

What's missing is new life. It's all around me, but I mean the life of husbandry. I came back to the farm via Wyoming and a place I know with a small herd of dairy goats. One was due to deliver, and I became completely absorbed in the goat-watch. She had reached her term—150 days—and hour by hour her behavior and conformation changed. I marveled at her readiness, her deep knack, the timing of it all.

Only my timing was wrong. I was on the road when her twins were born. They're females, and I hope to have a couple of their kids. They were on my mind when the birds began this morning. Over my coffee, I dog-eared the pages of a fencing catalog.

June 26

Thirty-five years ago, almost to the day, I made the same drive I'm making now, rising out of California and crossing Nevada on my way east. I was leaving home for graduate school and a future whose shape I couldn't begin to guess.

My dad chose the Plymouth Valiant I was driving. It had a shimmy at sixty-two miles per hour, and I had no faith in its radiator, for radiators had often failed our family. Climbing the Golconda Summit, I watched the needle in the temperature gauge climb, too. We crested the summit—the Valiant and I—just below boiling point.

It's hard to imagine the world in which that car was new. I think now of all the things I traveled without—credit card, cell phone, iPod, audiobooks—and the experience seems almost Conestogal, though it was anything but. The temptation is to jump to the end of the story—safe arrival in Princeton and the years since. But, as always, it's the passage that matters.

What I think about now is what I didn't feel then about the landscape I was crossing. I was just back from a year in London, and my head was stuffed with Dante and Virgil. It would never have occurred to me that if America is a kid bound across country for graduate school, it's also a pair of horses and a pipe corral in an indigo valley with a dust devil whirling up in the Nevada distance.

Now I wonder why, in 1975, I didn't turn off in the Starr Valley or make my way down into the Ruby Mountains and settle under the stars for a few nights, or perhaps for a lifetime. I wonder that even as I pass up the opportunity again. Turning north at Wells, I realize that I'm retracing an even older route—the road my family took when we moved to California from Iowa in 1966. As I bask in the late light on Route 93, heading toward Twin Falls, Idaho, I imagine passing a 1963 Ford Galaxie with two adults and four kids heading the opposite direction. Another hour, and I'm in Idaho, dropping down into well-watered valleys where the hay has just been cut and baled, hay of an almost theological quality standing in perfect, square bales, waiting to be stacked for winter.

July 2

I'm just home from a solo drive across country, accompanied by my thoughts and the implacable songs of Lori McKenna. I didn't solve any problems, for all my thinking, but I did a lot of looking. And, to use the wonderful old phrase, I'll tell you what. In America the rivers are full—the Yellowstone, the Cheyenne, the Missouri, the Rock, the Mississippi. They reach up into the boughs of the trees overarching them and sweep their shadows away downstream.

And everywhere I looked, all across the mountains and the plains, I saw grass of a kind you see only perhaps once in a generation, so thick and lustrous that it looks as though it had the texture of a beaver pelt. The high-pressure dome above me scattered the winds, sending the sunlight skittering over the grasses as though they were ripples on the waves at sea.

The cattle and horses were sleek and almost fatigued with good feeding. In western South Dakota, cows stood belly deep in a ranch pond, impersonating the kine in Constable's paintings. In the eastern part of the state, I came across an old barn sinking, prow high, in the ocean of grass.

I wanted to pull over and lie down in the thick of those pastures, watching the seeded heads of the grasses bending low in the wind above me. But I drove on, and noticed that northern Iowa, where silos were once the only tall landmarks on the horizon, has now given itself a certain grandeur by building towering windmills, mostly in pods of six.

On a trip this long, the driving sometimes grows weary. And yet rather than listening to books as I've done in the past, I found myself making up stories about characters based on the names on the exit signs I passed. My favorite, in eastern Iowa, is Galva Atkinson. In my mind she's tough as a pump handle but has cornflower eyes. In Illinois, I came across the wellborn but feckless Niles Plymouth. In Ohio, I contemplated the lovely Lorain Ferry, and in New York, at last, the sterling Frankfort Ilion, who was once a classicist but has since become a banker. And so, finally, all the way home again.

August 16

By the time I've made the first few passes across the middle pasture, the barn swallows have found me out. They come chiding out of the hayloft when I appear at the barn door but lose interest once I drive the tractor up the road. I make the turn into the pasture—bucket raised high to clear the gate—and send power to the big mower trailing behind me. The tractor shudders, and I shift into third, mower blades thrumming. Down go the burdock and milkweed and curly dock. Down go the thistles.

I come to the patches that give me particular pleasure—cutting across the hillside where wild strawberries grow or mowing the high, rank grasses out near the pond hole that never fills. But where the pleasure really comes from is hard to say. Is it the way the green of the pasture lusters up once it's mowed? Is it just the spreading neatness? Whatever it is, it feels jubilant, a jubilation embodied by swallows.

I mow alone at first. A vole slips out of a deep tuft of grass and runs to safety. A rabbit streaks out of the brambles. As I work my way through the thickest growth, a cloud of insects rises around me. Now there's one swallow with me; now there are two. And soon I can no longer count them, not because they're so many but because they're so fast.

I'm at the center of the insect cloud, and the swallows vector closer and closer. I can visualize them only in fragments—a rufous waistcoat, scything wings, the bluebottle back. Their flight is merciless, joyous. There's no athleticism here. This is merely life and death.

What I can't convey is the abruptness of the swallows' flight, the way they make me feel almost stationary. They dodge in and out of my periphery, as if the real game here were never to let me see them straight on. I cut the last swaths and turn for the barn, leaving the swallows at work behind me. I back the tractor in, kill the diesel, ease the hydraulics. A lone insect—a mothlike being—rises from my shoulder, and makes for the open air.

September 2

One day, I can hear the faint rustle of autumn coming. The next day I can't. One evening, summer leaks away into the cool night sky, and the next morning, it's back again. But there's headway through the season. Birdsong has gone, replaced by the bagpiping of the insect creation. I look out across the pasture as dusk begins and see a shining galaxy of airborne bugs. How would it be, I wonder, to have an awareness—a sentient feel—of the actual number of insects on this farm?

I ask myself a version of that question every day: "Have you ever really looked at…?" You can fill in the blank yourself. But every day I feel blinded by familiarity. I open the hive, which is filled with honey, and what I see are honeybees. Their particularity, even their community, escapes me, if only because I've been living with honeybees a good part of my life. I remember the old phrase "keep your eyes peeled," and maybe that's what I need, a good peeling, so all my senses revert to their original freshness.

Again and again, I find myself trying to really look at what I'm seeing. It happened the other afternoon, high on a nearby mountain. A dragonfly had settled on the tip of a pine bough. It clung, as still as only a dragonfly can be. Then it flicked upward and caught a midge and settled on the bough again, adjusting itself precisely into the wind. I see dragonflies quivering through the insect clouds above my pasture too. And what I always notice is that there's no such thing as really looking.

What I want to be seeing is invisible anyway—the prehistoric depth of time embodied in the form of those dragonflies, the pressure of life itself, the web of relations that binds us all together. I find myself trying to witness the moment when the accident of life becomes a continued purpose. But this is a small farm, and, being human, I keep coming up against the limits of what a human can see.

This morning I found a spider resting on the leaf of an oakleaf hydrangea, the axis of the spider's abdomen perfectly aligned with the axis of the leaf. What I noticed was the symmetry of their placement, the way spider and leaf resembled each other. What I wanted to notice was the spider's intent. If I could, I would have asked it, "What are you doing?" Or, better yet, "Who are you?" But all I could do was look—and notice that I was looking—and make the best of the sight I'd seen.

September 17

Why does the mounded hay in the horses' run-in shed look so inviting? Why does the chicken house feel like a clubhouse to me?—warm and tight and brightly lit, food and water and grit all at hand, a place where I could just settle in with the birds and enjoy the mild superiority of being human. I climb the ladder to the hayloft and the barn cat watches me warily from his redoubt in the hay bales. I feel like getting my sleeping bag and joining him.

Night comes, but the fog comes first, dragging the last light with it across the hilltops. The trees are bristling in a light breeze, and already the leaves have started to fall—just ones and twos so far, but already scorched into color by autumn. It's still too warm for the woodstove, the kind of evening that feels like summer in mourning, though without any real sadness. On a night like this, "grieving" sounds like the noise the wind would make if it got into the attic.

Real autumn is a long way off yet, no matter what the pumpkins say. They're starting to edge out the sweet corn at farm stands along the highway, their brightness almost preposterous in the fading light. I find myself wishing they weren't such emblems of Halloween, because the sight of them seems to jerk me six weeks forward. I'm not ready to be jerked forward in time. I want to consume the particulars of the day ahead of me one by one.

This is what I always say, and yet life never lets me mean it. I was away from the farm for two days this week, and it sprang ahead without me. The bees, uproarious around the hive-mouth when I left, are nowhere to be seen in the dusk, though I know they'll be out again in the morning.

I can't conceive what it means to be a bee. I don't know whether their labor feels like labor or whether necessity is joy to them. But I never walk past the hive without passing through a plume of honey-scent. And I never see the bees coming and going without wondering what so much kinship means.

Can they tell how tightly knit they are? Or is kinship to them as fundamental as gravity—the precondition of their existence? What I know is that I loved the education Merlin gives the young King Arthur in T. H. White's *The Once and Future King*, which was to be turned into one creature after another. I teach myself the same way every day I'm at the farm.

October 15

It's well before light, and I'm listening to the rain, watching every now and then the flicker of headlights coming down the hill. I no longer have custody of Ethel the Border terrier, so I'm up early on my own. She was itemized in a divorce settlement and now lives in Iowa, where I know she's happy. I hope she misses me, but I hope not nearly as much as I miss her.

Without her my attention seems to have spilled outward. I can feel the day coming and how different its rhythms are. Somehow there's more time for the horses, which is perhaps why Nell the mustang let me catch her when the farrier came the other day. At first she shied away, just to keep up appearances. But when the other horses had been trimmed she presented herself to my arms, and it was a much more beautiful day after that.

I have new chickens, layers eight weeks old. When they were chicks living under lights in the mudroom, I made a practice of picking them up one at a time, those that would let me. And now when I enter the poultry yard, I feel like a one-man midway at the chicken fair, birds standing in line waiting to be picked up. No good can come of lifting chickens. I can almost hear my dad thinking that, though he's gone now, too. And yet the birds churr and cluck, and I leave the yard happy.

The chicken house my dad and I built in the days after 9/11 has begun to sink on one end, thanks to the woodchucks. That gave me an excuse to buy a bottle jack, which I'll slip under the sill and jack the house back to level. That will make the place feel more trim, and it will keep water from running out of the chicken waterers, which matters once the freeze begins.

It's hard to explain where happiness comes from when so much has been lost and misplaced and set aside. But come it does. This is one of those mornings when I think I have a farm just to surround me while I work. I have this piece to finish and later there will be time for my new book.

The chickens will be darting in and out of the rain, the fall of hickory nuts will continue, and the horses will stand around an upended round bale in the run-in shed on the hill, looking for all the world as though they've got a game of three-handed pinochle going.

November 5

Just about now, I remember that the trees on this farm will be bare for the next six months. It always comes as a surprise. I'm surrounded by a hibernating forest. The maples and hickories have mulched themselves with their own leaves, and they seem to have gone rigid now that they carry so much less sail in the wind. Everything that can die back has done so. The last of the woodchucks have gone down their burrows. The tide of dormancy is rising all around me, and on a rainy day with the woodstove going, I wonder whether I'll sink or swim.

Even as the rain falls again and the temperature hovers in the forties, I can feel January in the back of my mind. I try hard to keep it out of my thoughts, as if incredulity might guarantee a mild winter. By the time the hard cold gets here I'll be inured to it, having haired up in my mind the way the horses are doing right now. But truthfully, I'm still back in mid-August somewhere, before the barn swallows vanished, before the pokeweed berries were ripe enough for the cedar waxwings, before the chipmunks gorged on the dogwood drupes.

This month more than any other, I slip in and out of season, never able to coincide with the calendar. I feel the slippage most when I'm indoors working, my thoughts almost anywhere but where I am. Where I am is facing south, looking into the tree-tops under a sky that's more than overcast. It's a squirrel-gray sky, a beech-bark sky, a sky as dark as a horseshoe right out of the box. It's no wonder my thoughts drift away.

But soon I'll put on my barn coat and work gloves and muck boots. And the minute I step outside, I'll step back into proper time. It feels as though the day suddenly sticks to me. The thought of January recedes because it's so purely November, the mud deep in the barnyard, the rain picking up again. I walk down to the barn and stand just inside the doorway, taking shelter with the tractor and my tools and all the implements of summer—the spade, the garden fork, the pig fence, and the chicken fences.

I'm filled, as always, with expectation. It's a look I see in the horses' eyes only at chore-time, when they know their grain is coming. But on a dark afternoon, rain falling, they stand in the middle of the pasture with no thought of the shelter they could take. Their posture is noncommittal. They're November horses, just the way they were June horses not so long ago.

November 24

I pull into the farm from the city well after nightfall but early in the evening. I turn off the headlights as I come up the drive. The moon hangs over the eastern hills like a hypnotist's watch. I drop a few things in the house, turn on the kitchen light, and wander out again to check on the animals.

I used to take a flashlight when I was new to this place. I no longer do, even on nights much darker than this one. My eyes adjust slowly, too slowly, but part of the pleasure of walking out in the night is feeling the adjustment, watching the flat opacity of my night blindness resolve into the three dimensions of the farm. All the nocturnal creatures are out and about and I'll never be one of them. Even the horses are more nocturnal than I am. They live in natural light year-round, and by the time I get home from the city, they're already a couple of hours into watching the night.

In summer, you can pretend the night is translucent and the Milky Way is emanating a warmth of some kind. But by late November, those illusions are past. The sun feels vigilant and benevolent, no matter how dim. And when it vanishes, just after four, it seems like the rising darkness is slowly becoming continuous with the deepest reaches of space. The feeling only intensifies as the weather gets colder and Orion rises in the sky.

The chickens are on their roost, pretending not to notice when I look in. The horses stand impassive in their pasture, though if I opened the gate and walked in, they would drift over to share their heat. Where the barn cat is, I have no idea, but he's so black that he would stand out on a night like this. I complete my rounds, and still my eyes haven't opened fully to the night.

I light a fire in the woodstove, put a few things away, remove a mouse from a trap in the pantry, and settle in to read in the kitchen. The night is too warm and still for the chimney to draw well. A rhomboid of light spills onto the deck, and at its edges I see a movement. It's an opossum, come up to investigate the cat-food dish. It walks up to the foot of the sliding glass door and peers in, surely unseeing in so much brightness.

Perhaps this is the opossum I met on the ladder going up to the hayloft a couple of months ago. It was a surprise to both of us. Now it stands in the light for another moment looking hopelessly disorganized, as opossums do, and then it wanders off into the darkness, where the seeing is so much better.

December 10

Out in one of the pastures lies a pocket knife with a serrated blade. I lost it at least ten years ago, but I think about it every time I walk the fence line, even though I've long since replaced it. Somewhere, too, there's a pair of lined work gloves, the ones I've used for the past six or seven winters. And where are my gaiters? Or, for that matter, the pair of flip-flops that vanished overnight?

This farm is a constellation of lost objects. They all know where they are, but they're keeping mum, the better to surprise me when they finally turn up. Finding a long-lost object brings an idiotic satisfaction. "There you are!" I heard myself saying yesterday when I stumbled upon a waterproof timer for the horse-tank heater. I wasn't looking for it, which is how I found it.

My dad had a basement woodshop with a pegboard wall for hanging hand tools—each in its special place. In practice, the wall was an index of what was missing. The problem isn't a lack of organization. It's the way one task turns into another. I go out to tighten a section of fence, set the hammer down in a conspicuous place, walk to the barn to get some wire, begin repairing something I notice while I'm there, and then it snows. Maybe I remember leaving the hammer by the fence. Maybe it turns up in April.

Living here is a constant exercise in problem solving. And that's the trouble with something that's gone missing. It's a problem with no solution. I prefer the kinds that work out in the end, like discovering that the broken stepladder I've kept for years makes a perfect chicken roost.

When it gets as cold as it is—five degrees one recent morning with half a foot of snow on the ground—all the problems change. I decide to switch implements on the tractor. Off goes the spear for moving round bales and on goes the back blade. No matter how solid or impressive a tractor looks, it's connected to its implements by several small pins which, when dropped in the snow, might never have existed in the first place.

But sometimes things work out just right. When the temperature plunged, the hydrant—a self-draining faucet—in the chicken yard froze up. I layered some insulation over a heat tape and plugged it in while the horses stood by, thumping their nearly empty tank. I thought it would be three days at least before the water was flowing. But when I went out to do chores that afternoon—wind chill at zero—the hydrant worked fine. It felt as good as it would to find that pocket knife.

199

December 30

I'm standing in the barnyard with the farrier. Remedy, the quarter horse, is getting his winter shoes. We're surrounded by vast heaps of plowed snow, the kind my friends and I loved to tunnel through when we were kids. It's a sparkling day, and for some reason I find myself thinking about a photograph we found after my father died. My grandfather is sitting on a high bank of snow, wearing work clothes, and he's holding up a fox terrier, which looks like it's ready to eat the camera. This is the home farm in northwest Iowa, probably 1936.

In the background is the barn where the draft horses lived. I don't know whether my grandfather was his own horseshoer, but I doubt it. So there must have come many days like the one I'm having now, standing in the cold beside a sleepy horse while a man with a damaged thumb and a sore back goes about his work. In all these years, the technology has hardly changed. Fire, steel, nails, rasp, hammer, anvil, and a pair of heavy chaps with a hoof knife in a leather pocket. A patient horse and an extra human to hold the lead rope.

I knew that farm long after the horses had been replaced by tractors. When I was older, I tried to get my dad to tell stories about what it was like growing up there during the Depression. He would sometimes talk about the blizzard of 1936, and he always talked about the kindly cunning of the draft horses, who loved to lean into him. But those days were always cloaked in a vagueness I never understood, as if the farm were a country from which he'd emigrated and long since put out of mind. I wanted the details, what the work was like, which chores were his, how June differed from January, how much pain and how much pleasure. I never got them.

So I look back at the old photos and try to imagine the life there. I think of another photo of my grandfather—face sun-blackened—holding my dad on his knee and a pup in the other arm. My dad's older brothers are there in ragged overalls, each one holding a well-chewed apple. In the background there's an octagonal brooder house and a long house for laying hens. What I wouldn't give to go back and see it all.

The closest I can come is to stand as quietly as Remedy does and wait for the farrier to finish. I close the gate behind him and send the horses thundering up the drive and into the breast-deep snow of the pasture. I hear the rooster crow as I carry an armload of firewood into the house.

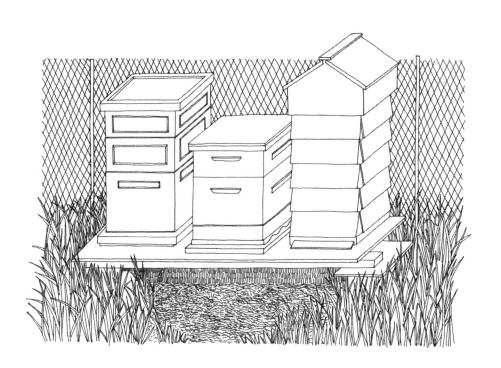

Year
TEN

February 10

Most days I see a male cardinal sitting in the hickory tree behind the house, waiting to forage beneath the bird-feeders. You don't really "see" a male cardinal. The world collapses to a carmine point that puts everything else out of focus, the hickory, the snow, the woodsmoke from the village down below. For its character—modest and more cautious than other birds—the cardinal is overdressed. But then what would living up to that plumage mean?

It would be nice if starlings came in ones and twos and were more like the cardinal in demeanor. We would suddenly see the ornateness, the exoticism of their feathering, which reminds me of darkly marbled endpapers in well-bound books. I've handled a starling skin—using its hackle feathers for tying trout flies—and each feather is a bit of the night sky with an iridescent galaxy shining near the tip.

But starlings don't come in ones and twos. They come in gangs and mobs and hordes. They mug the suet. They bicker over the oil-seed feeders. They bother even the squirrels. Their behavior is strictly self-referential—they fight only with each other and they fight all the time. The other birds look on, appalled, like hosts watching their dinner guests brawling across the table.

Starlings are capable of sleekness, but they often look bedraggled. Plus they have that child's drawing of a beak stuck in the middle of their faces.

The starlings arrived at the feeders a couple of weeks ago, and it's been mayhem since. I discovered that the Department of Agriculture's Wildlife Services killed 1,259,714 starlings in 2009 and dispersed another 7 million of the 200 million starlings in this country. They're all descended, as is well-known, from a few dozen birds released in 1890 by the American Acclimatization Society, which was devoted to introducing European species to America. Starlings are good intentions in the flesh, which says nearly everything about good intentions.

But they're here and I look for a reason to admire them, apart from their feathers. I notice that they waddle, more ducklike in their gait than any other bird at the feeders. Somehow this makes them seem less leather-jacketed and hoodlike, if not endearing. I think of their habit of poking that bill into the ground and prying it open with colossal jaw muscles, searching for prey, aerating the world as they go. But it's no use. They've de-nested billions of birds, and the porch where the feeders hang looks like a scene from Hitchcock.

Then one morning they're gone. The cardinal sits in the hickory. The chickadees come and go, taking a seed then pivoting quickly for a glance around. The woodpeckers are on the suet, ladder-backed and probing quizzically. The house sparrows—nineteenth-century imports themselves—move civilly among the fallen seeds as if to show they belong.

March 12

Again and again, I'm struck by the persistence of objects. I go out to do the chores wearing a blue plaid wool coat. I have no idea how old it is, because it's a hand-me-down, and yet every day there it is, waiting on its hook. I feed the horses and reflect, as I always do, that Remedy is thirty-three years old and still sultanic in his majesty. The sun comes up, and here we are everyday, all of us—animate and inanimate—persisting together.

There's nothing very surprising about it, any more than there is in the persistence of memory, which assures me that this is the same world I went to sleep in. And yet, for brief seasons, I can't help marveling at it. The farm and everything in it seems wonderfully solid, and it all reports for duty, unbidden, every day. Perhaps this is just a way of countering the other feeling I commonly have—that we've all been loaded aboard a planet streaking through time.

A rabbit has been eating the bark on the lower branches of the apple trees, which reminds me that now is pruning time—and that the trees are going on fourteen years old. The chickadees are suddenly singing their piping, two-note song. The snowpack is deflating. Nell is shedding great clumps of horse hair. Change is about to break out abruptly, persuasively. The woodshed, is almost down to nothing but chipmunk nests. Yet last week I burned a length of honey locust from a tree felled nearly a decade ago. It was still dense and orange. This week I burned a length from a sugar maple that was at least two hundred years old when it was felled, and the wood felt original, not a trace of decay. The house I live in was built mostly in the 1830s, and in the library there are a couple of quartos by John Dryden published in the late seventeenth century—the oldest objects on this farm that aren't rocks, earth, or trees. So I wake up and pretend that I persist too, that I'm as perdurable as that ancient sugar maple or the words of Dryden. The sunlight coming over the eastern ridge feels new and ancient, both. I put on my chore coat, slip on my muck boots, which are cracking with age, and go out to open the door to the chicken house my dad built a decade ago. The birds flutter to their nests in a second chicken house not far away. And when I go out later in the day, there will be something new and fresh, nine or ten eggs still warm from the hens that laid them.

April 1

After a long scentless winter—apart from the tang of woodsmoke in the air—I could suddenly smell the earth again one morning last week. It seems odd to call the scent fresh—it was darker and mustier than that—but fresh is how it felt. It hovered like a ground fog above the last rotting banks of snow, so fertile that the spring scent rising from the damp earth might be a growing medium.

When the snow slid back at last, revealing pasture and garden, it was like the retreat of a glacier, leaving everything mashed flat in its wake. The grass looked like it was waking from a long, sodden nap, and all but the stoutest plants—the yuccas even—had been bulldozed. It seemed as though almost every non-woody plant had been drawing on a common reservoir of terrestrial sap that ran dry over the winter. That new scent in the air is the reservoir refilling, saturating the soil.

Vole trails are still visible on what looks like a lawn of crushed velvet, and the ground isn't soft underfoot yet, except where the gophers have been digging, and there it's spongy and accepting. The only ice left anywhere is under the scattered hay where the horses fed in the middle pasture. Every time I walk across it I think of nineteenth-century icehouses packed with the winter's pond-ice and insulated with sawdust and straw—the inverse, somehow, of my hayloft still a third full of the hay of 2010.

This was a winter with casualties. The snow undid the bottom row of insulators on the electric fence one by one. I've lost track of the mice that wandered into my traps. Two losses leave me disheartened. One is the beehive. There was nothing stirring there on a sixty-degree day a couple of weeks ago, no bees on the aconites or snowdrops. There will be a mournful spring harvest as I clean out the hive and prepare it for a new colony next spring.

What worries me most is the barn cat, whom I haven't seen since the harshest days of early February. He'd been coming up to the house to eat on the deck, but I usually saw him up in the hayloft, watching warily as I tossed down bales, or basking in a wedge of sunlight in the run-in shed. In the heaviest snow, he waited on a low dogwood branch until he saw me coming, and then hid until I set out his food. I believe he's gone. He had a complicated route around the neighborhood, over the fields and across the road. So there's just a chance that one warm day I'll see him sitting on a fence rail.

April 21

Last weekend, I opened the hive of bees that died over the winter. For the past three years, I've left all the honey for the bees instead of taking some for myself, in hopes of making a hard season easier to bear. But in a winter as cold as this past one—and without a January thaw—it's possible for bees to cluster so tightly, trying to keep warm, that they're unable to move to their stores of honey only a few inches away.

I'd planned to take the hive apart in preparation for new bees. Instead, I found well over a hundred pounds of honey waiting to be harvested, honey in some sense bequeathed to me by the citizens of a vanished monarchy. Usually, beekeepers harvest honey in the fall. To be harvesting honey in the spring felt very odd, as if I'd started sugaring—a spring event—and somehow gone astray.

There's something unspeakably beautiful, at once frugal and profligate, in the sight of a frame full of honey just as the bees have left it, each cell carefully capped. Beekeepers usually try to take off honey just after it's been capped, but this was honey that had been capped last September, when the goldenrod was still in bloom. It had overwintered, aging and darkening as the days passed and the temperature dropped and its makers died. It's unlike any other honey I've ever harvested, somewhere between grade B maple syrup and molasses in color. Its taste has been affected only by the memory of losing the bees that made it.

The surprise was greater than simply finding unexpected honey. It was also the unexpected reawakening of the beekeeper in me, who has been dormant for several years. I've ordered three new packages of bees, and when they arrive at the end of May, they'll go in new hives designed to let the bees produce their own comb instead of building on a foundation of wax or plastic already embossed in a hexagonal pattern. It's a deliberate retreat from the familiar boxlike hives I've always used, which are really designed for large-scale honey production.

In fact, it's been a week of surprises. Honey is slowly filtering through sieves and waiting to be bottled. More honey is waiting to be removed from the frames and begin its filtering. Beeswax is waiting to be melted in the sun. And one evening, an hour before dusk, I looked out the window and there was the barn cat—last seen in January—sitting on the deck waiting for his milk. He looked at me as though wondering where I'd been, a question for which I have no good answer.

May 20

For the past thirteen years, my horses have gazed across a gravel road at a neighbor's pasture, where her horses stand, gazing back. Kinship, affinity, species recognition, herd instinct, longing—I don't know what to call this habit. But my neighbor and I are planning to move my horses into her pasture. She has plenty of extra grass, and my land can use a rest.

There will be some sorting out. I wonder where my neighbor's mule will come in the pecking order and whether her thoroughbred will defer to Remedy, who is the boss of my small herd. We'll see. What I really wonder is what my horses will think and feel—that's the only way I can put it—when they find themselves turned loose in a pasture they've spent such a long time contemplating. They've traveled widely over the years—to Montana, Wyoming, and Colorado—but to them, I suppose, that pasture across the road is thirteen horse-years away.

Their absence will give me a chance to do some refencing and to take down a couple of dead trees. I plan to cut up all my rotting post and rail fences into stove-lengths, which I'll cheerfully burn this winter. I can do some reseeding, and if I had a flock of sheep, I'd turn them loose in my pastures to eat the plants my horses won't eat. I imagine the whole farm shaking itself like a shaggy dog while the horses are across the road.

I wonder, too, how I'll take this move. The horses will be only a hundred yards up the road but mostly out of sight. The more I think about it, the more I realize how often I look at the horses, dozens of times a day. I gaze at them as steadily as they gaze at their neighbors across the road, and they communicate something to me every time I see them. Exactly what is hard to say, but they draw me out of myself again and again. My thoughts turn into the cowbirds wandering among the horses' hooves.

I look forward to walking up the road to see how the horses are doing, to see how the new herd is settling down. Will they be grazing in the far reaches of the new pasture? Or will they stand, all five of them, by the roadside fence, gazing back across the road at my empty pastures, wondering how this monumental change came to be?

June 14

Last week, the wind pulled apart a sugar maple on the edge of the pasture. It left a long, tapering wound on the side of the trunk, and on the ground a forking branch the size of a mature maple. Late one afternoon I began disassembling it with a chainsaw. I loaded my tools—saw, sharpener, logging chain, gas and oil—in the tractor bucket and put on my hearing protectors—orange plastic ear muffs—for the drive. Before I started the saw, I switched to a helmet with a face guard and built-in ear muffs.

I live in my own world on this farm, but when I put on hearing protectors I retreat to an even own-er world. Time after time, I've stepped off the tractor and started on some project without remembering to take off the muffs. I concentrate on what I'm doing and yet my thoughts go walkabout. Then I become aware of the pulmonary tide of my own breathing and realize I'm still wearing orange plastic ear muffs. Often as not, I choose to leave them on. I find it hard to explain why.

The best answer, I suppose, is that they heighten my sense of self-absorption, the feeling of dwelling in a task completely apart from the world I usually work in. But they also help me hear my body as it bends to the task, even as they distance me, aurally, from the task itself—the roaring of the chainsaw, the ringing of the T-post I'm pounding, the screaming of the table saw. And when they come off, it's like leaving self-consciousness behind and reentering the stream of events. I back the tractor into the barn, shut it down, and hang the ear muffs over the hydraulic lever. The first thing I hear is the barn swallows chastening me.

Years ago, this house had loose, single-pane windows. When the wind blew, they rattled and moaned. It was like living in the tree-tops. The windows have been replaced and now when a thunderstorm comes crashing in from the west, it spills its winds silently. I'm glad to be spared that sound, glad to wait it out in silence and discover what fell and what broke only after a good night's sleep.

June 30

Last week, there was a day I hesitate to call perfect only because I'd hate it if the truly perfect day had already come and gone in my life. I'd like it to remain somewhere ahead in my reckoning. But when that perfect day comes it will probably resemble the one last week. The western breeze had cleaned the sun and purified the light, which fell mote-less on the farm.

I recognized the day. It's the one that's inconceivable in midwinter. It's also the one in which midwinter itself is inconceivable—an antipodal day. The hive entrances were yellow with the pollen rubbed off as bees came and went, jodphured with the stuff. It was a woodchuck day too—all of them out, heads high, looking like grass-otters. As I walked up from the barn, a pair of blonde kit foxes—raised on my April chickens—spilled out of the culvert and scampered up the fence line.

Life—the thrust of living—seems raw and irrepressible on a day like that. Every niche, no matter how small, is fully occupied, no-vacancy signs visible everywhere. At dawn I walk through one spider trap after another, trailing silk by the time I get to the barn. Any object I move, I discover a colony of creatures behind it or under it or inside it. This is a farm of overlapping settlements and empires, and I plod through like Godzilla, undoing the work of the ant and earwig nations just by moving a five gallon bucket or a fence rail.

Chaotic as the life here feels—profligate and squanderous—I take refuge in it. It's what we have going for us—"we" meaning the kinship of all species. The strange part about being human is that "life" so easily comes to mean a quantity of time, an allotment of experience. We note that we're alive without feeling that we are, for a time, indomitable organisms sharing a planet with indomitable organisms of every other kind.

These are pure-sun, western-breeze thoughts, steam rising from compost. But on the day I mean, it seemed like a toss-up. Either everything was sentient along with me, or we were all sharing a vital insentience. I sat in the shade watching the bees come and go in the sunshine a few feet away, a nectared, pollened, purposeful cloud. That was the kind of day it was.

July 28

While the horses have been on vacation—staying across the road in a neighbor's pasture—my own pastures have grown into what looks like the first stage of abandonment. The grass is high, and so are the thistles and burdock. Here and there, sumac is trying to grow unnoticed. Several of the fences are down on purpose and in two of the pastures lie the trunks of dead sugar maples, cut into log lengths. They remind me of disjointed whale skeletons I saw on an island off the coast of southern Chile.

There's a surprising pleasure in the absence of a fence that has stood in place for more than a decade. I walk back and forth across the former fence lines just because I can. It reminds me that most of the figuring I've done in my head while living here has had to do with the layout of fences. I wish, in a way, they didn't have to go back up again. They may be my fences, but they constrain me as surely as they constrain the horses.

While the horses have been across the road, there's been no need to close the gates here. Anyone with large animals becomes fastidious about closing gates. I can, with effort, leave open the main gate to the barn while I'm moving branches to the burn pile or hauling logs with the tractor. But if I look out from the house and see the gate still open, I'm flooded with a sense of disarray. I know it's perfectly fine—the horses are behind other gates and other fences—and yet it feels as though something was left open in me.

So now it's time for a last grand mowing—taking out the weeds before they go to seed, cutting back the sumacs, mowing the fence lines themselves—and then up go the fences again, tighter and truer. But not just yet. I want to walk across this borderless farm a few more times, trying to understand why it feels so odd going from garden to pasture without having to step between the wires of a horse fence. Living here is such a mysterious affair.

September 9

I realize about now that most of the projects I started last spring when the snow melted either need finishing before the snow falls again or are the kind that can never really be completed, like cleaning the barn. Let me not depress you with a list of them. All I know is that instead of pounding the posts I need for a new fence around the yard or getting the garden ready for next spring, I've been gazing idly at small sailboats for sale on the web.

What attracts me isn't only the thought of sailing. It's how self-contained these vessels look, everything from a smart racing dinghy to a Nor'Sea 27 that looks like it just returned from a circumnavigation. A sailboat has no barn. It has no compost pile. Mildew can be a problem but not nettles or Japanese knotweed. I suppose one could keep a chicken or two aboard. But I'd have to draw the line at pigs, though I know from nautical narratives that pigs have done their fair share of sailing. There are sails and standing rigging to deal with and keeping the bottom barnacle-free, but can that be worse than stacking hay or splitting wood?

One thing holds me back. All the small sailboats I find myself looking at have trailers. That means they have tires. Nothing causes me more despair than seeing the condition of the tires on the trailers I already own. They rot in the rain and they rot in the sun. Oxygen seems to be bad for them. This is the trouble with even a small, avocational farm like mine. You set out to raise chickens and keep horses and end up with a collection of graying tires and small gas engines with fouled carburetors. Instead of looking at small sailboats I should be looking at oxen.

Perhaps the solution is to find a sailboat just too big to trailer. I can have it mounted on stands beside the barn, with a ladder reaching up to the cockpit. I'd light the cabin with kerosene and keep my sailing books and a few ragged mysteries on a simple wooden shelf. I might even hoist the jib and mainsail on quiet days. But mostly I'd go there when I need an escape from the farm I escaped to. I'd look up through the companionway and see the leaves turning, and I'd pretend not to hear the woodchucks whistling to each other.

October 7

Caterpillars have begun to appear outside my mudroom door. They look barely animate and thickly pelted, like moss creeping upward in individual inches. I wonder about the feel of black caterpillar fur, but some natural caution keeps me from touching them. Even so, they're a great improvement over the slugs and millipedes that crept up the door all summer long. The slugs looked like thick, muddy drops of gelatinous rain. There's no analogy for the millipedes.

Suddenly, after months of rain, there's a bright sky overhead. The chickens lie prostrate in blobs of sun. The flight of ladybugs seeking crevices everywhere will be coming soon. The milkweed has blown, and the sun now sets in the southwest corner of the pasture. Among humans, there's a sudden yearning for woodstove gaskets and logsplitters. We make last-minute calls to the chimney sweep, who's already booked until yuletide. I hold off on lighting that first fire, because once it's burning there's no turning back from the season ahead. The smell of woodsmoke will lead me by the nose into winter.

There's so much to be done, and yet it's tempting just to sit in the sun and listen to the hickory nuts falling. A flight of sugar maple samaras has already landed, ahead of the leaves. Chipmunks stop the heavy work of hauling hickory nuts in order to eat a maple seed here and there. They look almost improvident while doing so, as if they too wanted to bask in the sun. But then I've never seen a relaxed chipmunk. Nor have I ever seen one walk. They dart or freeze.

Every evening at dusk, five turkeys come down into the pasture from the woods. They begin as substantial beings—still enough light for that—but soon they become shadows, ghosting slowly across the clover and rye. I wait for them every evening. They confirm something for me, though I don't know what. They seem penitential, bringing a redeeming wildness with them.

I wish that when they catch sight of me, they'd stand and nod in my direction. But no. They lift their skirts and hasten through the gate until they find the spot far enough to resume their minute inspection of the pasture. I watch in hopes of being watched back.

November 10

Every now and then, I forget to turn off the lights in the barn, sometimes up in the hayloft, sometimes over the workbench or in a stall. I usually notice just before I go to bed, when the boundaries of the farm have drawn in close. That forgotten light makes the barn seem farther away than it really is—a distance I'm going to have to walk down and back before I can sleep. The weather makes no difference. Neither does the time of year.

I grew up in a landscape where nearly every farm had a yard light that shone all night long. I never understood why. Was it so a farmer, when he woke in the night, could look out at the tractor ruts or watch empty husks blowing past the corn crib? Was it to aid some wandering stranger? Or was it merely to posit one's existence, compressed as those farms were between a prairie of soil and a prairie of sky?

I always hated those lights. They impoverished everything they shone on. Far better the farms that lay dark until a light went on in the dairy barn at an impossibly early hour, a light shrouded by spiderwebs in the window-frame, a light nearly the color of a Jersey cow's milk. At that hour—no sign of dawn—it was impossible not to admire the quiet knowledge the cows carried with them. They would have milked themselves at that exact hour, and in that exact order, if they'd been able to and the humans in charge had overslept.

I don't have cows, and I don't have an all-night yard light either. Usually, after turning out that forgotten barn light, I sit on the edge of the tractor bucket and let my eyes adjust to the darkness outside. City people always notice the darkness here, but it's never very dark if you wait till your eyes owl out a little. I carry a flashlight, but I leave it off until I check on the chickens. Then I let only the dimmest edge of its luminescence show me the hens. Any more, and they stir on their roosts, looking fearful and resentful all at once.

I'm always glad to have to walk down to the barn in the night, and I always forget that it makes me glad. I heave on my coat, stomp into my barn boots, and trudge down toward the barn light, muttering at myself. But then I sit in the dark and remember this gladness, and I walk back up to the gleaming house, listening for the horses.

November 23

"It's raining," I think—and wonder what "it" is that's doing the raining. Ordinarily, that's just a linguistic question. But on a cold November day, when woodsmoke sinks from the chimney, it feels like a philosophical problem. It makes no sense to say the clouds are raining. It makes no sense to speak of "clouds" at all when the sky is so solidly, grayly felted. Out in the pasture, the horses stand, hair slicked, a hind leg cocked on each of them. I conclude that what's raining is the rain, a phrase that sounds like the opening of a grim, Anglo-Saxon lyric.

The trees are coming into their winter bareness. The fullness of their summer leaf seems almost imaginary now. The green they show is lichen on their branches. Against the hemlocks—dark as ever—the rain is obviously raining, falling in dim, straight lines. But the sugar maples on the far edge of the pasture have nothing to say about the rain, only the wind, which isn't absent but lying down, waiting to stir. This is the time of year when all the houses come out of the woods, edging closer to the roads as if for company.

On a day like this my thoughts are never far from the chickens. The red heat lamps are on in the brooder house, and when chore-time comes I'll look in through the window and watch the month-old chicks for a while before disturbing them with food and fresh water. One by one, they stand and stretch a wing and leg—the only balletic move a chicken makes—then settle back into the mass of bodies. They're always seeking thermal equilibrium, clustering tighter and edging closer to the heat as the temperature drops, dispersing and drifting away as it rises.

I do the same inside my house, sitting close to the woodstove, writing. The fire burns clean and hot, but this is the kind of day when there's sometimes a backdraft, a tuft of smoke venting out the air intake and into the kitchen with an audible puff. It rises and disperses leaving behind the scent of oak and maple burning, a scent so welcome and autumnal that it's almost bacon to the nose. The rain rains, the writer writes, the chickens brood, and the horses stand in the mist of their breath, all of us getting along as best we can.

December 28

Some days this month it hasn't been worth feeding the woodstove. The temperature hangs right at forty degrees like a picture on a nail. In October, forty feels like a reason to start a fire. Not in late December. But there's something disheartening about a cold woodstove, as if it were a conduit for cold air and bad spirits. So I light it anyway, for the warmth, for the light, for the company, and so that when I go outside to do chores there will be that burgee of smoke blowing sideways from the chimney.

Watching the fire, I think sometimes about two terrifying rooms in the basement of the Iowa farmhouse my dad grew up in. One was the coal room, the other the cob room. Coal went into the furnace, corncobs into the cookstove in the kitchen, but both rooms, when I first encountered them, had already fallen into disuse. In the coal room there was a darkness the eye couldn't penetrate. Next door, the cobs had settled into a heap that hadn't been disturbed in years. What frightened me I can no longer say, unless it was a glimpse into an abandoned way of living.

I think of it now because when I light the woodstove, I realize that I'm burning time. Handling the split logs, I notice their straightness or their irregularities. But when I feed them into the woodstove, I get one last, end-on glimpse of their tree rings. It's like feeding chapters of a biological chronicle into the fire one by one. Some of the split logs I'm burning today are as old as the memory of that Iowa farmhouse. Some are older still. Wind scatters the smoke instantly, and when the woodstove is cold again, I'll scatter the ashes.

There's no special virtue in burning wood. It's a way of keeping time in an otherwise hourless day. I have friends and neighbors who make an art of their woodpiles and kindling, whose mauls and axes are keen and bright. I used to think that one day I'd make a round Swedish woodpile, roofed with bark. What I have instead is a large, well-kept pile of things I used to think I'd do one day. It never rots. The chipmunks never nest in it. Every now and then, I actually do one of those things I thought I'd do one day. As it happens, sitting by the woodstove, burning time, is one of them.

Year

ELEVEN

ᔔ❧

January 13

Here's the thing about mice. They look at you with outrageous self-possession. I run across them everywhere on the farm, and they look up at me as if I'd just disrupted them in the act of reading a book in the privacy of their own home. Apart from the mice I find in traps and in the feed bin, I almost always come across them in their domesticity, a nest of shredded paper, fur, horsehair, or chicken feathers somewhere nearby. This week, I found a mouse living in the spare tire compartment of the car. It had turned the jack manual into a futon and was prepared to wait out the winter.

On their very small scale, the mice are working to return this house to nature, and I try my best to keep them from succeeding. It's an unequal contest. I never carry hickory nuts into the house, but from time to time I find one hidden in the toe of a work boot. Some days I wish I could leave my paper recycling to the mice. They'd do a good job of it, shredding it into illegibility, warming generations of mice to come. Hickories would eventually sprout in the mudroom and basement, raising the roof beams as they grew. If only mice ate rust.

This is how it always feels at the farm, as though nature is trying to pull my habitation apart. The farm is temporary shelter at best, even though the house has been standing, in one form or another, for more than two

217

centuries. Brambles tug at the fence wires. Soil rots the fence posts. Freeze and thaw work away at the stones in the foundation. Plants come tendriling over the railing and up the porch posts. Gravity does its insidious work. I wouldn't be surprised to learn that the farm is slowly sliding downhill.

There's no stasis, only change. And this winter, even the illusion of stasis—the deep cold, the settled snow—is missing. The sign at the farm supply store says, "Seeds Are In!" and everywhere I look I see people hoping to get the jump on spring while worrying that winter will get the jump on them. As for me, I write and read and do chores and whatever I can to stem the tide. I know that mice will be with us always.

March 8

There's a boat in the barn. I put it there last October, and yet it surprises me every time I go down to get a bale of hay. A previous owner called it the *Judy of Gloucester*—still painted on the stern—but its manufacturer called it a Typhoon, a name I like to think was taken from the novel by Joseph Conrad. You can pack a lot of daydreams, plans, and illusions into a forty-year-old sailboat only nineteen feet long in a barn 140 miles from the sea. I see the boat in my barn and I think of the Lyle Lovett song about "me upon my pony on my boat," a song that's all about illusion.

When the weather warms up, I'll begin restoring the *Judy of Gloucester*. It will be yet another of the things I'd never done until I came to this farm, like raising pigs. I imagine that one day I'll be far out at sea remembering those pigs. Or perhaps I'll be in the pigpen imagining all of us far out at sea together, like the pigs and the children on the pirate ship in Richard Hughes's novel, *A High Wind in Jamaica*. I don't know. It's hard to say how it will all work out. I like walking the length of the mast, which is lying on sawhorses in the barn, before I feed the animals. It's not exactly climbing into the crow's nest, but it will do for now.

Meanwhile, this is still an upland farm in early March. At evening, a rim of light behind the birches divides the blue of sky from the blue of twilit snow. There's a little summer, a little lingering, in that rim of light, but only for a moment. Then the rising moon runs across the pasture, and it's winter again. In the moon's light, the snow-worn hill by the barn looks like an old Appaloosa lying on its side, barely breathing, slowly shedding, its white flank blotched and speckled with dark.

When I was young, my father bought me the cheapest old car he could find, in hopes that restoring it would take my mind off other things.

We parked it in the garden and put the front end up on blocks. I never did restore that car, but I used to sit in it, angled toward the sky, when the moon was high. I haven't yet taken to sitting in the cockpit of the *Judy*, pretending to be a-sail when everything around me says I'm not. But I'm sure that day will come.

March 30

On fair days, I've been letting the chickens have the run of the farm. I come out of the house, and the birds are waiting at the chicken-yard fence like petitioners in Dostoevsky, but with boundless optimism instead of resignation and despair. I open the gate, and out they come, all thirty of them, except for the hens who are busy laying. It's a flock of many breeds—Appenzeller, Penedesenca, Orpington, Campine. They sound like the great, exploring sailors of a much earlier time, the discoverers of straits and continents.

I let them out because it so plainly makes them happy, and because their optimism is catching. Now and then a Welsummer or a Barnevelder strolls onto the deck and walks up to the sliding glass door. The chickens and I—and Ceilidh the Border terrier—look at each other with heads askew. The birds gaze into the house with one eye, then the other—they live in a monocular world, after all—and decide there's nothing of interest there. Then we all go back to work. I, at least, am happier for the encounter.

Why do I like these birds so much? It's not just the eggs and beautiful feathering, the crowing and the clucking. It's the instinctive chicken-ness of their behavior, the boundary, in every movement, between what's chicken and what's not. A hen raking backwards through winter's duff is a professional at work. Scratch, scratch, look around for predators, and what have we here? A foraging chicken feeds itself by finding surprises everywhere. It's such a bountiful view of the world.

And yet the eye of every chicken—even the calmest and most buxom of hens—is inherently skeptical. They seem poised between doubt and trust, never jaundiced, never dismayed. The world seems perfectly adjusted to their expectations. They take the world just as it is.

Light falls, and Ceilidh and I go out to do chores. I feed the horses and the chickens run among their legs looking for spilled grain and hayseeds. Everywhere, there are signs of their raking, leaves and plant-litter overturned. Before long, the birds are back in their yard, vanishing up the ramp to their house, all but the roosters, who keep a wary eye until the flock is in.

April 18

Doing without mud season shouldn't feel like a loss. Who misses mud? But here we are, coasting toward the end of April, and I haven't lost a boot to the suction of the barnyard swamp. I haven't had to cut drainage channels through the corral. Nor have I had to tractor through hub-deep primeval ooze while hauling a round bale to the run-in shed.

Forsythia and mud nearly always coincide. The mud persists even as the azaleas begin to blossom all over the county in a hideous color that might be called Importuning Pink. Usually, the mud abates as the tulips fade and the lilacs come out. In a well-drained garden, mud season makes it easy to do your spading, whether you plant your potatoes on Good Friday, as my uncle always does, or are merely preparing the earth for tomatoes to come.

What we have this year is intractable stuff, hard, powdery, and, lacking moisture, too light in color. What rain has fallen has barely laid the dust, and even a good storm now—a soaker—wouldn't raise the kind of mud I've come to expect over the years. Mud season is more complex than that. It needs frozen ground, good snowpack, and a sudden thaw. The mud of mud season isn't merely waterlogged dirt. It's upheaval, the amphibian earth changing shape before your eyes. It's the seed of spring in the corpse of winter.

Just now the maples carry immature leaves that look like small, folded bat wings, if bat wings were chartreuse. The metasequoia along the fence line is preparing to jump another foot or two in height. All the conifers are showing the first bright green of their intentions. Only the hickories—always late to the party—pretend that this ebullience is folly. Spring has to prove itself before a hickory will come into leaf.

It's the between time, even without enough mud to say so. The night-song of the peepers has faded, but the Canada goslings haven't hatched. Robins are here, but no catbirds or swallows. Goldfinches wear their breeding colors, but phoebes aren't yet nesting over the kitchen door. In the garden, the chives have a long head start on the asparagus. Mars is now high above, Orion subsiding, when Ceilidh the Border terrier and I take our last walk at night. We look at the sky, we sniff the air, and when we come back in our feet are perfectly dry.

May 20

I resent my lawn. It grows in the night. Right now, it's deep enough to hide a rabbit. I've thought about cutting paths through it, letting the rest of it grow wild. But lawn is more than a cultural legacy. It's a sensory legacy—the smell of cut grass and gas fumes, the geometric symmetry the mower leaves behind. As a kind of landscape art, it's just one step short of plowing. And yet it's a legacy I wish I'd never inherited.

I have no neighbors to tut over my unmowed lawn. The other organisms on the farm seem to love it. Ceilidh and I walk around the house at first light, and she grazes as she goes, dew gathering on her face. A turkey feeds beneath the apple trees. The unevenness of the grass gives spiders a richer undergirding for their webs. Another week and what I do when I mow won't be lawn care. It will be forestry.

Lawn seems especially arbitrary here. Beyond the fence it's pasture. And yet when I mow the pasture it doesn't become lawn. And if I parked one of the horses on the lawn, it wouldn't become pasture. The difference lies in the mixture of species. Lawn is meant to be monoculture, pasture not. Here the two converge.

Lawn mowing—like driving—is one of those long strands that reaches all the way back through my life. If anything, mowing is more primal. It's what young boys in small towns are supposed to do when they're not delivering newspapers. The most prosperous boys in my boyhood town—crew-cut twins and Future Farmers of America—ran a mowing business with mowers that gleamed like tiny new combines. When we moved to California, we discovered the true idolatry of lawn. In California, they edged the lawns. No one had heard of such a thing in Iowa.

I'll give it up, the lawn, and let the ferns and wild mint take over. But like so much else in our culture, lawn is a terribly hard habit to break. All the more because when I mow, I see the farms I knew as a child. Out in the fields, my uncles are driving their tractors, plowing. My aunts are all on riding mowers, zooming around the hydrangeas, the house, and the edge of the grove.

June 19

In early May, my neighbor and I moved my three horses across the gravel road to her summer pasture. Last year, it took a while before her animals—a thoroughbred and a mule—herded up with mine, but eventually they settled down into a single unit. This year, they did something unexpected. They ejected Remedy from the herd. My neighbor put salve on his bites. When I went to check on him the next morning, I found him standing alone in the shallow creek, as if his feet were hot. His head was to the fence, his tail to all the rest of the world.

I bought Remedy in Colorado when he was nineteen. Now he's thirty-four. He has ruled all the horses as long as I've owned him, wherever we've been, but not anymore. I walked him out of the creek and back to my place and put him in a paddock out of sight of the horses across the road. He was limping slightly, but now that limp has hardened into a deep and permanent hitch in his gait. He gets around as though he's used to the damage, but his orbit in the paddock has grown smaller and smaller. His eyes are bright. His coat gleams. His ears seem to have lengthened as he's aged, but they still twitch with attention.

Remedy has always been the youngest old horse I know, but thirty-four is terribly old for a horse. A wise equestrian friend told me that Remedy would let me know when he's ready to go. I've seen that moment in dogs and humans and known it for what it was, but never in a horse. I'm afraid I won't recognize it, that I'll let him down in dying. He's been such a powerful figure in my life, the remedy to a disabling fear that stole upon me unexpected one day. He has one more thing to teach me, and I hope I learn it well.

July 19

By the time you read this, I will have filled in Remedy's grave. The vet is coming Friday. I'd promised myself not to write about this, but then I met the man with the backhoe who's digging the grave. His name is Digger, lean, gray, wearing his spectacles low on his nose. I showed him the spot I had in mind in the lower garden. I asked him how much I'd owe him. His answer caught me deep inside. "Nothing," he said. "I've been doing this for free all my life."

I've kept this coming loss at a distance for as long as I can, said all the things you can say about an injured thirty-four year old horse and his time to go. They sound like compassion and common sense intertwined. But I wasn't prepared for the subtle, feeling gift Digger is giving me down in the lower garden as I write. I expected that Remedy would be himself right up till the end. I know, in the best sense, what to expect from horses. Digger reminded me that I don't always know what to expect from humans.

There's been a lot of dying on this farm. That's the nature of living with domesticated animals on the edge of the wild—and with pigs. The deaths add up over the years. I've seen again and again how forceful and how frail life is. Before I cover Remedy's body, I'll scatter the ashes of Buster, Angus, Tavish, and Darcy in the grave. The first few chickens that died, years ago, were sentimental losses. But sentimentality washes away, and then you come to the bedrock of grief.

The part I hate is that every death brings with it every other death, going all the way back through my life. In my experience, there's no segregating grief by species. Losing Remedy sets all the other losses echoing, animal and human alike. What differs isn't the feeling of grief itself—it's the afterlife. With pets—and pigs—there's an unalloyed incandescence. It's always more intense than I expect, but it also burns out quickly. With humans—well, you'll have to write your own sentence here. All I know is that when the vet comes tomorrow and her work is done, I'll be surrounded by the memory of everyone I've ever lost.

Coda

———

August 4

The other night I took the dogs for a walk in the pasture. It was a cloudless evening with low humidity, a rare event in this damp, northeastern summer. I always look at the stars when I'm outside in the dark, but all too often they're obscured by haze, even here in the country. Not that night. Cassiopeia, Corona Borealis, Lyra, the red light of Arcturus in the west, the diffuse band of the Milky Way arching overhead—their presence was overwhelming. And yet somehow when the stars look close to Earth it's easier to imagine how far away they really are. It was a warm July night, but I could almost feel the chill of space.

I've been watching the stars for nearly half a century now. Not much has changed up there. The sky is a memory in itself. I stared at the rings of Saturn and the moons of Jupiter through a small telescope of my own when I was a boy in Iowa. I spent part of a summer watching meteors while I was helping my family build a house in the foothills of the Sierra Nevada and part of a winter stargazing from the top of a mesa on the Hopi Reservation, where somehow the smell of cedar mingled with the light of the moon. The only thing that has changed in all that time—apart from a few new satellites crossing the sky—is the state of my knowledge.

The same could be said for the whole of humanity. Besides a supernova here and there or a comet fluttering past, the night sky visible to the naked eye has barely changed as long as our species has been looking at it, unlike the stories we use to describe what we see up there. Each human culture, separate in time or place, has lived under a different celestial roof. The metaphors for the heavens have changed over time, but not nearly as much as what we know about the universe itself.

. . .

Usually, the dates in the history of science seem abstract, almost equidistant in the past: 1543, 1632, 1905—it's all ancient history. But this time, I found myself weighing the dates of various discoveries—the ones that define our present idea of the age and dimensions of the universe—against the time-scale of my own life. I tried to picture what the universe looked like—or was thought to look like—around the year my dad was born, 1926, or the year I was born, 1952. I'm overwhelmed by the recentness of what we know.

Take something "everybody knows." Earth belongs to the solar system, and the solar system belongs to a galaxy called the Milky Way, which is about 100,000 light-years across. The Milky Way is one of perhaps a hundred billion galaxies in the observable universe, each containing perhaps a hundred billion stars. But until 1925, many astronomers believed, on the available evidence, that the Milky Way contained the whole of the observable universe, and that ours was thus the only galaxy. Astronomers had seen and cataloged plenty of galaxies—they were called nebulae in those days—but there was no way to know how far away they were.

In 1923, Edwin Hubble discovered a Cepheid variable star in the nebula called Andromeda. Thanks to Henrietta Leavitt's research on these stars, Hubble was able to calculate the distance to the Andromeda Galaxy, as we call it now. It was vastly more distant than anyone had guessed. By his calculations, Andromeda was 900,000 light-years away—well outside the Milky Way. In a sense, Hubble had turned the universe inside out.

Hubble was wrong about one thing. Andromeda is 2.2 million light years away, not 900,000. You can see it with the naked eye if you look just below and to the right of the constellation Cassiopeia on a dark, clear night. It's worth knowing that in another three billion years Andromeda will collide with the Milky Way. "Violently intersift" is perhaps a better way of putting it.

To a casual naked-eye observer on Earth it makes no practical difference whether the universe is the size of the Milky Way or much, much bigger.

226

In fact, it makes little difference whether we're looking up at stars scattered across empty space or at an empyrean of concentric crystalline spheres. The night sky overhead would look the same.

Or would it?

What we see when we look up into the darkness of a summer night isn't just a pattern of pinpoint lights. We're also looking up at the state of our knowledge and the contents of our imagination. Does our own galaxy encompass the whole observable universe? Or is it only one among a huge number of galaxies in a vastly larger universe? The difference is enormous. Both are theories. One was plausible before 1925. The other is true. The revolution in imagining who we are and where we are is Copernican.

In the years since, there have been many discoveries more astonishing, including Hubble's discovery, several years later, that the universe is expanding. But measuring that Cepheid variable in Andromeda fascinates me. It's tempting to construe its effect solely in human terms, to say, with a vainglorious sniff, that it diminishes the place of humans in the universe. Ah, well. There's no end to that. One of the central problems of cosmology all along has been getting a true sense of scale. The age of the universe, its size, its origin, whether it's static or expanding or contracting—these things are all interrelated, and they all depend on being able to measure distance accurately out to the far reaches of the universe. The more we know, the smaller we humans seem to loom against the universal backdrop. Luckily, what matters isn't how big or important we are. It's how interesting the universe is.

. . .

My maternal grandfather was born in the 1880s. He used to marvel that in his lifetime humans had gone from horse-drawn carriages to the moon. I like to think of it a different way. He was born about the time astronomers finally proved that the ether—the peculiar light-carrying substance through which all celestial bodies were supposed to move—doesn't exist. He was married around the publication of Einstein's theory of general relativity. He died a few years after Arno Penzias and Robert Wilson found the lingering echo of the Big Bang with a radio telescope in New Jersey. I don't imagine my grandfather was aware of any of these discoveries. And yet within his lifetime, the dimensions of the universe increased by a factor I'm not mathematician enough to work out. Call it ten to the plenty.

In 1931, Edwin Hubble concluded that the universe was 1.8 billion years old, a nonsensical number since geologists had already shown that the rocks on Earth are nearly twice that age. (Recent knowledge in itself!) In 1952, the scale of distance was recalculated with greater accuracy, and suddenly the age of the universe doubled to 3.6 billion years, much older but still a problematic figure. In 1955, the universe aged another 1.9 billion years overnight, again thanks to a clearer understanding of the things that shine in the dark. In the past eighty years the universe has expanded faster and aged faster—in the minds of humans—than it's doing in actuality. The current age of the universe, as measured in 2003, is now 13.7 billion years, give or take 200 million. That's another way of saying that the distance to the edge of the observable universe is 13.7 billion light-years.

What astronomers are seeing when they look at a galaxy like Abell 1835 IR1916—13.2 billion light-years away—is light (or radiation) that was emitted 13.2 billion years ago, light that's about three times older than the planet we live on. Imagine a galaxy just a little farther away, at the extreme edge of what astronomers can observe. Suppose it emits light even as you're reading this sentence. How far away will the edge of the observable universe be when that light reaches us? The answer is somewhere between 78 and 90 billion light-years. In fact, cosmologists have no idea how much of our universe lies beyond the threshold of observability. There's even sober speculation that we live in a multiverse, that our universe is merely one of a possibly infinite series of universes. One of the best arguments for the multiverse is the simple fact that we exist.

. . .

Science is mostly a tale of continuity. Scientists today are working within the same professional framework—the same idea about how they do what they do, what hypotheses are, what evidence is—as scientists did a century ago. That's the strength of the endeavor. The change from one picture of the universe to another is incremental, based on work that obeys the self-regulating, international standards of the scientific enterprise. But I find myself marveling at its discontinuity, too.

In 1920 there was one galaxy and now there are 100 billion.

In 1955 the universe was 5.5 billion years old. Now it's believed to be two and a half times older—an estimate with a much higher degree of precision.

For many years, the Big Bang was a conceptual possibility, the logical implication of an expanding universe. (What happens when you run the film of an expanding universe backwards?) But in 1965, Penzias and Wilson found an evenly diffused radiation permeating the sky, with a temperature of 2.7 degrees Kelvin. They had discovered the cosmic microwave background—residual radiation from the Big Bang.

The cosmic microwave background has been measured again and again, with greater and greater precision. Recent measurements support a theory of inflation first proposed by Alan Guth in 1979 and since refined. It says that at an unimaginably short time after the Big Bang, the universe experienced an abrupt inflation, doubling in size over and over again until inflation stopped an unimaginably short instant later. The result is the relatively smooth and geometrically flat universe we find ourselves living in.

Research suggests that the universe is made of 4 percent atoms (now called baryonic matter), 22 percent dark matter, and 74 percent dark energy. As an idea, dark matter first popped up in the 1930s. Dark energy is the thought of the past few years. No one knows what either of them is, except that without them the behavior of the universe makes no sense. It's worth remembering, too, that the modern idea of the atom—that is, the old-fashioned modern idea, well before quarks—only came together in 1932, when the neutron was discovered.

. . .

Someone, somewhere, is likely to be shouting, "Aha!" about now.

"You're saying that our so-called scientific knowledge is only a projection of sorts and that there's no scientific truth, only relativistic assumptions—culturally created ideas—about the universe around us. Isn't that what you're saying?"

Thanks for asking. The answer is no. Science is a cultural enterprise, like everything humans do, and it sometimes suffers from characteristically human flaws. But the evolution of what we know about the universe doesn't reveal the indeterminacy of science. It reveals the extraordinary intellectual and imaginative yields that a self-critical, self-evaluating, self-testing, experimental search for understanding can generate over time.

We know the universe to be a very different and in every way more amazing place than we did even a generation ago. We have no idea how much more surprising it will turn out to be, should we manage to survive as a species that's able to do science. If what you want from life is a constant, fixed, unchanging truth, then fresh news from science can only seem bewildering. But the unchanging truths that people cling to in this inconstant world tend to rest on unexamined and untestable assumptions. At their best they may be permanent ethical truths, which can't be contradicted by the open-ended possibilities of scientific exploration. At their worst, they're dogma.

The open-endedness of science isn't its failing. It is its very beauty. Each answer is merely the prelude to the next question, and you never know when you'll come upon an answer that forces you to rethink almost everything. This is as true in biology—itself overwhelmed by recent knowledge—as it is in cosmology. Yet many people can't help hoping for a final set of answers. "So how old is it really—and how big is it really?" they ask about the universe, with an emphasis on "really." The fact that the answer depends on when you happen to ask it—1931, 1955, 2003, today—seems to many people to imply that science has no answers worth giving.

But this is simply the bias inherent in living in the "now." Stated as a sentence, that bias goes like this: "We're here now, so we expect some answers." Think about the analogies meant to convey the immensity of time. They always end in the present. If the history of the universe is a clock, mankind emerges at eleven seconds to midnight, and then what? The clock stops at the current time, as if the game is over. But there's no time limit on the questions science asks, and there's little likelihood of a final set of answers. Humanity emerges, looks up at the stars, and soon there's a probe in space telling us that most of what exists is stuff we can't identify. Who would want it any other way?

. . .

Thinking about the recentness of what we know means thinking simultaneously about the strangeness of the past and the strangeness of the present—the reciprocal strangenesses that time brings about. I have a hard time trying to imagine the universe as it might have been in 1920—the whole of it packed into the Milky Way. But I have an equally hard time imagining what it was like being a hired hand on my grandfather's farm in 1920. The changes in the way we live loom far larger in our minds than changes in the theoretical model of a universe that most of us think about—if we think about it at all—only on dark, clear nights. But the changes go together.

At best, I'm the kind of cosmological reader who has to skip the math. As a result, my grasp on most of what astronomers have learned in my lifetime is largely aesthetic. I admire the finished painting, but I have no real conception of what it means to apply the paint. And for me, the old forms of knowledge are hard enough. Not the ones rooted in dogma, but the ones rooted in a practical application of what astronomers have learned over the years.

Understanding the motion of the moon through the sky is far more complicated than it sounds, as I've discovered from trying to sort it out.

Knowing how and why the universe is expanding doesn't change the
rules of celestial navigation any more than it changes the stories people
tell about the figures in the constellations. The recentness of what we know
doesn't annul the old knowledge; it transfigures it. Suddenly, what we used to
know is now part of the story of how we go about knowing things and no longer a description of the universe around us. But go out on a deep summer
night and there overhead are all the skies we've ever seen.

Appendix

Ocotber 28

On April 18, 1818, William Cobbett—a fifty-five-year-old Englishman living on a farm in North Hempstead, Long Island—wrote in his journal, "We have *sprouts* from the cabbage stems preserved under cover; the Swedish turnip is giving me *greens* from bulbs planted out in March; and I have some *broccoli* too, just coming on for use. *How* I have got this broccoli I must explain in my *Gardener's Guide*; for write one I must. I can never leave this country without an attempt to make every farmer a gardener."

As always, Cobbett was making a point. He did write a gardener's guide, called *The American Gardener*, first published in London in 1821. If you look up "Dandelion," you'll find this apparently peripheral note: "In the spring (June) 1817, when I came to Long Island, and when nothing in the shape of *greens* was to be had for love or money, *Dandelions* were our resource; and I have always, since that time, looked at this *weed* with a more friendly eye." Cobbett's point is this: once settled, he managed to have greens by April. The rest of Long Island could grow none by June. The secret? Hotbeds.

This is Cobbett all over: two parts practical knowledge, two parts rural economy—and one part self-satisfaction, a pleasure it's hard to begrudge him. A quick sketch of who and what Cobbett was when he decided "to make

233

every farmer a gardener" will allow you to enjoy his self-satisfaction too. Cobbett came to America in 1817 in what he called "self-banishment," fleeing the wrath of an English government that suspended *habeas corpus* in order to imprison its enemies more easily. Cobbett was the most important of them. By 1817, he had been writing *Cobbett's Weekly Political Register*, the only politically independent newspaper in England, for fifteen years, and he would continue to write it until a week before his death in 1835. That paper, published every Saturday, was the voice of political reform, and "among the great mass of people it became the most powerful journal in England," according to one of Cobbett's biographers.

Cobbett had lived in the New World before 1817. He came to New Brunswick in 1785 as a soldier. After his discharge and marriage in England, he returned with his wife, Nancy, to Philadelphia in 1792, "passing," as he says, "eight years there, becoming bookseller and author, and taking a prominent part in all the important discussions of the interesting period from 1793 to 1799, during which there was, in that country, a continual struggle carried on between the English and the French parties." Those vitriolic "discussions" were in ink. Cobbett's American pseudonym was Peter Porcupine. His vehicle was *Porcupine's Gazette*—in nearly all respects, but one, a precursor to *Cobbett's Weekly Political Register*. That one respect was the side he took.

Before 1800, Cobbett was an archconservative, a member of the English party trying to bring about closer ties between America and its parent country, a relationship still in tatters after the American revolution and made far worse by the French revolution and its consequences. But at home in England Cobbett found a corrupt government, a failing monetary policy, a venal Parliament, and a collapsing agriculture. He made a volte-face of stunning proportions and passed it off as consistency. He began to view the "weed" America, like the dandelion, with a friendlier eye. He began to clamor for reform of Parliament, to campaign against a national debt and a paper money that was bankrupting farmers and destroying the lives of farm laborers. And when he faced the near certainty of being imprisoned by the English government—it would have been his second political incarceration—he boarded ship with two of his sons and made America his refuge until the end of 1819.

This is the person you must imagine writing *The American Gardener*— nearly as famous a man as there was at the time in England or America. He is already, as William Hazlitt said in 1821, "unquestionably the most powerful political writer of the present day," and he's on the cusp of becoming, as Hazlitt also put it, "one of the best writers in the language." For the great period of Cobbett's work is about to begin. If Cobbett ever lay fallow, it was in the grave.

While he was in America, living on Long Island, Cobbett kept up his political barrage in the pages of the *Political Register*. On December 6, 1817, he began writing *A Grammar of the English Language, in a Series of Letters*, which was published in New York the following year. It is, as Hazlitt affirms, "as entertaining as a story-book," and it sold one hundred thousand copies by 1834 and remained in print at least until 1919, a fact that's all the more amazing when you remember that Cobbett began life as an unlettered plowboy. He wrote and published *A Year's Residence in the United States of America* and began work on *The American Gardener*. Still ahead lay some of his greatest books, published in quick succession in the early 1820s: *Cottage Economy*, a French grammar that was no less successful than his English grammar, and the first of the essays that became *Rural Rides*, a masterpiece of political and agricultural reporting.

. . .

It sounds as though Cobbett was dipped in printer's ink at birth and baptized with political ichor. But he was the child of a farm laborer and grew up in Hampshire during a period of agricultural prosperity. He had as many ideas as there were minutes in his day, which always began at four A.M. "He is like a young and lusty bridegroom," Hazlitt wrote, "that divorces a favourite speculation every morning, and marries a new one every night. He is not wedded to his notions, not he. He has not one Mrs. Cobbett among all his opinions." But there was a Mrs. Cobbett among his sentiments, and that was a love of the land, of farming, gardening, and the virtues of a prosperous rural life, no matter how poor in outward show.

Between 1793 and 1821 the small farmers and rural laborers of England forgot how to brew beer and bake bread and raise pigs, which are among the arts that Cobbett discusses in *Cottage Economy*. It seems incredible until you realize that we've lost similar kinds of knowledge just as quickly and completely in our own time. Knowledge of the land and how to live wisely and thriftily on it doesn't just lie there, dormant, like a crocus that renews itself in the first flush of spring. It must be cultivated, and it must be knotted, in practice, to the people who have cultivated it before us. In *Cottage Economy*, Cobbett tried to reconnect the rural men and women of 1821, defrauded of their agricultural birthright by England's disastrous wartime economy, with their elders, who were wise almost beyond remembering in the ways of the land.

This is a hard idea to get across—the notion that once upon a time, perhaps only a little while ago, people knew a better way of doing things. The small amount of humility needed to believe it is beyond us. The result is that we always exaggerate the simplicity, the uncouthness of the past. We assume that what people knew then isn't worth knowing now. Or, worse, we assume that those people, now in the grave, aren't really up to the demands of what we know. This is the peculiar wonder of Cobbett. He doesn't despise what his elders knew. Nor does he doubt the abilities of the present generation, unless they flee, as he writes in *Rural Rides*, "from the dirty *work* as cunning horses do from the bridle."

Cobbett found that America in 1817 was *"a country of farmers."* But it was also a country where the abundance of land overwhelmed the desire to garden on a single spot. "When large parcels of land are undertaken to be cultivated," Cobbett writes, "small ones are held in contempt; and, though a good garden supplies so large a part of what's consumed by a family, and keeps supplying it all the year round too, there are many farmers even in England, who grudge even a wheelbarrow full of manure that is bestowed on the garden." Cobbett's purpose in *The American Gardener* is nothing less than to teach the rudiments of gardening to American farmers and to inculcate the love of cottage gardens found among rural laborers in the England he grew up in.

So don't let yourself picture Cobbett seated at a desk, pen in hand, during the light of the day. Imagine, instead, that it's early, early morning, and he's dictating to one of his children before the sun comes up. After four hours of literary work, he turns to other business. He took over a long-abandoned house on Long Island, and he and his children restored the garden there. He raised pigs, oxen, chickens, sheep, ducks, and turkeys. And when that house burned down in the spring of 1819, he raised a tent, lined it with English newspapers, and camped out there for several months, dressed in "a shirt, a pair of nankin trowsers, yellow buckskin shoes and a broad-brimmed straw hat."

Nearly all of Cobbett's gardening advice is still good advice. It's impossible to improve on his description of how to prepare the soil for planting: "Make the ground rich, move it deep, and make it fine." He walks you through the double-digging of a garden plot, a task that hasn't changed since 1821. With the manure of cattle or horses and a little effort, you could still make a hotbed of the kind Cobbett describes, following his instructions to the letter, and it would yield just as Cobbett says it does. No one has ever written a better or clearer description of how to eat an artichoke. And if Cobbett's passions overflow from time to time—as they always did—they are excellent passions. To him, the locust (*Robinia pseudoacacia*) is the "most beautiful of trees and best of timber." To him, sea kale "is, unquestionably, (after the Asparagus,) the very best garden vegetable that grows." The geranium (the *pelargonium*, that is) "wants *hardiness only* to make it the finest flower-plant of which I have any knowledge." The cranberry "is one of the best fruits in the world. All tarts sink out of sight in point of merit, when compared with that made of the American Cranberry."

Cobbett urges the gardener to consider the neatness, the handsomeness with which he does things. Partly, this is for moral reasons. But Cobbett also urges neatness and beauty for practical reasons. "Next comes *the act of sowing*," he writes. "The more *handsomely* this is done, the *better* it is done. A handsome dress is *better* than an ugly one, not because it is warmer, or cooler, but because, liking it better, being more pleased with it, we *take more care of it*." Cobbett imagines the American farmer building a garden for the ages. When it comes to laying out the hawthorn hedge, "place *a line along very truly*; for, mind, you are planting for generations to come!" He describes how to make a rake-like tool for laying out drills, or rows, in the soil. If made, as he recommends, with white oak for the head and locust for the teeth, "every body knows, that the tools might descend from father to son to the fourth or fifth generation."

You may not choose to garden directly from the pages of *The American Gardener*, though generations of gardeners have done so. But in its pages you'll find another America, a place where the profusion of wild huckleberries on Long Island "gives rise to a *holiday*, called *Huckleberry Monday*," where fine laburnums bloom "between *Brooklyn* and the Turnpike gate." Best, of all, you'll find a rich helping of the genuine Cobbett. Thomas Carlyle described him as "the pattern John Bull of his century, strong as the rhinoceros, and with singular humanities and genialities shining through his thick skin." He's a man of genuine tenderness. "For, count our real pleasures," he writes; "count the things that delight us through life: and you will find, that ninety-nine out of every hundred are derived from women. To be the object of *no woman's* care or good wishes is a sentence the most severe that can be pronounced upon man."

And even if you don't end up making a hotbed or planting a hawthorn hedge, you'll still find yourself going down to the garden with Cobbett's words in mind. "Seasons wait for no man. Nature makes us her offers freely; but she will be taken at her word."

NOTE TO THE READER

Nearly all the pieces gathered in this book were first published, in slightly different form, on the editorial page of the *New York Times*, usually under the rubric "The Rural Life." I'm grateful to Andy Rosenthal—and his predecessor at the editorial page, Gail Collins—for their continued publication of the occasional editorial essay. I'm also grateful to my wonderful colleagues on the Editorial Board, who have been warm and supportive in good times and bad. I still owe an inexpressible debt to Howell Raines, who brought me to the *Times* when he ran the editorial page and who imagined there might be room on the page for something like "The Rural Life."

Other thanks? As always to Flip Brophy at Sterling Lord Literistic. To Roger Cohn, a longtime friend and editor who has given me room at Yale Environment 360. To my good friends and neighbors—who also happen to be excellent publishers and editors—Kevin and Jennifer Lippert. To the designers of this book, Paul Wagner and Benjamin English, and to the illustrator Nigel Peake for making such a handsome volume. To the neighbors around me in the country—farmers and friends—who have taught me and helped me and put up with me. And, most of all, to readers who bring this farm alive in their imaginations. I often wish I were living a life as thoughtful and deliberate as they suppose I do.

I owe one more inexpressible debt, and that is to Lindy Smith, who for a decade shared this farm and helped make it what it is. She knows better than anyone its joys and its sorrows.

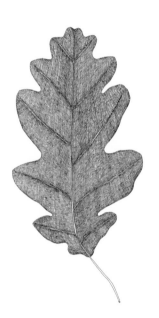